THE SELF

THE SELF

Explorations in Personal Growth

EDITED BY

CLARK E. MOUSTAKAS

Merrill-Palmer School, Detroit

WITH ASSISTANCE IN EDITING INDIAN PAPERS BY

SITA RAM JAYASWAL

University of Lucknow, Lucknow, India

Harper & Row, Publishers, New York and Evanston

Grateful acknowledgment is made to the following for permission to reprint selections included in this book:

Gordon W. Allport and the American Orthopsychiatric Association for "The Trend in Motivational Theory" by Gordon W. Allport, American Journal of Orthopsychiatry, January 1953, Copyright 1953 by the American Orthopsychiatric Association.

Andras Angyal and Duke University Press for "A Theoretical Model for Personality Studies" by Andras Angyal, Journal of Personality, September 1951, Copyright 1951 by Duke University Press.

Erich Fromm and Rinehart & Company, Incorporated for "Selfishness, Self-Love and Self-Interest" from Man for Himself: An Inquiry Into the Psychology of Ethics by Erich Fromm, Copyright 1947 by Erich Fromm.

Kurt Goldstein and the American Book Company for "The So-Called Drives" from The Organism by Kurt Goldstein, Copyright 1939 by American Book Company.

Island Press Co-operative, Inc. for "The Personality" from Self-Consistency by Prescott Lecky, edited and interpreted by Frederick C. Thorne, Copyright 1945 by Kathryn Lecky, 1951 by Island Press Co-operative, Inc.

C. G. Jung, Pantheon Books Inc., and the Bollingen Foundation for "The Development of Personality" from The Development of Personality by C. G. Jung, Copyright 1953 by the Bollingen Foundation.

Alfred A. Knopf, Inc. for "Fate and Self-Determination" from Will Therapy & Truth and Reality by Otto Rank, transl. from the German by Jessie Taft.

Copyright 1936, 1945, by Alfred A. Knopf, Inc.

The Macmillan Company for "Human Personality" from An Idealist View of Life by Sarvapelli Radhakrishnan, Copyright 1932 by The Macmillan Company; and "The World of Personality" from Personality by Rabindranath Tagore, Copyright 1918 by The Macmillan Company.

A. H. Maslow and Grune & Stratton, Inc. for "Self-Actualizing People" by A. H. Maslow from Symposium #1 1950 Values in Personality Research, edited by Werner Wolff, Copyright 1950 by Grune & Stratton, Inc.

Ross L. Mooney and the American Psychological Association, Inc. for "Groundwork for Creative Research" by Ross L. Mooney from the American Psychologist, September 1954, Copyright 1954 by the American Psychological Association, Inc.

W. W. Norton & Company, Inc. for "The Search for Glory" from Neurosis and Human Growth by Karen Horney, Copyright 1950 by W. W. Norton & Company, Inc.

The Philosophical Library for "The Meaning of 'To Make' and 'To Have' " from Existential Psychoanalysis by Jean-Paul Sartre, Copyright 1953 by the Philosophical Library.

Marie I. Rasey and Harper & Brothers for "Toward the End" from It Takes Time by Marie I. Rasey, Copyright 1953 by Harper & Brothers.

Carl R. Rogers and the Board of Trustees of Oberlin College for "What It Means to Become a Person" from Becoming a Person by Carl R. Rogers, Copyright 1954 by the Board of Trustees of Oberlin College.

TO DOROTHY LEE
who, being free
frees others to be

CONTENTS

THE CONTRIBUTORS

GORDON W. ALLPORT, a Professor of Psychology at Harvard University, has incorporated a personalistic, humanistic view in personality theory, as presented in his most recent book, *Becoming*.

ANDRAS ANGYAL, a psychiatrist and psychotherapist in private practice in Boston, has created a theoretical structure through which the individual personality may be fully realized.

ERICH FROMM, a psychoanalyst with deep interest in underlying human ethics, values, and intrinsic conscience, has written important books on the subject. His most recent, *The Sane Society,* is a continuation of the ideas in *Escape From Freedom.*

KURT GOLDSTEIN, a psychiatrist and neurologist in New York City, is currently interested in basic ideas for an organismic psychotherapy in the treatment of nervous disease. He has brought new meaning to the concept of health as the basic tendency toward self-actualization.

KAREN HORNEY (1885–1952) viewed inner strivings as positive, and created a psychoanalytic orientation which saw the individual as a continually growing person, responding to constructive cultural influences as well as neurotic trends in society.

CARL G. JUNG, of the Jung Institute for Analytical Psychology in Zurich, Switzerland, continues to present his unique ideas in personality theory and their relevance to a world view.

PRESCOTT LECKY (1892–1941) pioneered in the study of unity and self-consistency and developed the conception that the individual must define for himself the nature of that totality which he is. His work has become known to the world largely through the efforts of his students.

DOROTHY LEE is an anthropologist at the Merrill-Palmer school. Her conceptions of being and the self emerge from submersion into a personal experiencing of other cultures.

A. H. MASLOW, Professor of Psychology at Brandeis Universit , is the

ix

author of *Motivation and Personality*. Having devoted many of his earlier professional years to studying abnormal and deviant behavior, he is now especially interested in health as creativity and growth.

Ross L. Mooney, a Professor of Education at Ohio State University (Bureau of Educational Research), has been developing new and unusual principles and concepts of creative research.

Clark E. Moustakas, the editor of this volume, is a staff member of the Merrill-Palmer School. He is the psychologist in charge of play therapy with children, and in addition to psychotherapy with children and adults he supervises the clinical work of graduate students in child-centered play therapy and adult counseling.

Sarvepalli Radhakrishnan, Vice President of the Indian Republic, is interested in pure existence and absolute reality as Brahman philosophy. His striving has been toward unity and oneness of humanity and away from things that divide men, set them apart, and make them distrust one another.

Otto Rank (1884–1939) initiated many new and exciting developments in psychoanalytic theory and practice, and was among the first psychologists to stress the self-directive nature of growth.

Marie I. Rasey is a Professor of Education at Wayne University. Her merging of professional self and personal self enables her to express the meaning of learning and teaching. For many years she has dedicated herself to the potentialities of exceptional children at the Rayswift School.

Carl R. Rogers, Professor of Psychology and Executive Secretary of the Counseling Center, University of Chicago, initiated a basic philosophy of counseling and its application in a wide variety of settings. He is currently relating this philosophy to personal growth.

Jean-Paul Sartre, Existentialist philosopher, playwright, and editor of *Les Temps Moderne* in Paris, has expanded and elaborated the meaning of being from an existential point of view, as well as relating it to his own unusual approach to psychoanalysis.

David Smillie is a staff member at the Merrill-Palmer School. His chief interest currently is the construction of a theory of developmental psychology which includes human experience.

Rabindranath Tagore (1861–1941) dedicated his later life to encouraging peace throughout the world, calling upon nations to give up wars and exploitation and denouncing aggressive nationalism as a crime against humanity. He expressed principles of self-purification and self-realization in literary form, particularly in books of songs or lyric poetry.

FRANCES WILSON is a Professor in the Department of Child Development and Family Relations at Cornell University. Her current work is focused chiefly toward releasing potentials for aesthetic growth through art experience that encourages uniqueness and individuality.

PREFACE

Concern for the self with all its contributing attributes and potentials is rapidly becoming a central focus of contemporary psychological inquiry. More and more the interest is in the understanding of health and creativity as the exploration, expression, and realization of human talents. There is a gradual but definite movement throughout the world to understand individual well-being more fully.

Until recently study of abnormality, deviation, and illness have dominated psychological and psychiatric investigations. But conventional Freudian concepts, evocative as they are in attempting to explain hidden dynamics, have proved less than totally effective in application to healthy behavior, and frequently fail to correspond to actual behavioral patterns as seen in reality.

The selection of recent writings in this book portrays the fundamental unity of personality and presents a framework for understanding healthy behavior. The emphasis is on knowing, exploring, and actualizing the self. The various papers represent unique theories of personality. The fact that so many people in different fields are arriving independently at the same theoretical conclusions proves their significance more effectively than any argument could. In these papers are referented many disciplines, arts, and schools of psychiatric, psychological, and philosophic thought which seem to be converging (and all at one point in time) upon an understanding of the self which is essentially the same in all cases. The approaches and vocabularies are different, yet a clear and fresh kernel of common awareness and positive insight into the self is coming to characterize current knowledge of the human individual.

My own experience in editing these papers has been an unusual one. The book started as an anthology or symposium, to help me and others know more about the self. As I worked with the material, I realized I cannot know *about* the self. I can only *know* the self. I believe this knowing of the self has been the nature of my experience with this volume, not an experience of the various writings but a true experiencing of the persons through their writings.

What started out to be a "collection of papers" on the self became an exciting, satisfying, and at times painful and exhausting experience. What began as an approach to point to for others, became a journey in feeling-insights and in broadened perspective for myself. My search led me to experience anew, and reaffirm, values I had known in Dorothy Lee's discussion of being, and the significance in valuing sheer being in itself. It also led me to reaffirm Maslow's portrayal of the self-actualizer and his unyielding trust in intrinsic nature; Marie Rasey's sensitive, personal account of her own growth as a teacher, and the inherent brotherhood of life; Gordon Allport's elaborations of the destructive tendencies in analysis, and the inadequacies of past histories; Prescott Lecky's pioneering studies of self-consistency and his proclamation that resistance is health. Also Andras Angyal's poetic perceptions of the person as an organized patterned process with tendencies toward increased autonomy; and Karen Horney's belief that, given a chance, the individual tends to develop his human potentialities.

I had intended to use a different paper of Carl Rogers to point to what had been a significant experience for me, but as usual, Rogers' empathic nature brought me to another "discovery" which fitted movingly into my own experience as a psychotherapist. He expressed more fully my own experiencing of feeling all the way to the limit. I recognized for myself that empathy was not enough, that the other person must be fully *experienced*. Rogers' emphasis on the open self met my own stress on *true* experience and touched off a new orientation for me.

Another phase in my search began when I "rediscovered" the works of Fromm, Rank, and Goldstein. I had remembered vividly Erich Fromm's discerning passages on man's ineradicable striving to be himself, but in my earlier "experience" I was unready, unable to perceive the impact or meaning of the indivisibility between self and other and between unique and universal, with all the implications this has for personal and world growth.

Rank, I thought I had "studied" carefully, but I had truly experienced little of his penetrating discussion of self-determination. And Goldstein's lucid presentation of the so-called drives put into words what I have felt to be true, that mere discharge or release of tensions cannot be characteristic of healthy life. This emphasis, along with his discussion of decentering, opened new vistas of thought and potential insight. With Jung, it was a different matter. My perception of Jung was dim and partial. I cannot say I "rediscovered" Jung, for he had never really "existed" for me. Then his paper on personality came as a complete revelation. Here was Jung speaking for me a meaningful language which I could feel, touch, perceive, know in my own experience. His discussion of the inner voice of man, the essential creativity of potential man, the personality as being, were especially meaningful. His declaration that "what was *good* made what is *better* evil," was something I needed to do further thinking with. This work encouraged me to go "back" to re-read and "out" to explore more fully his more recent papers.

Then there was my investigation of existentialism which proved stimulating and challenging, giving me a different and unusual perspective as well as a feeling that here was material appropriate to an exploration of personal growth. Yet I was unable to find just the *right* paper until I happened upon Sartre's "The Meaning of 'To Make' and 'To Have': Possession," with its view of possession as an internal bond of being, a unique reality of possessor and possessed.

At this point Maslow's unpublished paper, "Personality Problems and Personality Growth," arrived and made me keenly aware of what it means to be human and how it becomes necessary to develop problems in loud protest against the crushing of one's psychological bones, of one's true nature, in reaction to "adjustment." It was Maslow's reference to Fromm's intrinsic unconscious that took me back to Fromm and the full realization that moral values were intrinsic to man's existence, and not solely the product of parental teaching.

Maslow also led me to Mooney and Wilson. Mooney has deeply and sensitively expanded and extended my beginning awareness of the possibilities for creative research in personal experience and personal growth. Mooney has also pointed the way to scientific inquiry along the dimensions of openness, self-realization, control, and aesthetic value. Frances Wilson, with her enthusiasm and fire, literally moved me through exciting explorations. It seemed so clear to me that even while she wrote, she was groping for meaningful expressions and developing ideas, becoming. She helped me to discover being in art experience in a deeper way than I have ever considered, though my own work with children in play therapy has given me moments of complete silence and reverie and absorption in their art expressions. She showed me how true art expression is in self-exploration and utterance; to *use* art in any way is to violate its nature and make it into what it is not.

Dr. Jayaswal, of the University of Lucknow, introduced me to the Indian writings on the self. It was difficult to select from the papers he sent me the two included in this volume, but for me they expressed most clearly what I could perceive as substantial and real. Tagore, in his quiet, contemplative manner, opened new vistas of meaning with poetic insights on the false nature of abstraction, analysis, and sameness. He gave me much to contemplate on and hope for in his view that life is here to express the eternal in us; that the reality of the world belongs to man; and that man can express his infinity in everything around him. Radhakrishnan further extended and elaborated my perception of being and becoming in his emphasis that the individual and his world coexist and subsist together. Subject and object are one in experience, and uniqueness and universality grow together until the most unique becomes the most universal.

My experience with David Smillie was again something new. For while I was on a journey of my own of self-growth through others, he was trying to find a way for himself to express two reality viewpoints. Even while his "immanent orientation" was taking form, falling into a configuration or pattern, his ideas were in a constant state of transition. Each day a more elaborated, truer picture of his own self-experience was taking form. I felt privileged to be able to live this experience with him as he frequently "sent" me to more fully consider my own immanent self and the direction of the journey of this book. I remember one day he said that he did not know how his immanent orientation would turn out when he began to explore his thoughts. He let his perceptions, his meanings, simply emerge from him as he touched the keys of the typewriter. But there were many agonizing moments later when he saw that though new thoughts sprang from him, the words did not always adequately express his experience.

All of these papers are for me deeply personal, exploratory, aesthetic, creative. One sees the personality of the individual in and through his writing, and the groping, searching nature of the persons. I view them as explorations in personal growth, of real people. To me the book has come to be a natural, spontaneous, creative expression of self as totality. It stresses the positive, healthy, growing potentials of the individual. It indicates the essential equality of intrinsic nature and its expression in uniqueness and variation, in differences. It presents the self as unified, consistent expression, as unique, personal experience, undifferentiated and undivided. The self is explored or expressed in personal conviction and discovery, as being and becoming. My valuing of intrinsic nature, individuality, and true experience has been strengthened.

This book was unplanned and without purpose, unless one conceives the "growing self" as purposive. Yet it contains something unified, whole in my experience, as I have tried to set forth in the concluding pages. It does not contain all the essential explorations of personal growth. I am hoping many more will be brought to my attention and make it possible for me to further discover meaning — of intrinsic nature, being, and becoming — through the experience of others.

If the reader wishes to have a more detailed picture of the basic theme, I suggest he turn to the concluding summarizing chapter.

I have, for the sake of readability, taken the liberty of deleting from some of these essays material not relevant to the theme of the book. Since this has been done with the permission of the authors and publishers, I have omitted ellipses where the deletions occur.

I wish once again to express my thanks to the various contributors acknowledged on the copyright page for their kind permission to use this material. I must thank, also, the following authors for permission to use their unpublished papers: A. H. Maslow, for "Personality Problems and Personality Growth"; David Smillie, for "Truth and Reality from Two Points of View"; and Frances Wilson, for "Human Nature and Aesthetic Growth." And Dorothy Lee for permission to use "Being and Value in a Primitive Society," originally published in The Journal of Philosophy.

I would like further to thank A. H. Maslow for his guiding inspiration throughout the many transformations of the book.

And finally, I must express heartfelt acknowledgment to Mrs. Pauline Park Wilson Knapp, Director (and the Merrill-Palmer School), whose philosophy incorporates principles of growth which make this kind of exploration possible, and to Betty Moustakas, my wife, who lived it with me.

CLARK E. MOUSTAKAS

THE SELF

TRUE EXPERIENCE AND THE SELF

CLARK E. MOUSTAKAS

Experience is true to the person when he is himself alone. In such experience perception is unique and undifferentiated. The individual is free to discover and express his potentialities. In true experience every expression is creative, the creation of the person one is and is becoming. There is only the exploring, spontaneously expressing self, finding satisfaction in personal being.

There are no goals to pursue, directions to follow, or techniques to use. There is the growing, experiencing self, significance and meaning in personal experience, and exploration and discovery. True experience may be understood through empathy in communal living or in self-expression or utterance. But it cannot be communicated. To communicate the self is to abstract from it, speak of its aspects or parts and thus do violence to it. Communication represents or symbolizes the self. It distinguishes, compares, and characterizes. Communication is used to influence and often to change. Communication requires explanation, analysis, description, and clarification. It must make what is known by one person common to be understood. The self is not its symbol or external behavior. The self is itself alone existing as a totality and constantly emerging. It can be understood only as unique personal experience. Self-expression is not persuasive and is without special purpose or function. The self is undifferentiated in time and space. It is being,

3

becoming, moving, undivided from the world of nature or the social world.

True being is self and other, individual and universal, personal and cultural. It cannot be understood by comparison, evaluation, diagnosis, or analysis. Such an approach breaks up an experience and violates its nature.

From the beginning the human person wants to feel that his who-ness is respected and his individuality is treasured. Too often the person is respected for what he represents in intelligence, achievement, or social status. This distorts the real nature of the person and interferes with human understandingness. It blocks the potential forces that exist within the person for creativity, for unique, peculiar, and idiosyncratic expression.

True growth, actualization of one's potential, occurs in a setting where the person is felt and experienced as sheer personal being. In such an atmosphere the person is free to explore his capacities and to discover for himself meanings and values of life consistent with the self.

In spite of all the advances in tests and measurements and in analyzing human behavior, understanding the person from his own point of view, in the light of his own unique experience, is the most real way of knowing him. More and more we are realizing that the self-expression of the individual in true experience is complete in itself. To see the person as he sees himself is the deepest way to know him and respect him.

Even the growing evidence, however, has not helped us to feel more trust in individual self-expression. The tendency remains to rely heavily on external measures. Recently Allport [2]* reported a series of studies in which the great need for food among men on a starvation diet failed to be uncovered on tests given these men. The number of food associations actually declined with longer periods of fasting. No one would question the importance of strong hunger

---

* Notes refer to numbered bibliographies at the end of each chapter.

in motivating behavior, yet it could not be determined without approaching the men directly and asking them to tell about this important need.

Adler [1] once wrote that the only people who really know human nature are those who have experienced the worth and value of others through their own empathy. Correspondence of perceptual experience is perhaps the best basis for understanding what an experience means to another individual, but without such similarity of perception we can still know the meanings that experiences have for others through listening with objectivity and warmth, through attempting to understand the essence of the experience through the perceptions of the other person. Objectivity as used here refers to seeing what an experience is for another person, not how it fits or relates to other experiences, not what causes it, why it exists, or for what purpose. It is an attempt to see attitudes and concepts, beliefs and values of an individual as they are to him, not what they were or will become. The experience of the other person as he perceives it is sufficient unto itself, true and of value as itself, understood in terms of itself.

Knowing the content of individual experience does not explain the unique meaning or totality any more than knowing that a tree has a trunk and branches tells how it will be perceived by the different people who see it. The "facts" regarding human behavior have little meanings in themselves. It is the manner in which they are perceived and known that tells how they will be expressed in behavior. Experiments at the Hanover Institute have shown that we do not get our perceptions from the things around us, but that our perceptions come from us.[7] There is no reality except individual reality and that is based on a background of unique experience.

It sometimes requires complex and thorough examination to diagnose tuberculosis, cancer, or a heart ailment in an individual, but knowing the presence of such a serious illness does not tell what it will mean in the life of an individual or his family. A group of physicians may find it easy to communicate with each other regarding the nature of an illness, but difficult to talk to patients when they have not taken into account the perceptions the patient has of his illness. To the extent that physicians fail to consider the personal experiences and meanings of the individual, they do not understand the full nature of the illness and often talk in authoritative terms disclosing their lack of real knowledge. These physicians show complete faith in the object or the part which has medical significance but little recognition of the person as a unique, special individual who in some ways is unlike any other person who has had a painful disease. When the physician doubts the impact of the individual's self-perception on his illness, he distrusts the potential curative powers within the person and his striving for health. This threatens the strength of being and self-confidence of the individual.

Facts regarding human living gain their full value when examined in the context of unique individual experience. Most experts are expert in pointing out facts, in making evaluations and diagnoses, but when they fail to recognize that facts gain their meaning in a personal context and these meanings differ for different individuals, then they fail to understand fully the true nature of the fact. When experts discard the individual's discrete experiences as insignificant, they often make generalizations about human growth and development which contradict the true nature of the person. Or they give recommendations which are inconsistent with the individual's purposes and values and interfere with his growth. These recommendations based on "facts" cannot be accepted and utilized and sometimes frighten and disturb the person.

In the final analysis the individual must know for himself the totality that he is. He alone has had touch with all his experiences. He alone knows his feelings and thoughts and what his experiences mean to him. The meaning depends on the values involved in the situation, event, or experience and these values come from the person's personal background. The individual alone can tell the true meaning of his experience.

There is a tendency among analytic people to see an individual in terms of someone else — his father, mother, or siblings. This approach distorts the real nature of the person and interferes with valid understanding of him. One does not recognize the otherness of a person as a reality by projecting into him someone else or by abstracting out of him transferred feelings and attitudes. And when one sees in a person his father or mother or anyone else, one ignores the person as he really is. Angyal[3] regards this as a fundamental disregard for and destructive attitude toward the other person. He points out that real understanding of the other person is not some sort of shrewd analysis which has a keen eye for the weaknesses of people but a deep perception of the core, of the essential nature of the other person as he is.

All psychological phenomena can be understood as illustrative of the single principle of unity or self-consistency.[8] When the individual is free to be himself his acts are always consistent with his values. No matter what we are told, our own perceptions of ourselves will always seem substantial and solid to us.[11] Resistance is a way for the individual to maintain consistency of self in the light of external pressure. It is a healthy response, a sign that the will of the individual is still intact. It is an effort by the individual to sustain the integrity of the self. When the individual submits without wanting to submit, he is weakened and unable to function effectively. Conformity blocks creativity while freedom and spontaneity foster growth.

Rank[10] stressed the importance of positive will expression. He believed that the denial of will expression is the essence of neurosis. His aim was to strengthen will, not weaken it. In the light of external pressures (attempts to frighten and even terrify the person, to force him to submit to symbols, standards, and values outside himself) which, yielded to, may mean disintegration of self and destruction of will, the individual must often call upon the forces within himself, follow his internal cues, awareness, and direction, maintain his position and assert himself in order not to seriously distort his essence, his being. When the individual submits while the very core of his existence cries out against submission, the health and stability of the person is seriously impaired and he is often unable to think, decide, or act. Sometimes he becomes the expectations, convictions, and values of others.

It is within the nature of the individual to actualize himself and become whatever he is meant to be, to explore his individual potential as fully as possible.[5, 6] He will resist all attempts to change him that threaten his perception of self, and will respond favorably to situations which permit him to express and explore his potentials. The individual will not respond to stimuli which are inadequate to him. Such stimuli can be effective only if they are very strong and force themselves upon him. Then the person is driven into a catastrophic situation not only because he is unable to react adequately but also because he is shocked and disturbed, sometimes so severely he is unable to react at all.[5] Thus when we force an individual to behave according to external values, when we impose our convictions on the other person, we impair his creativity and his will to explore and actualize.

Maintenance of the real self is of primary significance for the individual. It is the most stable consistent value in his life. The real self is the central core within each individual which is the deep source of growth.[6] To operate in terms of the persons we are is natural, comforting, and satisfying. It permits us to be creative, to utilize our capacities.

It is not possible to accept the other person and at the same time openly reject his values and ideas. Such a concept is antithetical to the consistency of self. We cannot separate the individual from his behavior and say that we accept him but do not accept his behavior.

This type of distinction is possible when the self is viewed in terms of categories instead of holism or unity. Individuals do not see themselves in categories. Behavior is self.

Sometimes people are forced to reject the behavior of another person and, therefore, to reject the person. This rejection may be less severe if one focuses on the behavior itself. However, by rejecting the behavior of the person, one cannot escape a rejection of the person himself. Even though this is so, if the rejection occurs only occasionally in a relationship and it is limited to the behavioral act while at the same time the feelings are recognized and accepted, a general attitude of acceptance can still exist and be conveyed.

In the face of drastic action that will markedly affect the behavior of the person, can the individual continue to be silent and objective or must he express his own convictions? Must he live by whoever he is? Integrity of the self is the main source of strength in the individual. To be untrue to oneself, dishonest, or insincere may result in self-impairment. When the self is threatened and endangered, continued attempts completely to accept the other might eventuate in a disorganization of oneself. Two teachers may be able to listen and accept one another's opposing approaches within the same school system as long as administrative changes which will affect their work are not contemplated. Two teachers with varying philosophies and ideas may be able to work effectively in adjacent rooms, but if they had to work with the same group of children at the same time, it would be difficult for them to accept one another's methods and work harmoniously.

The following principles summarize the basic approach and recognition of the self in true experience and the creation of human understandingness.

1. The individual knows himself better than anyone else.

2. Only the individual himself can develop his potentialities.

3. The individual's perception of his own feelings, attitudes, and ideas is more valid than any outside diagnosis can be.

4. Behavior can best be understood from the individual's own point of view.

5. The individual responds in such ways as to be consistent with himself.

6. The individual's perception of himself determines how he will behave.

7. Objects have no meaning in themselves. Individuals give meanings and reality to them. These meanings reflect the individual's background.

8. Every individual is logical in the context of his own personal experience. His point of view may seem illogical to others when he is not understood.

9. As long as the individual accepts himself, he will continue to grow and develop his potentialities. When he does not accept himself, much of his energies will be used to defend rather than explore and to actualize himself.

10. Every individual wants to grow toward self-fulfillment. These growth strivings are present at all times.

11. An individual learns significantly only those things which *are* involved in the maintenance or enhancement of *self*. No one can force the individual to permanent or creative learning. He will learn only if he wills to. Any other type of learning is temporary and inconsistent with the self and will disappear as soon as threat is removed.

12. Concepts, ideas, symbols, and events can be denied or distorted but experience is experienced in the unique reality of the individual person and cannot be untrue to itself. If it threatens the maintenance or enhancement of self, the experience will be of little relevance or consequence to the individual though it may temporarily stifle further growth.

13. We cannot teach another person directly and we cannot facilitate real learning in the sense of making it easier. We can make learning for another person possible by providing informa-

tion, the setting, atmosphere, materials, resources, and *by being* there. The learning process itself is a unique individualistic experience. It may be a difficult experience for the individual person even if it has significance for the enhancement of self.

14. Under threat the self is less open to spontaneous expression; that is, is more passive and controlled. When free from threat the self is more open, that is, free to be and to strive for actualization.

The educational situation which most effectively promotes significant learning is one in which (a) the threat to the self of the learner is at a minimum while at the same time the uniqueness of the individual is regarded as worthwhile and is deeply respected, and (b) the person is free to explore the materials and resources which are available to him in the light of his own interests and potentiality.

Most research studies on the self have been highly structured and intellectualized. An increasingly narrow definition is emerging. Descriptions imply and sometimes clearly state that a definition of self is self. Statements an individual can make about himself or that someone else makes about him are tabulated and the score an individual receives is interpreted as an expression of the individual's self. These reports abstract the self into such parts as "self-concept," "negative-self," "inferred-self," and "ideal-self." The self finally becomes limited to verbal statements and categories. Viewing the self as categories, characteristics, and in other abstractive ways makes such studies possible, but they do not enrich our understanding of the experience of self. Thus conceptions of self are shared, communicated, and conveyed in words but the natural, spontaneous immanence of self is somehow lost.

The self is not its definition or description but rather the central being of the individual person. The self is not definable in words. Any verbal analysis tends to categorize or segment the self into communicable aspects or parts. The self can only be experienced. Any attempt to convey its meaning verbally must be based on function or structure and on language which can be partially understood. Therefore comparison, relatedness, and association to situations and events are required in a communicable definition of self. When the self is understood only in words the experience of the self is lost. The self as experienced involves the totality of the individual. It is a natural, automatic, and complete expression, only partially available to verbal communication. Understanding of self is possible through unqualified perception and empathy, that is, human presence and being.

When the focus is placed on words of the self rather than on the self itself, the unique perception of the individual person as expressed in the totality of his behavior is not really understood. In such a setting the opportunity for fuller expression of uniqueness and individuality is threatened. When we attempt to abstract from our experience facts, knowledge, and information we tend to focus on limited aspects of experience which will have relevance to another person, which can be conveyed in precise words. In that way, we tend to close the possibility for fuller impact, meaning, and significance of experience as it influences us naturally and automatically in the pursuit and exploration of our potentialities.

Fromm [4] has emphasized that the duty to be alive is the same as the duty to become oneself. Somehow we do not have faith that if we simply permit a person to explore his interests in his own way he will become a truly human person. We fear that the individual will develop antisocial tendencies, emerge as inadequate, or become socially destructive. Autonomy is regarded with suspicion or distrust or simply interpreted and categorized as resistant behavior. We feel we have to condition the person, teach him directly, keep after him to socialize him and make him behave like others. We do not trust ourselves or have enough confidence that our own personal experiences with children will provide a healthy basis for social growth. We do not accept our own being, we do not own the self, when we act on external standards, judgments, and expectations.

We seem satisfied when the child is like others and troubled when he turns out to be different.

Individuality must be encouraged, not stifled. Only what is true and therefore of value to society can emerge from individual interests, that is, expressions of one's true nature. All children may need love, safety, belongingness, acceptance, and respect as basic conditions to their growth, and when these conditions are provided by the human environment, growth will occur naturally through the person's potential. Adults may offer resources, make available opportunities, and give information and help when it is meaningful to the child, but to force standards, social values, and concepts on the child is to stifle his potential creativity and difference.

Relations must be such that the person is free to affirm, express, actualize, and experience his own uniqueness. Adults help to make this possible when they show they deeply care for him, respect his individuality, and accept the child's being without qualification. To permit the person to be and become is not to promote selfishness, but to affirm the person's truly human self.

Somehow we must remove the beliefs that make men mistrust themselves and each other. Being given the opportunity to grow and to actualize one's self provides the best basis for interacting with others, and within the framework of groups and society. When individuals are free to operate in terms of their real selves, they do not violate the trust that is conveyed to them. Under such an atmosphere, individual integrity is maintained and fostered and society is enriched. We must not accept as intrinsic an antagonism between individual interests and social interests. Maslow[9] has strongly emphasized that this kind of antagonism exists only in a sick society. But it need not be true. Individual and social interests are synergetic, *not* antagonistic. Creative individual expression, that is, expression of one's own intrinsic nature, results in social creativity and growth which in turn encourage and free the individual to further self-expression and discovery.

REFERENCES

1. Adler, Alfred. *Understanding Human Nature.* New York: Greenberg, Publishers, Inc., 1927.
2. Allport, Gordon W. The Trend in Motivational Theory. *American Journal of Orthopsychiatry,* 23:107-119 (1953).
3. Angyal, Andras. "A Theoretical Model for Personality Studies." *Journal of Personality,* 20:131-141 (1951).
4. Fromm, Erich. *Man For Himself: An Inquiry Into the Psychology of Ethics.* New York: Rinehart and Company, Inc., 1947.
5. Goldstein, Kurt. *Human Nature: In the Light of Psychotherapy.* Cambridge: Harvard University Press, 1940.
6. Horney, Karen. *Neurosis and Human Growth.* New York: W. W. Norton & Company, Inc., 1950.
7. Kelley, Earl C. *Education for What Is Real.* New York: Harper & Brothers, 1947.
8. Lecky, Prescott. *Self-Consistency: A Theory of Personality.* Frederick C. Thorne, ed. New York: Island Press, 1951.
9. Maslow, A. H. The Instinctoid Nature of Basic Needs. *Journal of Personality,* 22:326-347 (March 1954).
10. Rank, Otto. *Will Therapy.* New York: Alfred A. Knopf, 1936.
11. Rogers, Carl R. *Client-centered Therapy.* Boston: Houghton Mifflin Company, 1951.

II THE SO-CALLED DRIVES

KURT GOLDSTEIN

We have to deal with a difficult problem here. The pertinent discussion in psychiatric literature is in a state of confusion, making it difficult to obtain any orientation on this basis. Therefore, let us look at some phenomena in pathology and see what we can learn from observations on patients concerning the essential problem in question, namely: Toward what are the drives driving?

DRIVES AS RELEASE OF TENSION — A PATHOLOGICAL PHENOMENON

Observations in patients present us with a phenomenon important for the theory of drives. The sick person has the tendency to avoid catastrophic reactions, because these are even more dangerous for him than for normals. He is not able to bear them, and he is hindered by them to a much higher degree than normals in the execution of performances. He therefore tries to avoid them. Many peculiarities of patients are understandable only from this condition. Catastrophic situations are especially favored by abnormal tensions in any field. In pathology abnormal tensions occur relatively often in single fields, because reactions tend to take place in isolated parts and because the process of equalization is disturbed. Therefore the sick organism tends especially to remove abnormal tensions, and seems to be *governed by the drive to do that*. For example, the sick suffering from a tension in the sex sphere seem

15

to be forced, above all, to release this tension. From such observations arose the idea that it is the real goal of all drives to alleviate and to discharge the tension, and to bring the organism into a state of nontension, i.e., *it is the goal of the drive to release itself.*

In the state of isolation, as in sick people, the discharge of tension is in the foreground: the tendency to *remove* any arising tension prevails. In sound life, however, the result of the normal equalization process is the *formation* of a certain level of tension, that which makes possible further ordered activity.

The tendency to discharge any tension whatsoever is an expression of a defective organism, of disease. It is the only means of the sick organism to actualize itself, even if in an imperfect way. Such a state is possible only with the support of other organisms. It will be remembered what we have said about the fact that the life of a sick organism, its entire existence, depends upon other organisms. This shows clearly that life under such conditions is not normal life, and that mere discharge or release of tensions cannot be a characteristic of normal life.

The "Drive for Self-Preservation" — A Pathological Phenomenon

The basic tendency of the sick organism is to utilize the *preserved* capacities in the best possible way, considered in relation to the normal nature of the organism concerned. The behavior of patients is to be understood only from such a viewpoint. We can say an organism is governed by the tendency to actualize as much as possible its individual capacities, its "nature" in the world. This nature is what we call the psychosomatic constitution, and as far as considered during a certain phase it is the individual pattern, the "character" which the respective constitution has attained in the course of experience. This tendency to actualize its nature, to *actualize "itself," is the basic drive, the only drive by which the life of the organism is determined.* This tendency undergoes in the *sick* human being a characteristic change. The patient's scope of life is reduced in two ways: (1) He is driven to utilize his *preserved* capacities in the best possible way. (2) He is driven to maintain a certain state of living, and not to be disturbed in this condition. Therefore sick life is very bare of productivity, development, and progress, and bare of the characteristic particularities of normal organismic and especially human life. Frequently, the law of maintaining the existent state — the self-preservation — is considered as the basic law of life. I believe such a concept could arise only because one had assumed as a starting point the experiences in abnormal conditions or experimental situations. The tendency to maintain the existent state is characteristic for sick people and is a sign of anomalous life, of decay of life. The tendency of normal life is toward activity and progress. For the sick, the only form of self-actualization which remains is the maintenance of the existent state. That, however, is not the tendency of the normal. It might be that sometimes the normal organism also tends primarily to avoid catastrophes, and to maintain a certain state which makes that possible; but this takes place under inadequate conditions and is not at all the usual behavior. Under adequate conditions the normal organism seeks further activity.

Only One Drive: Self-Actualization

Normal behavior corresponds to a continual change of tension, of such a kind that over and again that state of tension is reached which enables and impels the organism to actualize itself in further activities, according to its nature.

Thus, experiences with patients teach us that we have *to assume only one drive, the drive of self-actualization,* and that the goal of the drive is not a discharge of tension. Under various conditions different actions come into the foreground. They seem to be directed toward different goals, and they thereby give the impression of independently existing drives. In reality, however, these different actions occur in accordance with the various capacities which belong to the nature of the organism, and occur in accordance with those instrumental processes which are then necessary prerequisites of the self-actualization of the organism.

The concept of different, separate drives is based especially upon two groups of observations — observations on young children, and on animals under experimental conditions. That is, observations are made under circumstances which represent a decentering of the functioning of the organism. They are derived from a condition which we have characterized as favoring an abnormal "coming into relief" of activities corresponding to the functioning of isolated parts of the organism.

DISCHARGE OF SPECIAL TENSION — A PHENOMENON OF DEFECTIVE CENTERING

Let us first consider the observations in children. We often have the impression that the actions of infants, in the beginning of life, are directed toward the goal of discharging a tension. Tension and removal of tension can be observed in the whole behavioral aspect of the child in pertinent situations. In a situation of hunger or thirst the child appears governed by the desire to release those tensions corresponding to the phenomenal goals — for instance, sucking. In another example, the child appears satisfied only if he can grasp the object by which he is stirred up. But we should never forget that such descriptions of the behavior of children always lack certainty. More accurately stated, *we do not know anything definite about the child's reactions, about what is really the stimulus for the child, about the desires or needs by which it is driven, and by what reactions they are released.* Let us look at some facts. For instance, there is the first turning-to movement of the head, which we believe can be explained as simple equalization. Here we might assume as the essential factor of the process the release of a tension produced by the stimulus. It may be that in such reactions the infant also experiences some tension and the release of it. The situation changes, however, when the infant becomes more mature. Then the character of the head-turning is totally different.

It is difficult to say how many of the reactions of the infant are reactions of "single tension release." I like to regard the first grasping reactions of the baby as such an equalization phenomenon — as long as the grasping is restricted to objects placed in the hand of the baby, and the baby tends to hold the object without doing something else with it. The Moro response is a phenomenon of that kind.[1,2] If the interpretation of these reactions is correct, namely, that we have to deal with release phenomena, then we may speak here of *a drive for release* of a tension produced by a stimulus. However, to speak of a drive for release would state nothing concerning the character of drives in general. In the mentioned examples we are faced with phenomena under inadequate conditions — that is, during the stage of *immaturity* of an organism. We have no right to conclude from such observations anything about the natures of drives in adult life. One could say: The infant itself does not tend to grasp, but his hand separately grasps if it is stimulated, without the organism as a whole being concerned in the activity. In the case however where the infant tends to grasp the object if it is not placed in his hand, and then tries to use it in a way which corresponds to his capacities, we have to do not only with a discharge of a tension but also with the organism's tendency to come to terms with the object — not only with a reaction of a part of the organism but with a performance of the whole organism. What impulse in the infant might be satisfied by this action is difficult to say, but we are certainly not faced merely with a discharge of a tension. The same might be the case in sucking. Here especially, we seem to be justified in speaking of a release of a tension in one field. But are we sure that the sucking, with its effect — the intake of food — relieves only a desire for food? Perhaps it would be possible to describe the situation in the following way: The desire is only a partial aspect of a feeling of deficiency of the whole organism, which makes its activities, i.e., its self-actualization, impossible; and the sucking and the intake of food are the means of bringing the whole organism into a condition where it is able to perform again, corresponding to its nature. Then we should not speak of a special drive, but of a special condition of the entire organism. Such a description would be supported by facts. The observations of the infant lead us to assume that sucking is dependent upon the condition of the whole organism. It changes, corresponding to the changes of the condition of the whole organism. We could describe the whole phenomenon as a tension of the organism in general, which disturbs its functioning and finds its special expression in the desire for food. Thus the sucking act, as an action of the entire organism, brings the organism again into the state of being able to perform normally as a whole. Then we would have to consider, as the goal of the drive, the tendency to come into a condition in which the organism can perform normally, i.e., corresponding to its nature. The sucking movements would be suited to return the organism to this condition, because they are means for removing a certain disturbance. In that case we would have to deal not with a special drive and the release of it, but with a tendency to remove a condition which makes any adequate performance impossible. We would have to deal not with a discharge of any tension, but with the tendency to self-actualization that renders necessary, under certain conditions, some characteristic actions. We would have to deal with an action which is only one phase in the activities of the organism, that is, with activities that correspond to the process of actualization of its nature.

I cannot prove that the situation in children is of the type I have tried to characterize. However, I think that our explanation has at least the same degree of probability as the usual theory of drives, and I am inclined to assume that my interpretation rests more on facts. Be that as it may, our example illustrates that we have to be very careful in any derivation of a theory of drives from the behavior of children. It is so difficult to obtain a real insight into the condition in children that ultimate certainty here is not to be realized. Therefore we should be cautioned against drawing upon observations in children in considering the behavior of adults with regard to possible existence of drives.

This criticism must also make us cautious if we try to build up a theory of drives. We have to deal here with a condition of uttermost isolation, and all facts which are found in this state are liable to the above-mentioned fallacies of experimental observation under special conditions.

The impression of drives arises because the organism is governed at one time by one tendency, at another time by another; because one or the other tendency in the given condition becomes more important for self-actualization. This is especially the case when the organism is living under inadequate conditions. If a human being is forced to live in a state of hunger for a long time, or if there are conditions in his body which produce a strong hunger feeling so that he is urged to relieve this feeling, the self-actualization of his whole personality is disturbed. Then he appears as if under a hunger drive. The same may be the case with sex.

A normal organism, however, is able to repress the hunger feeling or the sex urge if it has something very important to do, the neglect of which would bring the whole organism into danger. The behavior of a normal individual is to be understood only if considered from the viewpoint that those performances are always fulfilled that are most important for the organism. That presupposes a normal centering of the organism and a normal, adequate environment. Because these conditions are not always fulfilled, even in normal life, the organism might often appear to be governed transitorily by a special tendency. In this case we have to deal not with a normal situation, but with an emergency situation, one which gives the impression of a special, isolated drive. This is particularly to be found if the organism is not allowed to actualize one or the other potentialities for an abnormally long time, as for example if the reception of food is hindered a long time. Then the harmonious attitude of the organism to the outer world might be thrown out of gear. The individual is thereby driven to fulfill that potentiality because only in this way can the existence of the organism be guaranteed. We are confronted here with a behavior where only those activities prevail that are important for mere existence in situations of danger. But these are not the activities by which normal behavior can be understood.

From our discussion, I think we are in no way forced to assume the existence of special drives. I believe the facts that are taken as foundations for the assumption of different drives are more or less abstractions from the natural behavior of the organism. They are special reactions in special situations, and represent the various forms in which the organism as a whole expresses itself.

The traditional view assumes various drives which come into the foreground under certain conditions. We assume only one drive, the drive for self-actualization of the organism; but we are compelled to concede that under certain conditions the tendency to actualize one potentiality is so strong that the organism is governed by it. Superficially therefore, our theory may not appear so much in conflict with others. However, I think there is an essential difference. From our standpoint, we can understand the latter phenomenon as an abnormal deviation from the normal behavior under definite conditions; but the theory of separate drives can never comprehend normal behavior without positing another agency which makes the decision in the struggle between the single drives. That means: Any theory of drives has to introduce another, a "higher" agency. We must reject this auxiliary hypothesis as unsuitable to solve the problem. "The tendency of the organism to actualize itself" always confronts us with the same answer. We do not need the drives.

POTENTIALITIES ("CAPACITIES") AND SELF-ACTUALIZATION, TENDENCY TO PERFECTION.

We reject the theory of drives from still another point of view: If one of these potentialities,* or one which we can abstract from the whole of the organism, is taken as a distinct faculty we fall into the errors of faculty psychology. This isolation changes the capacity, exaggerates it in the same way as every behavioral aspect is changed when isolated from the rest of the organism. And starting from the phenomena to be observed in such situations of isolation, we can never understand the behavior. False concepts arise, such as the determining importance of single drives, sex or power, etc. A judgment about such phenomena as sex and power is to be made only if one considers them outside of their appearance in isolation and looks at their appearance in the natural life of the organism where they present themselves as embedded in the activities of the *organism as a whole*. With this approach to the problem, the way (most often obstructed by some preconceived idea of isolated drives) is free for new investigations. That should be the essential outcome of our critique.

What are usually called drives are tendencies corresponding to the capacities and the nature of the organism, and the environment in which the organism is living at a given time. It is better that we speak of "needs." The organism has definite potentialities, and because it has them it has the need to actualize or realize them. The fulfillment of these needs represents the self-actualization of the organism.

The needs are further determined by the situation in which the organism has to realize itself. The intensity with which one or the other potentiality is realized depends on its significance for the self-realization of the organism in the given moment. A comparison between the potency of different needs can therefore not be estab-

* Henceforth the terms potentiality and capacity will be used interchangeably.

lished without the consideration of the particular situation. It seems to me doubtful whether it is really possible to assume a fixed hierarchy of needs. Certainly the organism will be forced to satisfy the physiological needs if he is in danger of perishing; under such circumstances no other needs may be effective. But that would be a special situation, one that does not correspond to the normal life of the organism. When there is, for self-realization, the necessity to fulfill another need, then even the physiological needs may not come to the fore.

Thus we come to the solution: we do not need to assume different drives; we can even omit the term "drive"; it is sufficient to understand the coming to the fore of different needs by determination of the particular form of self-realization.

REFERENCES

1. Goldstein, K., Landis, C., Hunt, W., and Clark, F. "Moro Reflex and Startle Pattern." Archives of Neurology and Psychiatry, 40:322-327 (1938).
2. Goldstein, K. "A Further Comparison of the Moro Reflex." Journal of Psychology, 6:33-42 (1938).

III THE TREND IN MOTIVATIONAL THEORY

GORDON W. ALLPORT

Motivational theory today seems to be turning a corner in the road of scientific progress. In attempting to characterize this change in direction I wish to pay special attention to the problem of psychodiagnostic methods. For the successes and failures of these methods can teach us much about psychodynamic theory.

Let us start by asking why projective methods are so popular in both diagnostic practice and research. The answer, I think, is to be found in the history of motivational theory during the past century. All of the major influences have pressed in a single direction. Schopenhauer, with his doctrine of the primacy of the blind will, had little respect for the rationalizations invented by the individual's intellect to account for his conduct. Motives, he was sure, could not be taken at their face value. Darwin followed with his similar anti-intellectual .emphasis on primordial struggle. McDougall refined the Darwinian stress on instinct, retaining in his horme the flavor of Schopenhauer's will, Darwin's struggle for survival, Bergson's *élan*, and Freud's libido. All these writers were irrationalists — confident that underlying genotypes in motivation should be sought rather than the surface phenotypes. All of them were reacting against the naïve intellectualism of their predecessors and against the rationalizations offered by self-justifying mortals when called on to account for their conduct. Among these irrationalists who have dominated Western psychology for the past century Freud, of course, has been the leading figure. He, like the others, correctly perceived that the mainsprings of conduct may be hidden from the searchlight of consciousness.

In addition to irrationalism modern dynamic psychology has developed another earmark: geneticism. The original instincts laid down in our nature are regarded as decisive or, if not, then the experiences of early childhood are held to be crucial. At this point, the leading nondynamic school of thought, stimulus-response psychology, joins forces with geneticism. Stimulus-response theorists agree with instinct psychologists and psychoanalysts in viewing adult motives as conditioned, reinforced, sublimated, or otherwise elaborated editions of instincts, drives, or of an id whose structure, Freud said, "never changes."

Not one of these dominating theories of motivation allows for an essential transformation of motives in the course of life. McDougall explicitly denied the possibility; for our motivational structure is laid down once and for all in our equipment of instincts. New objects may become attached to an instinct through learning, but the motive power is always the same. Freud's position was essentially identical. The concept of "sublimation" and of shifting object "cathexis" chiefly accounted for whatever apparent alterations occur. Stimulus-response psychology is likewise geared to the assumption of remote control operating out of the past. We respond only to objects that have been associated with primary drives in the past, and we do so only in proportion to the degree that our responses have been rewarded or gratified in the past. From the stimulus-response point of view the individual can hardly be said to be *trying* to do anything at all. He is simply *responding* with a complex array of habits that somehow were rewarded year before last. The prevailing dictum that motivation is always a matter of "tension reduction" or of "seeking equilibrium" is consistent with this point of view, but scarcely consistent, I think, with all the known facts.

This prevailing atmosphere of theory has engendered a kind of contempt for the "psychic surface" of life. The individual's conscious report is rejected as untrustworthy, and the contemporary thrust of his motives is disregarded in favor of a backward tracing of his conduct to earlier formative stakes. The individual loses his right to be believed. And while he is busy leading his life in the present with a forward thrust into the future, most psychologists have become busy tracing it backward into the past.

It is now easy to understand why the special methods invented by Jung (forty years ago), Rorschach (thirty years ago), and Murray (twenty years ago) were seized upon with enthusiasm by psychodiagnosticians. At no point do these methods ask the subject what his interests are, what he wants to do, or what he is trying to do. Nor do the methods ask directly concerning the subject's relation to his parents or to authority figures. They infer this relationship entirely by assumed identifications. So popular is this indirect, undercover approach to motivation that many clinicians and many university centers spend far more time on this type of diagnostic method than on any other.

Occasionally, however, a client may cause the projective tester consternation by intruding his unwanted conscious report. The story is told of a patient who remarked that a Rorschach card made him think of sexual relations. The clinician, thinking to tap a buried complex, asked him why. "Oh, because," said the patient, "I think of sexual relations all the time anyway." The clinician scarcely needed a Rorschach card to find out this motivational fact.

Still it is probably true that most psychologists prefer to assess a person's needs and conflicts by going the long way around. The argument, of course, is that everyone, even a neurotic, will accommodate himself fairly well to the demands placed upon him by reality. Only in an unstructured projective situation will he reveal his anxieties and unmasked needs. "Projective tests," writes Stagner, "are more useful than reality situations for diagnostic purposes." [16] To my mind this uncompromising statement seems to mark the culmination of a century-long era of irrationalism, and therefore of distrust. Has the subject no right to be believed?

Fortunately, the extensive use of projective methods at the present time is yielding results that enable us to place this technique in proper perspective, and to correct the one-sided theory of motivation upon which their popularity rests.

Let us consider first the wartime research conducted with thirty-six conscientious objectors who lived for six months on a semi-starvation diet.[5] Their diet was so rigorously meager that on the average they lost one quarter of their initial body weight in the course of the six months. The food need was agonizingly great; their incessant hunger most poignant. Unless occupied with laboratory or other tasks they found themselves thinking of food almost constantly. Typical daydreaming is reported by one subject as follows: "Today we'll have Menu No. 1. Gee, that's the smallest menu, it seems. How shall I fix the potatoes? If I use my spoon to eat them I'll be able to add more water. . . . If I eat a little faster the food would stay warm longer — and I like it warm. But then it's gone so quickly." Now the curious thing is that while these men were clearly obsessed by their food drive, and all their energy seemed directed toward its fulfillment, yet on projective tests the need failed to appear. The investigators report that among the tests used (free word association, first letters test, analysis of dreams, Rorschach, and Rosenzweig's P-F Study) only one gave a limited evidence of the preoccupation with food, viz., the free association test.

Here is a finding of grave significance. *The most urgent, the most absorbing motive in life failed completely to reveal itself by indirect methods.* It was, however, entirely accessible to conscious report. Part of the explanation may be that the subjects turned in relief to laboratory tasks to forget for a while their obsessive motive. They responded to the projective tests with heaven knows what available, habitual associational material. The failure of night dreams to reveal a significant amount of wish fulfillment is somewhat more perplexing. It can scarcely be ascribed to a defensive mental set. But both types of result suggest a possible law: Unless a motive is repressed it is unlikely to affect distinctively the perception of, and responses to, a projective test. It is too early to tell whether this is a valid generalization, but it is a hypothesis well worth testing.

Other studies on hunger seem to yield supporting evidence.[11, 15] Their trend suggests that on projective tests the number of explicit food associations actually declines in longer periods of fasting, apparently because the motive itself gradually becomes completely conscious and is not repressed. It is true that instrumental associations (ways of obtaining food) continue to appear in the subject's word-responses as the state of hunger grows. This finding, however, is quite consistent with the hypothesis, since while hunger is fully conscious, the subject in the experimental situation is prevented from seeking satisfaction, and thus is still repressing his instrumental action-tendencies.

Another revealing line of evidence comes from the research of J. W. Getzels.[6] This investigator utilized two forms of a sentence completion test — one couched in the first person and one in the third. His pairs are of the following type:

When they asked Frank to be in charge he ——
When they asked me to be in charge I ——

When Joe meets a person for the first time he usually ——
When I meet a person for the first time I usually ——

In this experiment, of course, the items were randomized. In all there were twenty diagnostic items of each type. The subjects were sixty-five veterans, twenty-five diagnosed as well adjusted; forty were psychoneurotic cases discharged from service with a disability involving personality disorder.

It turned out that to a highly significant degree the well-adjusted men gave *identical* responses to the first and to the third person completions. If we assume that the third-person sentence is a "projective method" then the results obtained by this method for well-adjusted subjects squared almost perfectly with the results obtained from the direct, first-person questioning. The psychoneurotics, on the other hand, to a highly significant degree varied their responses. They said one thing when queried directly (e.g., "When they asked me to be in charge I agreed") and another on the projective item (e.g., "When they asked John to be in charge he was afraid"). The first-person completion is so direct that in the psychoneurotic it invokes the mask of defense and elicits a merely conventionally correct response.

Thus the direct responses of the psychoneurotic cannot be taken at their face value. The defenses are high, the true motives are hidden and are betrayed only by a projective technique. The normal subjects, on the other hand, tell you by the direct method precisely what they tell you by the projective method. They are all of a piece. You may therefore take their motivational statements at their face value, for even if you probe you will not find anything substantially different.

This research adds weight to the tentative judgment we formed in the case of the starving subjects. It is not the well-integrated subject, aware of his motivations, who reveals himself in projective testing. It is rather the neurotic personality, whose façade belies the repressed fears and hostilities within. Such a subject is caught off guard by projective devices; but the well-adjusted subject gives no significantly different response.

There is, however, one difference between the two researches. The starving subjects actually *avoided* any betrayal of their dominant motive in the projective tests. The well-adjusted veterans, on the other hand, gave essentially the *same* type of response in both direct and in projective testing. It may be that the dissimilar nature of the tests used in the two situations accounts for this difference in results. But this detailed difference need not detain us here. What seems to be important is the implication of these researches that *a psychodiagnostician should never employ projective methods in the study of motivation without at the same time employing direct methods*. If he does not employ both methods he will never be able to distinguish a well-integrated personality from one that is not. Nor will he be able to tell whether there are strong conscious streams of motivation that are entirely evading the projective situation (as in the case of the starving subjects).

The trend of evidence that I have presented seems to indicate that a normal, well-adjusted individual with strong goal-directedness may on projective tests do one of two things: (1) either give material identical with that of conscious report — in which case the projective method is not needed; or (2) give no evidence whatever of his dominant motives. It is only when emotionally laden material that is contradictory to conscious report, or to other results of direct assessment, comes forth in projective responses that we find special value in projective testing. And we shall never know whether or not a neurotic situation prevails unless we use both diagnostic approaches and compare the yield.

Consider for a moment the diagnosis of anxiety. Using various responses on the Rorschach and TAT cards the clinician might infer a high level of anxiety. Now this finding taken by itself tells us little. The subject may be the sort of person who is enormously effective in life because he harnesses his anxiety to performance. He may know perfectly well that he is a harried, worried, bedeviled over-achiever. Anxiety is an asset in his life, and he has enough insight to know the fact. In this case the yield by projective methods is matched by the yield from direct methods. The projective technique was not really needed, but it does no harm to use it. Or, as in our starvation cases, we might find that projective protocols reveal no anxiety, while in actuality we are dealing with a person who is as harried, worried, and bedeviled as our first subject but who effectively controls his jitters. In this case we assume that his large measure of control enables him to tackle the projective tests with some mental set unrelated to his anxious nature. But we may also find — and here is where projective methods have their uses — that an apparently bland and calm individual, denying all anxiety, reveals profound disturbance and fear in projective performances. It is this type of dissociated nature that projective tests help to diagnose. Yet they cannot do so unless direct methods also are employed.

In speaking so frequently of "direct" methods I have referred chiefly to "conscious report." To ask a man his motives, however, is not the only type of "direct" method that we may employ. It is, however, a good one — especially to start with.

When we set out to study a person's motives we are seeking to find out what that person is trying to do in this life, including of course what he is trying to avoid, and what he is trying to be. I see no reason why we should not start our investigation by asking him to tell us the answers as he sees them. If the questions in this form seem too abstract they can be recast. Particularly revealing are people's answers to the question, "What do you want to be doing five years from now?" Similar direct questions can be framed to elicit anxieties, loyalties, and hostilities. Most people, I suspect, can tell what they are trying to do in this life with a high degree of validity, certainly not less on the average than the prevailing validity of projective instruments. Yet some clinicians disdain to ask direct questions.

But by "direct methods" I mean also to include standard pencil-and-paper measures, such as the Strong Interest Inventory and the recently revised Allport-Vernon-Lindzey Study of Values. Now it often happens that the yield on such instruments is not what would come from the subject's conscious report. The subject may not have known, for example, that compared with most people his pattern of values is, say, markedly theoretical and aesthetic, or far below average in economic and religious interest. Yet the final score on the Study of Values is itself merely a summation of a series of separate conscious choices that he has made in forty-five hypothetical situations. While his verbal report on the pattern as a whole may be faulty, yet this pattern not only squares with all his separate choices, but is known on the average to have good external validity. People with certain patterns of interests as measured by the test do in fact make characteristic vocational choices and do in their daily behavior act in ways that are demonstrably consistent with the test results.

To sum up: direct methods include the kind of report that is elicited in careful interviews, whether it be of the simple psychiatric variety, the sort employed in vocational or personal counseling, or in nondirective interviewing. Autobiographic methods when employed at their face value are likewise direct. So too are the results of any kind of testing where the final scores represent a sum or pattern of a series of conscious choices on the part of the subject.*

The currently fashionable term *psychodynamics* is often equated explicitly with psychoanalytic theory. Projective techniques are con-

---

* For the purposes of the present argument this simplified discussion of "direct" and "indirect" techniques is adequate. Psychodiagnosis requires, however, a much more discriminating classification of the methods currently employed, and of the "levels" or organization that each normally taps. An excellent beginning is Rosenzweig's proposal that three classes of methods be distinguished, each adapted in principle to tapping three levels of behavior.[14] What he calls *subjective* methods require the subject to take himself as a direct object of observation (questionnaires, autobiographies). *Objective* methods require the observer to report on overt conduct. *Projective* methods require both subject and observer to "look the other way," and the diagnosis is based on the subject's reaction to apparently "ego-neutral" material. Broadly speaking, Rosenzweig's subjective and objective procedures correspond to what I here call "direct" methods, and projective procedures to "indirect" methods.

Especially noteworthy is the author's statement that the significance of projective methods (e.g., his own P-F Study) cannot be determined unless the subject's projective responses are examined in the light of his subjective and objective responses.

sidered psychodynamic because they are thought to tap deepest layers of structure and functioning. We have already indicated reasons for doubting the sufficiency of this assumption. Many of the most dynamic of motives are more accurately tapped by direct methods. At the very least the discoveries by projective techniques cannot be properly interpreted unless they are compared with discoveries yielded by direct methods.

Devotees of psychodynamics often say that no discoveries are of value unless the unconscious is explored. This dictum we find in the valuable book by Kardiner and Ovesey, *The Mark of Oppression*,[9] dealing with the seriously disordered and conflictful motivational systems of Negroes in a northern city. Unless I am greatly mistaken, however, the authors discover little or nothing about their cases through psychoanalytic probes that is not evident in the manifest situation. The conscious handicaps of a Negro in our society, the economic misery, the deteriorated family situations, the bitterness and despair, constitute a painful psychodynamic situation in individual lives that in most instances receives no further illumination when depth analysis is employed.

Most of the psychodynamic evidence given by Kardiner and Ovesey concerning their cases is, in fact, drawn from straightforward autobiographical report. Their use of this method is acceptable and their findings highly instructive. But their theory seems to me out of line with both the method actually used and the findings obtained. Psychodynamics is not necessarily a hidden dynamics.

This point is well made by the psychiatrist J. C. Whitehorn,[17] who correctly holds that psychodynamics is a general science of motivation. Into its broad principles one may fit the specific contributions and insights of psychoanalysis. But psychoanalysis itself is by no means the sum and substance of psychodynamics. Whitehorn insists that the proper approach to psychotic patients, especially to those suffering from schizophrenic or depressive disorder, is through such channels of their normal interest systems as remain open. It is not the region of their disorder that requires primary attention, but those psychodynamic systems that still represent sturdy and healthy adaptations to reality. In Whitehorn's words, the therapist should seek "to activate and utilize the resources of the patient and to help him thereby to work out a more satisfying way of life with a less circumscribed emphasis upon these special issues." (p. 40)

Sometimes we hear it said that psychoanalytic theory does not do justice to psychoanalytic practice. What is meant is that in the course of therapy an analyst will devote much of his time to a direct discussion with his patient of his manifest interests and values. The analyst will listen respectfully, accept, counsel, and advise concerning these important, and *not* buried, psychodynamic systems. In many instances, as in the cases presented by Kardiner and Ovesey, the motives and conflicts are taken at their face value. Thus the method of psychoanalysis as employed is not fully sustained by the theory that is affirmed.

Nothing that I have said denies the existence of infantile systems, troublesome repressions, or neurotic formations. Nor does it deny the possibility of self-deception, rationalization, and ego defense. My point is merely that methods and theories dealing with these aberrant conditions should be set in a broad conception of psychodynamics. The patient should be assumed insightful until he is proved otherwise. If you asked a hundred people who go to the icebox for a snack why they did so, probably all would answer, "Because I was hungry." In ninety-nine of these cases we may — no matter how deeply we explore — discover that this simple, conscious report is the whole truth. It can be taken at its face value. In the hundredth case, however, our probing shows that we are dealing with a compulsive over-eater, with an obese seeker after infantile security who, unlike the majority of cases, does not know what he is trying to do. It is peace and comfort he is seeking — perhaps his mother's bosom — and not the leftover roast. In this case — and in a minority of all cases — I grant we cannot take the evidence of his overt behavior, nor his account of it, at their face value.

Freud was a specialist in precisely those motives that cannot be taken at their face value. To him motivation resided in the id. The conscious, accessible region of personality that carries on direct transactions with the world, namely the ego, he regarded as devoid of dynamic power.

It is a misfortune that Freud died before he had remedied this one-sidedness in his theory. Even his most faithful followers tell us now that he left his ego psychology incomplete. In recent years many of them have labored to redress the balance. Without doubt the principal current in psychoanalytic theory today is moving in the direction of a more dynamic ego. This trend in theory is apparent in the work of Anna Freud, Hartmann, French, Horney, Fromm, Kris, and many others. In a communication to the American Psychoanalytic Association, Kris points out that the attempt to restrict interpretations of motivation to the id aspect only "represents the older procedure." Modern concern with the ego does not confine itself to an analysis of defense mechanisms alone. Rather it gives more respect to what he calls the "psychic surface." Present psychoanalytic techniques, he tells us, tend to link "surface" with depth." [10] In a similar vein Rapaport [13] has argued that a measure of true autonomy must now be ascribed to the ego.

To illustrate the point at issue we might take any psychogenic interest of maturity, for example the religious sentiment. Freud's handling of the matter is well known. To him religion is essentially a neurosis in the individual, a formula for personal escape. The father image lies at the root of the matter. One cannot therefore take the religious sentiment, when it exists in a personality, at its face value. A more balanced view of the matter would seem to be this: *sometimes* one cannot take this sentiment at its face value, and *sometimes* one can. Only a careful study of the individual will tell.

In a person in whom the religious factor serves an obviously ego-centric purpose — talismanic, bigoted, self-justificatory — we can infer that it is a neurotic, or at least immature, formation in the personality. Its infantile and escapist character is not recognized by the subject. On the other hand, in a person who has gradually evolved a guiding philosophy of life where the religious sentiment exerts a generally normative force upon behavior and confers intelligibility to life as a whole, we infer not only that this particular ego formation is a dominant motive but that it must be accepted at its face value. It is a master motive and an ego ideal whose shape and substance are essentially what appear in consciousness.[1]

Let us consider a final example. It is well known that most boys around the ages of four to seven identify with their fathers. They imitate them in many ways. Among other things they may express vocational aspirations for daddy's job. Many boys when grown do in fact follow their father's footsteps.

Take politics. Father and son have been politicians in many families: the Tafts, Lodges, Kennedys, La Follettes, Roosevelts, to mention only a few. When the son is at a mature age, say 50 or 60, what is his motivation? Is he working through his early father identification or is he not? Taken at its face value the interest of the son in politics now seems to be absorbing, self-contained, a prominent factor in his own ego structure. In short, it seems to be a mature and normal motive. But the strict geneticist would say: "No, he is now a politician because of a father fixation." Does the geneticist mean that an early father identification started him in a political direction of interest? If so, the answer is yes, of course. All motives have their origin somewhere. Or does he mean, "This early fixation now, today, sustains the son's political conduct"? If so, the answer is normally, no. The political interest is now a prominent part of the ego structure, and the ego is the healthy man's source of energy. To be sure, there may be cases where a person mature in years is still trying to curry father's favor, to step into his shoes, to displace him with the mother. A clinical study of a second-generation politician may conceivably show that his behavior is compulsively father-identified. In such a case his daily conduct is in all probability so compulsive, so ungeared to realistic situational needs, so excessive, that the diagnosis can be suspected by any skilled clinical observer. But such instances are relatively rare.

To sum up: we need in our motivational theory to make a sharper distinction between infantilisms and motivation that is strictly contemporary and at age.

I am fully aware of my heterodoxy in suggesting that there is in a restricted sense a discontinuity between normal and abnormal motivation, and that we need a theory that will recognize this fact. Discontinuities are distinctly unpopular in psychological science. One theory of abnormality tells us that we are merely pleased to regard the extremes on our linear continuum as abnormal. Further, some culture theorists insist that abnormality is a relative concept, shifting from culture to culture and from one historical period to another. Likewise, there are many borderline cases which even the most experienced clinician could not with confidence classify as normal or as abnormal. Finally, and most important, is the fact that in many normal people one can by scratching deeply enough find *some* infantilism in their motivation.

Granted all these familiar arguments, there is still a world of difference — if not between normal and abnormal people — then between the healthy and unhealthy mechanisms involved in the development of motivation. What we call integrative action of the nervous system is basically a wholesome mechanism that keeps motivation up to date. It tends to bring about an internal consistency and a reality testing among the elements entering into motivational patterning. Effective suppression is another healthy mechanism, not only harmless to the individual but making possible the arrangement of motives in an orderly hierarchy.[4, 12] With the aid of effective suppression the individual ceases to act out infantile dramas.

Insight, a clear self-image, and the little understood factor of homeostasis may be mentioned among the balancing mechanisms.

As Getzels' experiment shows, direct and projective performances in healthy people are all of a piece. A further test of normality — unfortunately one psychologists have not yet developed — may lie in the harmony of expressive behavior (facial expression, gestures, handwriting) with the individual's fundamental motivational structure. There is evidence that discoordination between conscious motives and expressive movement is an ominous sign.[3] This lead for research should be followed through.

In unhealthy motivation, unbalancing mechanisms have the upper hand. There is always some species of dissociation at work. The individual represses ineffectively; repressed motives erupt in autistic gestures, in tantrums, in nightmares, in compulsions, perhaps in paranoid thinking. Above all, self-knowledge is lacking in large regions of the life.

My point is that normally the balancing mechanisms have the upper hand. Sometimes, in certain badly disordered lives, the unbalancing mechanisms take over. Occasionally too, we find them operating in a segmental way in lives that are otherwise healthy. When the clash in mechanisms is marked, diagnosis is then aided by the use of projective techniques. But when there is essential harmony within the personality system projective methods will teach us little or nothing about the course of motivation.

From what has been said it is clear that a satisfactory conception of psychodynamics will have the following characteristics: (1) It will never employ projective methods nor depth analysis without allowing for a full diagnosis of motives by direct methods as well. (2) It will assume that in a healthy personality the great bulk of motivation can be taken at its face value. (3) It will assume that normal motivation of this order has a present and future significance for the individual that is by no means adequately represented by a study of his past life. In other words, it will allow that the present psychodynamics of a life may in large part be functionally autonomous, even though continuous with early motivational formations (*The Nature of Personality*,[2] esp. pp. 76-113). (4) It will at the same time retain the epochal insights of Freud and others to the effect that infantile fixations frequently occur, and that we do well to check on conscious report and to supplement direct methods by indirect.

Before such an adequate conceptualization can be achieved there is one current dogma in motivational theory that demands reexamination. I refer to the oft-encountered statement that all motives aim at "the reduction of tensions." This doctrine — found in instinctivism, psychoanalysis, and in stimulus-response psychology — operates to keep us on a primitive level of theorizing.

We cannot, of course, deny that basic drives seem to seek "reduction of tension." Oxygen need, hunger, thirst, elimination are examples. But these drives are not a trustworthy model for all normal adult motivation. Goldstein remarks that patients who seek only tension reduction are clearly pathological. They are preoccupied with segmental irritations from which they seek relief. There is nothing creative about their interests. They cannot take suffering, or delay, or frustration as a mere incident in their pursuit of values. Normal people, by contrast, are dominated by their "preferred patterns" of self-actualization. Their psychogenic interests are modes of sustaining and directing tension rather than escaping it.[7]

We should, I think, agree with Goldstein that tension reduction is not an adequate statement of the functioning of mature psychogenic motives. At the time of his inauguration as president of Harvard, James Bryant Conant remarked that he was undertaking his duties "with a heavy heart but gladly." He knew he would reduce no tensions by committing himself to the new job. Tensions would mount and mount, and at many times become almost unbearable. While he would in the course of his daily work dispatch many tasks and feel relief, still the over-all commitment — his total investment of energy — would never result in any equilibrium. Psychogenic interests are of this order; they lead us to complicate and strain our lives indefinitely. "Striving for equilibrium," "tension reduction," "death wish" seem trivial and erroneous representations of normal adult motivation.

Recent years, as I have said, have brought a wholesome turn in theorizing. Few authorities on war neuroses, for example, wrote in terms of tension reduction. They spoke rather of "firm ego structure" or "weak ego structure." Grinker and Spiegel [8] say, "As the ego becomes stronger the therapist demands increasing independence and activity from the patient." (p. 94)

After successful therapy these and other writers sometimes remark, "The ego now seems in full control." In such expressions as these — and one encounters them with increasing frequency — we meet post-Freudian ego psychology again. True, the flavor of these theoretical statements varies. Sometimes they still seem close to the conception of the ego as rationalizer, rider, and steersman. But often, as in the statements just quoted, they go far beyond. They imply that the ego is not only normally able to avoid malignant repression, chronicity, and rigidity, but that it is also a differentiated dynamism — a fusion of healthy psychogenic motives that can be taken at their face value.

There is no need to take fright at the conception of an "active ego." As I see the matter, the term "ego" does not refer to a homunculus, but is merely a shorthand expression for what Goldstein calls "preferred patterns." The term means that normally healthy personalities have various systems of psychogenic motives. They are not limitless in number. Indeed in a well-integrated adult they may be adequately indicated on the fingers of two hands, perhaps one. What a person is trying to do persistently, recurrently, as a function of his own internal nature, is often surprisingly well focused and well patterned. Whether these leading motives are called desires, interests, values, traits, or sentiments does not greatly matter. What is important is that motivational theory — in guiding diagnosis, therapy, and research — should take these structures fully into account.

REFERENCES

1. Allport, G. W. *The Individual and His Religion.* New York: The Macmillan Company, 1950.
2. ——, *The Nature of Personality: Selected Papers.* Cambridge: Addison-Wesley Publishing Company, 1950.
3. Allport, G. W., and Vernon, P. E. *Studies in Expressive Movement.* New York: The Macmillan Company, 1933.
4. Belmont, L., and Birch, H. G. "Re-Individualizing The Repression Hypothesis." *Journal of Abnormal and Social Psychology,* 46:226-235 (1951).
5. Brozek, J., Guetzkow, H., Baldwin, M. V., Cranston, R. "A Quantitative Study of Perception and Association in Experimental Semi-Starvation." *Journal of Personality,* 19:245-264 (1951).
6. Getzels, J. W. *The Assessment of Personality and Prejudice by the Methods of Paired Direct and Projective Questionnaires.* Unpublished Thesis. Cambridge: Harvard College Library, 1951.
7. Goldstein, K. *Human Nature in the Light of Psychopathology.* Cambridge: Harvard University Press, 1940.
8. Grinker, R. R., and Spiegel, J. P. *War Neuroses.* Philadelphia: Blakiston Company, 1945.
9. Kardiner, A., and Ovesey, L. *The Mark of Oppression.* New York: W. W. Norton & Company, 1951.
10. Kris, E. "Ego Psychology and Interpretation in Psychoanalytic Therapy." *Psychoanalytic Quarterly,* 20:15-30 (1951).
11. Levine, R., Chein, I., and Murphy, G. "The Relation of the Intensity of a Need to the Amount of Perceptual Distortion: A Preliminary Report." *Journal of Psychology,* 13:283-293 (1942).
12. McGranahan, D. V. "A Critical and Experimental Study of Repression." *Journal of Abnormal and Social Psychology,* 35:212-225 (1940).
13. Rapaport, D. "The Autonomy of the Ego." *Bulletin of the Menninger Clinic,* 15:113-123 (1951).
14. Rosenzweig, S. "Levels of Behavior in Psychodiagnosis with Special Reference to the Picture-Frustration Study." *American Journal of Orthopsychiatry,* 20:63-72 (1950).

15. Sanford, R. N. "The Effect of Abstinence from Food upon Imaginal Processes." *The Journal of Psychology*, 2:129-136 (1936).
16. Stagner, R. "Homeostasis as a Unifying Concept in Personality Theory." *Psychological Review*, 58:5-17 (1951).
17. Whitehorn, J. C. "Psychodynamic Considerations in the Treatment of Psychotic Patients." *University of Western Ontario Medical Journal*, 20:27-41 (1950).

IV A THEORETICAL MODEL FOR PERSONALITY STUDIES

ANDRAS ANGYAL

In this paper I shall present a particular model which I have advocated previously for the formulation of a theory of personality,[1] reformulating certain aspects of this theoretical orientation and illustrating my points with pertinent examples taken mainly from the field of psychotherapeutic theory and practice.

Personality may be described most adequately when looked upon as a unified dynamic organization — dynamic, because the most significant fact about a human being is not so much his static aspect as his constituting a specific *process:* the life of the individual. This process, the life of the person, is an organized, patterned process, a Gestalt, an organization. A true organization presupposes an organizing principle, a unifying pattern. All part processes obtain their specific meaning or specific function from this unifying over-all pattern. Therefore it seems plausible that a tentative phrasing of the nature of this total pattern — the broad pattern of human life — may serve as an adequate model for the formulation of the problems pertaining to the study of personality.

The over-all pattern of personality function can be described from two different vantage points. Viewed from one of these vantage points, the human being seems to be striving basically to assert and to expand his self-determination. He is an autonomous being, a

44

self-governing entity that asserts itself actively instead of reacting passively like a physical body to the impacts of the surrounding world. This fundamental tendency expresses itself in a striving of the person to consolidate and increase his self-government, in other words to exercise his freedom and to organize the relevant items of his world out of the autonomous center of government that is his self. This tendency — which I have termed "the trend toward increased autonomy" — expresses itself in spontaneity, self-assertiveness, striving for freedom and for mastery. In an objective fashion this tendency can be described as follows: the human being is an autonomous unity that, acting upon the surrounding world, molds and modifies it. His life is a resultant of self-determination on the one hand and the impacts of the surrounding world, the situation, on the other. This basic tendency, the trend toward increased autonomy, expresses the person's striving from a state of lesser self-determination (and greater situational influence) to a state of greater self-determination (and lesser situational influence).

Seen from another vantage point, human life reveals a very different basic pattern from the one described above. From this point of view the person appears to seek a place for himself in a larger unit of which he strives to become a part. In the first tendency we see him struggling for centrality in his world, trying to mold, to organize, the objects and the events of his world, to bring them under his own jurisdiction and government. In the second tendency he seems rather to strive to surrender himself willingly to seek a home for himself in and *to become an organic part of something that he conceives as greater than himself*. The superindividual unit of which one feels oneself a part, or wishes to become a part, may be variously formulated according to one's cultural background and personal understanding. The superordinate whole may be represented for a person by a social unit — family, clan, nation — by a cause, by an ideology, or by a meaningfully ordered universe. In the realm of aesthetic, social, and moral attitudes this basic human tendency has a central significance. Its clearest manifestation, however, is in the religious attitude and religious experience.

I wish to state with emphasis that I am not speaking here about a tendency which is an exclusive prerogative of some people only, e.g., of those with a particular religious bent or aesthetic sensitivity, but of a tendency that I conceive as a universal and basic characteristic in all human beings.

These two tendencies of the human being, the tendency to increase his self-determination in his expanding personal world, and the tendency to surrender himself willingly to a superordinate whole, can be summed up by saying that the human being comports himself *as if he were a whole of an intermediate order.* By this I mean a "part-Gestalt" like, for example, the cardiovascular system, or the central nervous system, each of which is a *whole,* an organization of many parts, but at the same time a *part* with regard to its superordinate whole, the body. The human being is both a *unifier,* an organizer of his immediate personal world, and a *participant* in what he conceives as the superordinate whole to which he belongs.

The basic human attitude that makes man behave as a part of a larger whole reflects itself also in his "horizontal relationships," that is in his relationship to the other "parts," to other persons. Were man's behavior determined exclusively by his urge for mastery, his attitude toward others could be only as toward means to his ends. Experiencing others as coparticipants in a larger whole brings, however, another facet of his nature into manifestation. To avoid the coining of some outlandish term, we call this basic relation "love." In common usage this word has been badly misused to denote not only cheap sentimentality but even relationships that are actually founded on exploitation, possessiveness, helplessness, and similar destructive attitudes. The basic nature of love consists in a recognition of the *value* and acceptance of the *otherness* of the loved "object" while at the same time one experiences an essential *sameness* that exists between oneself and what one loves.

To recognize and to accept the otherness of a person means to respect him as a valuable being in his own right, in his independence. This attitude is incongruous with any idea of possessiveness or any tendency to use him as means to an end, be this in the form of exploitation, domination, possessiveness, or some other attitude. In other words, it is incongruous with the nature of love to try to reduce the loved person to "an item in one's personal world," or to try to make him comply with one's demands, or to try to exert power over him in whatever way. Love has to be recognized as a basic human attitude which is quite distinct from and irreducible to man's self-assertive tendencies.

The recognition and acceptance of the otherness of the person implies, furthermore, an *understanding* of him. There can be no real love without understanding of the other person, only some sort of deceptive feeling based on an illusion. One does not recognize the otherness of a person as a reality by projecting into him one's fantasies, however flattering they may be. And when one sees in a person one's mother or father or anyone else, one ignores the person as he really is. In the last analysis this is a fundamental disregard for and destructive attitude toward the other person. The understanding of the other person — as we are now using this expression — is not some sort of shrewd "practical psychology" which has a keen eye for the weakness of people, but a deep perception of the core, of the essential nature of the other person. In love this essential nature of the other person is experienced as a value, as something that is very dear to one. Love is not "blind" but visionary: it sees into the very heart of its object, and sees the "real self" behind and in the midst of the frailities and shortcomings of the person.

Love has a second basic component which is complementary to respect for the otherness of its object: the experience of a certain fundamental belongingness and *sameness* between lover and the loved. Experientially, this is not "identification," that is, an identity that is more or less artificially created, but an existing identity that is *acknowledged*. Man behaves in certain fundamental respects *as if* he were a part, a shareholder in some kind of superordinate unit, in some kind of commonwealth. When two persons love one another they clearly or dimly have the feeling that something greater is involved therein than their limited individualities, that they are one in something greater than themselves or, as the religious person says, they are "one in God." *

Without such an implicit orientation all interests of a person would be centered in himself alone as an individual. He, as an isolated entity, would be facing an alien world and his reaching beyond himself would be only to possess, master, and govern the surrounding world. He would compete with other people or he would calculatingly cooperate with them, but he would not love them. In order to love, it is essential that a man come out of his shell, that he transcend his individuality, that he "lose himself." Somehow this self-abandonment is the precondition to a broadened existence in loving. One rejoices in the characteristic ways, in the real being, beyond the surface of pretense, of the other; one suffers in the other's misfortunes and in his misdeeds: therein one gains a whole new life with its joys and sorrows. One is enriched through a vital participation in another life without wanting, however, to possess the other person. The significant truth is expressed in the paradox that the one "who loses his life [of isolation], will gain it [in a broadened existence]." The paradox is resolved by recognizing that man functions as a part of a large whole. He has a life as a part — and that is all he has, as long as he remains in his self-enclosure. But it is possible for him to have a greater life, the life

* This statement does not have to be understood in a theological sense. In this context it is not our concern, e.g., whether or not the "superordinate whole" is reality or not; we state only that man appears to function *as if* he were or would experience himself as a part of a superordinate whole.

of the whole, as it is manifested in himself, in the other "parts," and in the totality.

I have described the over-all pattern of personality functioning as a two-directional orientation: *self-determination* on the one hand and *self-surrender* on the other. The first is the adequate attitude toward the items within one's individual world, the second, toward the greater whole toward which one behaves as a part. A particularly important aspect of this second orientation is the "horizontal" relatedness of the parts to other parts within the whole. I spoke in some detail of love because I believe — largely in agreement with current clinical views — that this is the crux of the entire problem of personality and of interpersonal relationships.

Actual samples of behavior, however, cannot be ascribed exclusively to one or the other orientation. It is only in the counterfeit, the unhealthy, behavior that one or the other of these basic orientations is partially obliterated; in a well-integrated person the behavioral items always manifest both orientations in varying degrees. Instead of conflicting, the two orientations complement each other. As in the tendency toward increased autonomy, one strives to master and govern the environment, one discovers that one cannot do this effectively by direct application of force, by sheer violence, but can do it by obedience, understanding, and respect for the laws of the environment — attitudes that in some way are similar to those of loving relationships. Similarly, bringing one's best to a loving relationship requires not only capacity for self-surrender but also a degree of proficient mastery of one's world, resourcefulness, and self-reliance, without which the relationship is in danger of deteriorating into helpless dependency, exploitation, possessiveness, etc.

The central point of the model which we suggest here for the study of personality is the assumption that the total function of the personality is patterned according to a double orientation of self-determination — self-surrender. In the study of personality as in any other scientific field, model building has its sole justification in its

practical applicability, that is, in its suitability for interpretation of
the pertinent phenomena and for the formulation of meaningful
problems. I have chosen the problem of the neuroses as a testing
ground and I hope to demonstrate that the suggested model is useful for clarification of pertinent problems. Needless to say, only a
few outstanding aspects of this broad field can here be touched upon,
but this consideration may suffice to give a first impression as to the
usefulness of the suggested frame of reference.*

I suggest the following thesis: The backbone of neurosis consists
in a disturbance of the two basic tendencies that we have assumed
as forming the over-all pattern of personality functioning. The two
cardinal disturbances on which the neurosis rests consist, first, in the
person's *loss of mastery* over his own fate, and second, what is
rather generally accepted as a basic factor in the neuroses, namely
anxiety. Loss of mastery is another expression for impairment of the
capacity for self-determination; anxiety, as we will try to show, is
related to the impairment of the capacity for self-surrender and the
capacity for love. These points may be best demonstrated by quickly
surveying some of the crucial points in the development of a
neurosis.

Although we have only vague and inferential knowledge of the
infant's subjective experiences, there is sufficient evidence for assuming that his self and the world are not clearly distinguished, but
rather blend into a single totality. This differentiation may be near
zero in the prenatal life; it is small in the early days of infancy and
usually is not quite complete even in adulthood — witness ubiquitous wishful thinking and other autistic phenomena. The gradual
birth of individuality may be largely a matter of maturation, but it
is also stimulated and precipitated by *painful* contacts with the
surrounding world. The hurtfulness of some objects of the environ-

* This nucleus of a model can be broadened and made more detailed. I have
made efforts in this direction in the previously quoted book and also in "The
Holistic Approach in Psychiatry." [2]

ment and their frustrating resistance and independence in regard to one's wishes, so to say their disobedience, are impelling experiences to the recognition of their otherness.

These pains and frustrations — even the pain of being born into an uncomfortable world — are possibly not traumatic in themselves. Their chief significance seems to lie in their hastening both the birth of individuality and the experience of an outside world that is distinct from oneself. And with the birth of individuality the stage is set, the *human situation* is created. Here for the first time the opportunity is given to the person to manifest and unfold his essential nature. The experience of separateness from the surrounding world, which is governed by forces outside oneself, supplies the impetus to strive for mastery over the environment. At the same time, the experience of oneself as a separated, limited individual gives one the feeling of incompleteness and the urge to seek for a larger life to be part of and to participate lovingly in other lives. The experience of one's separateness represents both the necessity and the opportunity for the person to manifest his basic tendencies.

The real traumatizing factors are those which prevent the person from expressing these basic tendencies. In the neurotic development there are always a number of unfortunate circumstances which instil in the child a self-derogatory feeling. This involves on the one hand a feeling of weakness which discourages him from the free expression of his wish for mastery, and on the other hand a feeling that there is something fundamentally wrong with him and that, therefore, he cannot be loved. The whole complicated structure of neurosis appears to be founded on this secret feeling of worthlessness, that is, on the belief that one is inadequate to master the situations that confront him and that he is undeserving of love.

The traumatizing circumstances which condition this loss of self-confidence and of self-respect are many. They have been rather carefully explored by therapists who deal with neuroses. It will be sufficient here to call to mind some of the most common factors.

1. The *over-protective attitude* of an insecure, anxious parent tends to convey to the child a feeling that he lives in a world that is full of dangers, and with which he is inadequate to cope. When a parent does too much for the child, he is telling him by implication that he is incapable of doing things by himself.

2. When the parent is too eager for the child to do well and is *excessively* critical of him, he is likely to instil in the child the feeling that "something must be very wrong with me; I can't do anything right."

3. When parents distort and exaggerate the child's achievement, when they cast him into a *superior role* and have great expectations of him, they plant the seed of self-derogation in still another way. Deep down the child knows that the parents' picture of him is untrue, and measuring himself by these excessive and often fantastic standards, he secretly begins to feel worthless.

4. The too many "don'ts" which the child hears tend to create in him the feeling that those things which he *most wants* are the things that are forbidden and *evil*. This easily can give rise in him to a secret conviction that he is a fundamentally evil person.

5. The ways in which children are being treated without *understanding* and without *respect* are many, and these are likely to create in the child the feeling that he just does not matter in this adult world, that he is of no account, that he is worthless. Often one wonders why the child accepts the verdict that he is worthless, instead of blaming the parent for being so obviously lacking in understanding, so wrong and selfish. The answer suggests itself that the child needs so much to feel that he has "good parents" that he tenaciously adheres ot this belief and would rather assume himself to be evil or worthless than give up the idea that he has good parents.

The whole complex of self-derogation can be roughly — and admittedly somewhat artificially — divided into a feeling of inadequacy and the feeling of being unloved. The first leads to an impairment of self-determination, the second to the impairment of the capacity to love.

One important way in which the self-determination of a person may be impaired is by trading the birthright of mastery over his own destiny for the mess of pottage of protection — and dependency. In addition to the assumption of his weakness, an overevaluation of the power of his parents and of the protection which they can give induces the child to make this fatal bargain. The terms of the bargain are set, at least by implication: "You are weak and helpless against the world which is full of dangers; if you are good, if you do what we want you to do, and don't follow your impulses, we will take care of you and protect you."

Another circumstance that may induce a child to give up or "escape" from his freedom is the exploitation by the adult of the child's loving nature. This is often done by holding up to the child the suffering his behavior may cause to others: "You may do it if you want to, but mother will be hurt"; or more directly: "What you do shortens my life"; "You put another nail in my coffin," etc. Particularly vicious and destructive is the influence of the "self-sacrificing mother," who holds up to the child the many sufferings, deprivations, and unhappinesses which she has had to endure for the child, implying the tremendous ingratitude that a self-assertion of the child against her wishes would mean.

In response to these and similar emotional insults the child is gradually led to deny himself, to hide his spontaneous impulses — which he assumes to be evil — and to pretend to be or to try to be someone else, a more impressive and a more desirable person. This step is literally suicidal, and it is born out of extreme despair. Indeed, only an extreme despair of any possibility of living in reality can induce a person to content himself with appearances, with the impression he makes. The exaggerated importance and value given to any external trappings with which a person may decorate himself is equivalent to declaring one's naked self worthless. If one basks in some sort of reflected glory, one declares one's real being to be ignominious.

All these various roads lead to loss of spontaneity, initiative, and genuineness. The child loses originality, which should not be the privilege of a few but a rightful heritage of everyone. The neurotic person experiences himself as a straw in the wind who cannot act under his own power but has to *wait for things to happen,* who is a "victim of circumstances" and whose fate depends on good or bad "breaks."

The discussion of another basic disturbance, the impairment of the person's capacity to love, leads us into the problem of anxiety. It seems to me that the original word-meaning that suggests constriction, being narrowed in (*Beengung*), expresses best the essential nature of anxiety. A person who feels weak and unlovable and surrounded by an alien and unfriendly world, will draw in his feelers and will surround himself with some protective shell. This shell, however, limits him and narrows him in to such an extent that he can barely move or breathe. We propose to define anxiety as this condition of the person. It seems preferable to use the term in this sense, as a "psycho-physically-neutral" term (William Stern), denoting a condition of the person which may or may not be consciously experienced. This usage would avoid the confusing issues of unconscious anxiety and such manifestations of anxiety that are conscious but not characterized by anxious feelings. Anxiety is not a mental phenomenon but a state of limitation of life. When we have sufficient information about a person's mode of living we can determine whether his life is a narrowed one or not; that is, we can determine the presence and degree of the condition of anxiety, independently of the presence and degree of anxious feelings.

Anxiety is dynamically related to fears in a twofold manner: it is born out of fears and it leads to fears. It is fear that makes the person erect his defenses with the resultant state of constriction or anxiety. The person's impulses, however, rebel against the enclosure, against the limitation, and threaten to break through the wall of defenses. This threat from within is experienced in those nameless fears, fears without a conscious object, which one usually refers to as "anxiety."

This narrowed-in condition of anxiety paralyzes the effectiveness of the person in dealing with his environment. He does not really dare to venture into the outside world, but looks out upon it from behind his defenses with suspicion, fear, apprehension, envy, and hatred. The most destructive aspect of anxiety, of this self-enclosure, is however the loss of the capacity or rather the loss of the freedom to love. For love presupposes that instead of anxiously standing watch over one's safety, one dares to go out of oneself, to abandon oneself, to venture out in order to participate in the life of others and in a larger life of which he feels himself a part. It is the nature of the human being that he finds fulfillment only in a broadened existence, and that for him life confined to the limits of one's individuality in segregation from others is worthless. He can find happiness and peace only if he loves, that is, participates in life outside the confines of his individuality; and only if he is loved, that is, received into and held fast and dear by another life.

Summing up this sketch of the origin of the neuroses, we have assumed that certain traumatizing experiences create in the child a derogatory picture, a feeling of the worthlessness of his self. This feeling of worthlessness has two components: first, the feeling that one is inadequate, too weak to cope with the environment; and second, the feeling that one is unloved and unworthy of love. These then lead to an impairment of the person's self-determination on the one hand, and to anxiety with the loss of capacity to love on the other. Neurosis represents a complicated interlocking system of maneuvers that are designed to maintain life in a human sense in spite of the fact that the person is wounded at the very core of his nature. This hypothesis of the origin of the neurosis I believe is more in agreement than at variance with many of the current views on the subject.

This view is also in good agreement with certain current theories of therapy. There are several psychotherapeutic factors to which, in general, a particularly important curative effect is ascribed. We shall mention only two such factors for further illustration of the main points of this paper: first, the patient's expression of anger in the therapeutic setting, and second, the positive relationship of the therapist to the patient.

The expression of angry feelings toward the therapist is assumed to have a beneficial therapeutic effect on the patient. This expression should be, however, more than just "blowing off steam," a catharsis. The patient's experience that he can express anger toward the therapist without being rejected or punished for it — important as it is — is not in itself the crucial therapeutic experience, but only preparatory to it. On the basis of a series of observations I am persuaded that not all forms of angry expressions are therapeutically valuable, but only certain kinds with well-defined differential characteristics. An outburst of anger, if it is not more than a blind expression of impotent rage, does not produce therapeutic effects, but is likely to leave the patient ashamed and guilty and worse off than before. The therapeutically effective anger is always a courageous expression and often clearly expresses the feeling that one would rather die than continue to live in fear and trepidation, tolerate injustice, etc. Such anger says emphatically: "I won't stand for it!" Daring to take this final aggressive stand makes one regain respect for oneself. And therein lies the therapeutic effect of this type of anger: it tends to abolish the feeling of inadequacy which is one component of self-derogation and which in turn is the foundation for the neurosis.

Even more fundamental is, however, the therapist's persistent attitude toward the patient, expressed in respect for him as a person of value, in understanding, in confidence that the patient can be saved, in sincere desire and devoted effort to help him to live a happier life. When the patient reaches the point of being able to trust the sincerity of the therapist's attitude, he will no longer be able to uphold completely the fiction of being unloved and unworthy, undeserving of love. And with this the other foundation of his neurosis begins to crumble.

The above examples, taken from the dynamics and therapy of the neuroses, may serve to illustrate the degree of usefulness and applicability of the model that was proposed here for the study of personality. It is not claimed that this brief exposition proves anything definitely, but perhaps it is sufficient to give a first impression of an avenue of approach which may be worth while to follow.

REFERENCES

1. Angyal, A. *Foundations For a Science of Personality*. New York: Commonwealth Fund, 1941.
2. Angyal, A. "The Holistic Approach in Psychiatry." *American Journal of Psychiatry*, 105:178-182 (1948).

V   SELFISHNESS, SELF-LOVE, AND SELF-INTEREST

ERICH FROMM

The doctrine that love for oneself is identical with "selfishness" and an alternative to love for others has pervaded theology, philosophy, and popular thought; the same doctrine has been rationalized in scientific language in Freud's theory of narcissism. Freud's concept presupposes a fixed amount of libido. In the infant, all of the libido has the child's own person as its objective, the stage of "primary narcissism," as Freud calls it. During the individual's development, the libido is shifted from one's own person toward other objects. If a person is blocked in his "object-relationships," the libido is withdrawn from the objects and returned to his own person; this is called "secondary narcissism." According to Freud, the more love I turn toward the outside world the less love is left for myself, and vice versa. He thus describes the phenomenon of love as an impoverishment of one's self-love because all libido is turned to an object outside oneself.

These questions arise: Does psychological observation support the thesis that there is a basic contradiction and a state of alternation between love for oneself and love for others? Is love for oneself the same phenomenon as selfishness, or are they opposites? Furthermore, is the selfishness of modern man really a concern for himself as an individual, with all his intellectual, emotional, and sensual potentialities? Has "he" not become an appendage of his socioeconomic role? Is his selfishness identical with self-love or is it not caused by the very lack of it?

Before we start the discussion of the psychological aspect of selfishness and self-love, the logical fallacy in the notion that love for others and love for oneself are mutually exclusive should be stressed. If it is a virtue to love my neighbor as a human being, it must be a virtue — and not a vice — to love myself since I am a human being too. There is no concept of man in which I myself am not included. A doctrine which proclaims such an exclusion proves itself to be intrinsically contradictory. The idea expressed in the Biblical "Love thy neighbor as thyself!" implies that respect for one's own integrity and uniqueness, love for and understanding of one's own self, can not be separated from respect for and love and understanding of another individual. The love for my own self is inseparably connected with the love for any other self.

We have come now to the basic psychological premises on which the conclusions of our argument are built. Generally, these premises are as follows: not only others but we ourselves are the "object" of our feelings and attitudes; the attitudes toward others and toward ourselves, far from being contradictory, are basically conjunctive. With regard to the problem under discussion this means: Love of others and love of ourselves are not alternatives. On the contrary, an attitude of love toward themselves will be found in all those who are capable of loving others. Love, in principle, is indivisible as far as the connection between "objects" and one's own self is concerned. Genuine love is an expression of productiveness and implies care, respect, responsibility, and knowledge. It is not an "affect" in the sense of being affected by somebody, but an active striving for the growth and happiness of the loved person, rooted in one's own capacity to love.

To love is an expression of one's power to love, and to love somebody is the actualization and concentration of his power with regard to one person. It is not true, as the idea of romantic love would have it, that there is only the one person in the world whom one could love and that it is the great chance of one's life to find that one person. Nor is it true, if that person be found, that love for him (or her) results in a withdrawal of love from others. Love which can only be experienced with regard to one person demonstrates by this very fact that it is not love, but a symbiotic attachment. The basic affirmation contained in love is directed toward the beloved person as an incarnation of essentially human qualities. Love of one person implies love of man as such. The kind of "division of labor," as William James calls it, by which one loves one's family but is without feeling for the "stranger," is a sign of a basic inability to love. Love of man is not, as is frequently supposed, an abstraction coming after the love for a specific person, but it is its premise, although genetically it is acquired in loving specific individuals.

From this it follows that my own self, in principle, must be as much an object of my love as another person. The affirmation of one's own life, happiness, growth, freedom, is rooted in one's capacity to love, i.e., in care, respect, responsibility, and knowledge. If an individual is able to love productively he loves himself too; if he can love only others he can not love at all.

Granted that love for oneself and for others in principle is conjunctive, how do we explain selfishness, which obviously excludes any genuine concern for others? The selfish person is interested only in himself, wants everything for himself, feels no pleasure in giving but only in taking. The world outside is looked at only from the standpoint of what he can get out of it; he lacks interest in the needs of others, and respect for their dignity and integrity. He can see nothing but himself; he judges everyone and everything from its usefulness to him; he is basically unable to love. Does not this prove that concern for others and concern for oneself are unavoidable alternatives? This would be so if selfishness and self-love were identical. But that assumption is the very fallacy which has led to so many mistaken conclusions concerning our problem. Selfishness and self-love, far from being identical, are actually opposites. The selfish person loves himself not too much but too little; in fact he hates himself. This lack of fondness and care for himself, which is only one expression of his lack of productiveness, leaves him empty and frustrated. He is necessarily unhappy and anxiously concerned to snatch from life the satisfactions which he blocks himself from attaining. He seems to care too much for himself but actually he only makes an unsuccessful attempt to cover up and compensate for his failure to care for his real self. Freud holds that the selfish person is narcissistic, as if he had withdrawn his love from others and turned it toward his own person. Rather it is true that selfish persons are incapable of loving themselves either.

It is easier to understand selfishness by comparing it with greedy concern for others, as we find it for instance in an oversolicitous, dominating mother. While she consciously believes that she is particularly fond of her child, she has actually a deeply repressed hostility toward the object of her concern. She is overconcerned not because she loves the child too much, but because she has to compensate for her lack of capacity to love him at all.

This theory of the nature of selfishness is borne out by psychoanalytic experience with neurotic "unselfishness," a symptom of neurosis observed in more than a few people who usually are troubled not by this symptom but by others connected with it, like depression, tiredness, inability to work, failure in love relationships, and so on. Not only is unselfishness not felt as a "symptom"; it is often the one redeeming character trait on which such people pride themselves. The "unselfish" person "does not want anything for himself"; he "lives only for others," is proud that he does not consider himself important. He is puzzled to find that in spite of his unselfishness he is unhappy, and that his relationships to those closest to him are unsatisfactory. He wants to have what he considers are his symptoms removed — but not his unselfishness. Analytic work shows that his unselfishness is not something apart from his other symptoms but one of them, in fact often the most important one; that he is paralyzed in his capacity to love or to enjoy anything; that he is pervaded by hostility against life; and that behind the façade of unselfishness a subtle but not less intense self-centeredness is hidden. This person can be cured only if his unselfishness too is interpreted as a symptom along with the others so that his lack of productiveness, which is at the root of both his unselfishness and his other troubles, can be corrected.

The nature of unselfishness becomes particularly apparent in its effect on others and most frequently, in our culture, in the effect the "unselfish" mother has on her children. She believes that by her unselfishness her children will experience what it means to be loved and to learn, in turn, what it means to love. The effect of her unselfishness, however, does not at all correspond to her expectations. The children do not show the happiness of persons who are convinced that they are loved; they are anxious, tense, afraid of the mother's disapproval, and anxious to live up to her expectations. Usually, they are affected by their mother's hidden hostility against life, which they sense rather than recognize, and eventually become imbued with it themselves. Altogether, the effect of the "unselfish" mother is not too different from that of the selfish one; indeed, it is often worse because the mother's unselfishness prevents the children from criticizing her. They are put under the obligation not to disappoint her; they are taught, under the mask of virtue, dislike for life. If one has a chance to study the effect of a mother with genuine self-love, one can see that there is nothing more conducive to giving a child the experience of what love, joy, and happiness are than being loved by a mother who loves herself.

Having analyzed selfishness and self-love we can now proceed to discuss the concept of self-interest, which has become one of the key symbols in modern society. It is even more ambiguous than selfishness or self-love, and this ambiguity can be fully understood only by taking into account the historical development of the concept of self-interest. The problem is what is considered to constitute self-interest and how it can be determined.

There are two fundamentally different approaches to this problem. One is the objectivistic approach most clearly formulated by Spinoza. To him self-interest or the interest "to seek one's profit" is identical with virtue. "The more," he says, "each person strives and is able to seek his profit, that is to say, to preserve his being, the more virtue does he possess; on the other hand, in so far as each person neglects his own profit he is impotent." * According to this view, the interest of man is to preserve his existence, which is the same as realizing his inherent potentialities. This concept of self-interest is objectivistic inasmuch as "interest" is not conceived in terms of the subjective feeling of what one's interest is but in terms of what the nature of man is, objectively. Man has only one real interest and that is the full development of his potentialities, of himself as a human being. Just as one has to know another person and his real needs in order to love him, one has to know one's own self in order to understand what the interests of this self are and how they can be served. It follows that man can deceive himself about his real self-interest if he is ignorant of his self and its real needs and that the science of man is the basis for determining what constitutes man's self-interest.

The modern concept of self-interest is a strange blend of two contradictory concepts: that of Calvin and Luther on the one hand, and on the other, that of the progressive thinkers since Spinoza. Calvin and Luther had taught that man must suppress his self-interest and consider himself only an instrument for God's purposes. Progressive thinkers, on the contrary, have taught that man ought

* Spinoza, *Ethics*, IV, Prop. 20.

to be only an end for himself and not a means for any purpose transcending him. What happened was that man has accepted the contents of the Calvinistic doctrine while rejecting its religious formulation. He has made himself an instrument not of God's will but of the economic machine or the state. He has accepted the role of a tool not for God but for industrial progress; he has worked and amassed money but essentially not for the pleasure of spending it and of enjoying life but in order to save, to invest, to be successful. Monastic asceticism has been, as Max Weber has pointed out, replaced by an inner-worldly asceticism where personal happiness and enjoyment are no longer the real aims of life. But this attitude was increasingly divorced from the one expressed in Calvin's concept and blended with that expressed in the progressive concept of self-interest, which taught that man had the right — and the obligation — to make the pursuit of his self-interest the supreme norm of life. The result is that modern man lives according to the principles of self-denial and thinks in terms of self-interest. He believes that he is acting in behalf of his interest when actually his paramount concern is money and success; he deceives himself about the fact that his most important human potentialities remain unfulfilled and that he loses himself in the process of seeking what is supposed to be best for him.

The deterioration of the meaning of the concept of self-interest is closely related to the change in the concept of self. In the Middle Ages man felt himself to be an intrinsic part of the social and religious community in reference to which he conceived his own self when he as an individual had not yet fully emerged from his group. Since the beginning of the modern era, when man as an individual was faced with the task of experiencing himself as an independent entity, his own identity became a problem. In the eighteenth and nineteenth centuries the concept of self was narrowed down increasingly; the self was felt to be constituted by the property one had. The formula for this concept of self was no longer "I am what I think" but "I am what I have," "what I possess." *

In the last few generations, under the growing influence of the market, the concept of self has shifted from meaning "I am what I possess" to meaning "I am what you desire me." ** Man, living in a market economy, feels himself to be a commodity. He is divorced from himself, as the seller of a commodity is divorced from what he wants to sell. To be sure, he is interested in himself, immensely interested in his success on the market, but "he" is the manager, the employer, the seller — and the commodity. His self-interest turns out to be the interest of "him" as the subject who employs "himself," as the commodity which should obtain the optimal price on the personality market.

The "fallacy of self-interest" in modern man has never been de-

---

* William James expressed this concept very clearly. "To have," he says, "a self that I can care for, Nature must first present me with some object interesting enough to make me instinctively wish to appropriate it for its own sake. . . . My own body and what ministers to its needs are thus the primitive object, instinctively determined, of my egoistic interests. Other objects may become interesting derivatively, through association with any of these things, either as means or as habitual concomitants; and so, in a thousand ways, the primitive sphere of the egoistic emotions may enlarge and change its boundaries. This sort of interest is really the meaning of the word *mine*. Whatever has it, is, eo ipso, a part of me!" *Principles of Psychology* (New York: Henry Holt and Company, 2 Vols., 1896), I, 319, 324. Elsewhere James writes: "It is clear that between what a man calls *me* and what he calls *mine*, the line is difficult to draw. We feel and act about certain things that are ours very much as we feel and act about ourselves. Our fame, our children, the work of our hands, may be as dear to us as our bodies are, and arouse the same feelings and the same acts of reprisal if attacked. . . . In its widest possible sense, however, a man's Self is the sum-total of all that he can call his, not only his body, and his psychic powers, but his clothes and his house, his wife and children, his ancestors and friends, his reputation and works, his land and horses and yacht and bank account. All these things give him the same emotions. If they wax or prosper, he feels triumphant, if they dwindle and die away, he feels cast down — not necessarily in the same degree for each thing, but in much the same way for all." *Ibid.*, I, 291-292.

** Pirandello in his plays has expressed this concept of self and the self-doubt resulting from it.

scribed better than by Ibsen in *Peer Gynt*. Peer Gynt believes that his whole life is devoted to the attainment of the interests of his self. He describes this self as:

> The Gyntian Self!
> — An army, that, of wishes, appetites, desires!
> The Gyntian Self!
> It is a sea of fancies, claims and aspirations;
> In fact, it's all that swells within my breast
> And makes it come about that I am I and live as such.*

At the end of his life he recognizes that he had deceived himself; that while following the principle of "self-interest" he had failed to recognize what the interests of his real self were, and had lost the very self he sought to preserve. He is told that he never had been himself and that therefore he is to be thrown back into the melting pot to be dealt with as raw material. He discovers that he has lived according to the Troll principle: "To thyself be enough" — which is the opposite of the human principle: "To thyself be true." He is seized by the horror of nothingness to which he, who has no self, cannot help succumbing when the props of pseudo self, success, and possessions are taken away or seriously questioned. He is forced to recognize that in trying to gain all the wealth of the world, in relentlessly pursuing what seemed to be his interest, he had lost his soul — or, as I would rather say, his self.

The deteriorated meaning of the concept of self-interest which pervades modern society has given rise to attacks on democracy from the various types of totalitarian ideologies. These claim that capitalism is morally wrong because it is governed by the principle of selfishness, and commend the moral superiority of their own systems by pointing to their principle of the unselfish subordination of the individual to the "higher" purposes of the state, the "race," or the "socialist fatherland." They impress not a few with this criticism because many people feel that there is no happiness in the

---

* *Loc. cit.*, Act V, Scene I.

pursuit of selfish interest, and are imbued with a striving, vague though it may be, for a greater solidarity and mutual responsibility among men.

We need not waste much time arguing against the totalitarian claims. In the first place, they are insincere since they only disguise the extreme selfishness of an "elite" that wishes to conquer and retain power over the majority of the population. Their ideology of unselfishness has the purpose of deceiving those subject to the control of the elite and of facilitating their exploitation and manipulation. Furthermore, the totalitarian ideologies confuse the issue by making it appear that they represent the principle of unselfishness when they apply to the state as a whole the principle of ruthless pursuit of selfishness. Each citizen ought to be devoted to the common welfare, but the state is permitted to pursue its own interest without regard to the welfare of other nations. But quite aside from the fact that the doctrines of totalitarianism are disguises for the most extreme selfishness, they are a revival — in secular language — of the religious idea of intrinsic human powerlessness and impotence and the resulting need for submission, to overcome which was the essence of modern spiritual and political progress. Not only do the authoritarian ideologies threaten the most precious achievement of Western culture, the respect for the uniqueness and dignity of the individual; they also tend to block the way to constructive criticism of modern society, and thereby to necessary changes. The failure of modern culture lies not in its principle of individualism, of self-interest, but in the deterioration of the meaning of self-interest; not in the fact that people are too much concerned with their self-interest, but that they are not concerned enough with the interest of their real self; not in the fact that they are too selfish, but that they do not love themselves.

If the causes for persevering in the pursuit of a fictitious idea of self-interest are as deeply rooted in the contemporary social structure as indicated above, the chances for a change in the meaning of self-interest would seem to be remote indeed, unless one can point to specific factors operating in the direction of change.

Perhaps the most important factor is the inner dissatisfaction of modern man with the results of his pursuit of "self-interest." The religion of success is crumbling and becoming a façade itself. The social "open spaces" grow narrower; the failure of the hopes for a better world after the First World War, the depression at the end of the twenties, the threat of a new and immensely destructive war so shortly after World War II, and the boundless insecurity resulting from this threat, shake the faith in the pursuit of this form of self-interest. Aside from these factors, the worship of success itself has failed to satisfy man's ineradicable striving to be himself. Like so many fantasies and daydreams, this one too fulfilled its function only for a time, as long as it was new, as long as the excitement connected with it was strong enough to keep man from considering it soberly. There is an increasing number of people to whom everything they are doing seems futile. They are still under the spell of the slogans which preach faith in the secular paradise of success and glamour. But doubt, the fertile condition of all progress, has begun to beset them and has made them ready to ask what their real self-interest as human beings is.

This inner disillusionment and the readiness for a revaluation of self-interest could hardly become effective unless the economic conditions of our culture permitted it. I have pointed out that while the canalizing of all human energy into work and the striving for success was one of the indispensable conditions of the enormous achievement of modern capitalism, a stage has been reached where the problem of production has been virtually solved and where the problem of the organization of social life has become the paramount task of mankind. Man has created such sources of mechanical energy that he has freed himself from the task of putting all his human energy into work in order to produce the material conditions for living. He could spend a considerable part of his energy on the task of living itself.

Only if these two conditions, the subjective dissatisfaction with a culturally patterned aim and the socioeconomic basis for a change, are present, can an indispensable third factor, rational insight, become effective. This holds true as a principle of social and psychological change in general and of the change in the meaning of self-interest in particular. The time has come when the anesthetized striving for the pursuit of man's real interest is coming to life again. Once man knows what his self-interest is, the first, and the most difficult, step to its realization has been taken.

VI FATE AND SELF-DETERMINATION

OTTO RANK

Here we can define self-determination as a voluntary and conscious creating of one's own fate. This means to have no fate in an external sense, but to accept and affirm oneself as fate and fate-creating power. This inner fate includes self-determination also, in the sense of the pleasurable will struggle with ourselves, the conflict which we affirm as long as we interpret it as consciously willed self-creation, and not neurotically as the force of stronger supernatural forces or earthly authorities. Everything depends on how this unavoidable self-creation of our own fate is perceived in our feeling and interpreted by our consciousness, and this again is determined by whether we have essentially an outer or inner ideal in terms of which we want to create ourselves and our fate. It is here that the interplay of will, feeling, and thinking is translated into action which forms and transforms the outside reality. The true self reveals itself in none of these spheres, however, but always only in the other self, that which we want to be, because we are not, in contrast to that which we have become and do not want to be. Accordingly therapy, which shifts to suit the momentary experience, cannot rest on the firm foundation of psychological truth. The manifest truth is the real of the moment, and as such constructive as long as it remains illusionistic, while the immediately latent represents the psychically true, which is always interpretative and as such inhibiting and destructive.

The creative expression of the personality in real experience, with all the deception of its emotional displacement and denial, is constructive. Self-knowledge (introspection) is and remains destructive with all its content of truth. We here strike the problem of the neuroses as a problem of consciousness. If, instead of seeking for the causes of the illness of the neurotic, we only ask ourselves about the causes of good health in other people, it is evident that it all rests on lack of understanding, misunderstanding, ignorance of their own psychology — in short on illusions. The knowledge of the average man about his own psychic processes and motivation proves to be so false that it works really only in its complete spuriousness, in an illusion troubled by no kind of knowing. Reality is always emotionally false, exactly like the manifest dream content, but, as this reveals, is equally constructive — that is, contains illusionistic elements and mechanisms which are necessary for real living. Therefore there can be neither a natural scientific nor an intellectual scientific psychology, but only a will and feeling psychology which works destructively in itself if it is not philosophically oriented, that is, aimed at epistemology and ethics. For the therapy follows from the fact that it can be grounded not on the psychological truth of the individual but on his reality experience, on the dynamic expression of personality. Accordingly, the patient needs reality personified in the therapist, who represents the only therapeutic agent, namly the human counter-will, which by virtue of its own psychic truth can bring the neurotic sufferer back to real living. This experience expresses itself in all the reality illusions of projection and personification, until the patient through and in the leaving experience accomplishes the great sundering of ties, and separates himself as an individual from the other and all that he personifies. This is the really human step, away from all that binds, to the essential self of the individual, while all former ones in the neurotic were directed by a compensatory clinging to his bonds as guilt reaction to the will to freedom and independence.

This step from the fated to the self-determining attitude in the therapeutic experience does not work egocentrically or tend to alienate from reality, if the individual strives for the acceptance of himself as fate-determining instead of an acceptance of reality as fate. The whole emphasis of experience is changed from the battle against a real fate which has created him, to the acceptance of his own willing individuality which not only creates its own reality but also affirms that which is given, in terms of self-determination. While the average man perceives himself really and adapts reality to his ego, that is, makes it acceptable through all the previously mentioned illusions, the neurotic perceives himself as unreal and reality as unbearable, because with him the mechanisms of illusion are known and destroyed by self-consciousness. He can no longer deceive himself about himself and disillusions even his own ideal of personality. He perceives himself as bad, guilt-laden, inferior, as a small, weak, helpless creature, which is the truth about mankind, as Ædipus also discovered in the crash of his heroic fate. All other is illusion, is deception, but necessary deception in order to be able to bear one's self and thereby life. The neurotic type represents a declaration of bankruptcy in human self-knowledge, as he destroys not only the unreal will justification of the religious projection and the real justification attempts of earthly authority and love ideals but also his own ethical ideal formation through his too-strong guilt consciousness. We recognize in him the human type who in an attempt at ethical justification masks even the ideal formation of his own individual ego. The weak, dependent, evil ego recognizes itself in him as the helpless creature which must justify itself through the creator, no matter whether it relates to a cosmic creator like the occidental God, an individual creator like the father of a family, or finally the self-creating personality who interprets his own individual ego as ideal, and as such puts it in place of real and unreal symbols of authority.

The modern neurotic type has thus completed the human process of internalization which reaches its peak in psychological self-knowledge, but also is reduced to an absurdity. He needs no more knowing; only experience and the capacity for it may yet be able to save him. Therefore it is of no consequence whether we call his knowledge psychologically true or false. The essential fact is that it contains a self-interpretation which is opposed to experience. In this sense one cannot say that the neurotic interprets falsely and psycho-analysis correctly; they merely interpret differently, but the fact remains that both are forced to interpret. Also it makes no difference whether it is correctly or falsely motivated, since there is no general criterion but only the fact that, in general, life must be interpreted and that the interpretation must be believed, that is, accepted as illusion.

The neurotic of today, however, already burdened with psycho-analytic knowledge, can no longer accept therapeutically even a natural science illusion, having already destroyed the religious and personal ones on which it rests, with the mounting consciousness of guilt. He is helped not by more knowing but only by willing, not by knowledge of his fate but by the living of his self-determination. This is no longer possible through the creation of new illusions, either real or spiritual, even if they appear in the guise of natural science ideology, in itself a continuation of disillusioning, or in the form of broader knowledge, but only in terms of the acceptance of the self, of the individuality as given, yes, as the only reality of which a doubt is not possible. Since the individual actually feels himself as real in the constructive separation experience, he trusts himself again to will without being obliged to justify this will in the other morally or to react with guilt to it. Yes, he can even give up having to justify his will ethically in his own ideal, if he accepts this ideal in a creative experience as his own real self. The average man always plays a role, always acts, but actually plays only himself — that is, must pretend that he plays, in order to justify his being; the neurotic, on the contrary, refuses this acting, this pretending, and yet is unable to be himself without will justification. With the impossibility of acting, this hypocritical rationalizing of the will falls away, but the neurotic is unable to put it through on his own responsibility. However, in dynamic therapy, as he can no longer assign this justifying role to others there remains to him only the solution of not pretending to play what he is, but really to be it; in other words, to accept himself as he is. Then self and ideal coincide, and are perceived as real, while the outer reality becomes material for the assertion of will and a therapeutic means of guilt-unburdening. In both avenues of expression we find a new source of guilt to be sure, but this can never be overcome intellectually, as it is the consequence of will itself and can only be continuously expiated in creative experience, where it works as individual guilt, not as neurotic guilt-consciousness.

In the therapy of the individual neurotic we deal therefore not with knowledge or ignorance, nor with the need for an "other" or "better" knowing, but with willing, to which knowing in the beginning serves as rationalization and only later opposes itself inhibitingly. The freedom of the will, to which the individual must attain, relates first of all to the self, the individuality; so to will this, as it is, forms the goal of constructive therapy while all forms of educational therapy wish to alter the individual in terms of a given ideology as he ought to be. From the latter viewpoint the individual must accept this ideology as authoritative, that is — believe; from the former, he must first believe in himself instead of being measured by the yardstick of any ideology in terms of which he perceives himself as bad and inferior. This feeling or rejection in relation to an unattainable ideal designates the individual as neurotic, while the creative man who perceives the rejection of the contemporary ideology first in terms of people, affirms himself as an individual, as different, and then creates a new ideology for himself which, corresponding to the level of consciousness attained, always works constructively for a definite phase, whether it be in heroic, artistic, or philosophic terms. For all constructiveness is temporary and limited, yes, it consists just in working out and affirming the new aspect of consciousness as immediately manifested in the eternal will-guilt conflict. The earlier this new aspect can be recognized and the more intensively it can be affirmed, the more it can be utilized constructively. This is valid for the therapeutic situation as well as for experience in general, which it represents psychically.

In one important point, however, the therapeutic experience differs from real experience. The latter is essentially an outer, the therapeutic an inner, experience which may be made external and concrete only far enough for the patient to recognize and accept it as his own self in the analytic reality created by him. In this sense the individual therapy of the neurosis is philosophical, which Freud will not admit because he thinks in the medical ideology in which he has grown up. But he himself has found that the neurosis presents not a medical but a moral problem, and accordingly the therapy is not casual but constructive, that is, a process which enables the sufferer to reach a level of development which he cannot attain alone, whose necessity, however, is laid down in terms of continuing self-consciousness. The patient needs a world view and will always need it, because man always needs belief, and this so much more, the more increasing self-consciousness brings him to doubt. Psychotherapy does not need to be ashamed of its philosophic character, if only it is in a position to give to the sufferer the philosophy that he needs, namely, faith in himself.

VII THE WORLD OF PERSONALITY

RABINDRANATH TAGORE

It is a well-known fact that our dreams often flow in a measure of time different from that of our waking consciousness. The fifty minutes of our sundial of dreamland may be represented by five minutes of our clock. If from the vantage of our wakeful time we could watch these dreams, they would rush past us like an express train. Or if from the window of our swift-flying dreams we could watch the slower world of our waking consciousness, it would seem to recede away from us at a great speed. In fact if the thoughts that move in other minds than our own were open to us, our perception of them would be different from theirs, owing to our difference of mental time. If we could adjust our focus of time according to our whims, we should see the waterfall standing still and the pine forest running fast like the waterfall of a green Niagara.

So that it is almost a truism to say that the world is what we perceive it to be. We imagine that our mind is a mirror, that it is more or less accurately reflecting what is happening outside us. On the contrary, our mind itself is the principal element of creation. The world, while I am perceiving it, is being incessantly created for myself in time and space.

The variety of creation is due to the mind seeing different phenomena in different foci of time and space. When it sees stars in a space which may be metaphorically termed as dense, then they are close to each other and motionless. When it sees planets, it sees them in much less density of sky and then they appear far apart and moving. If we could have the sight to see the molecules of a piece of iron in a greatly different space, they could be seen in movement. But because we see things in various adjustments of time and space therefore iron is iron, water is water, and clouds are clouds for us.

It is a well-known psychological fact that by adjustment of our mental attitude things seem to change their properties, and objects that were pleasurable become painful to us and vice versa. Under a certain state of exultation of mind mortification of the flesh has been resorted to by men to give them pleasure. Instances of extreme martyrdom seem to us superhuman because the mental attitude under the influence of which they become possible, even desirable, has not been experienced by us. In India, cases of fire-walking have been observed by many, though they have not been scientifically investigated. There may be differences of opinion about the degree of efficacy of faith cure, which shows the influence of mind upon matter, but its truth has been accepted and acted upon by men from the early dawn of history. The methods of our moral training have been based upon the fact that by changing our mental focus, our perspective, the whole world is changed and becomes in certain respects a different creation with things of changed value. Therefore what is valuable to a man when he is bad becomes worse than valueless when he is good.

When the mind of a person like Walt Whitman moves in a time different from that of others, his world does not necessarily come to ruin through dislocation, because there in the center of his world dwells his own personality. All the facts and shapes of this world are related to this central creative power, therefore, they become interrelated spontaneously. His world may be like a comet among stars, different in its movement from others, but it has its own consistency because of the central personal force. It may be a bold world or even a mad world, with an immense orbit swept by its eccentric tail, yet a world it is.

But with Science it is different. For she tries to do away altogether with that central personality, in relation to which the world is a world. Science sets up an impersonal and unalterable standard of creation. Therefore at its fatal touch the reality of the world is so hopelessly disturbed that it vanishes in an abstraction where things become nothing at all. For the world is not atoms and molecules or radioactivity or other forces, the diamond is not carbon, and light is not vibrations of ether. You can never come to the reality of creation by contemplating it from the point of view of destruction. Not only the world but God Himself is divested of reality by Science, which subjects Him to analysis in the laboratory of reason outside our personal relationship, and then describes the result as unknown and unknowable. It is a mere tautology to say that God is unknowable, when we leave altogether out of account the person who can and who does know Him. It is the same thing as saying that food is uneatable when the eater is absent. Our dry moralists also play the same tricks with us in order to wean away our hearts from their desired objects. Instead of creating for us a world in which moral ideals find their natural places in beauty, they begin to wreck the world that we have built ourselves, however imperfectly. They put moral maxims in the place of human personality and give us the view of things in their dissolution to prove that behind their appearances they are hideous deceptions. But when you deprive truth of its appearance it loses the best part of its reality. For appearance is a personal relationship; it is for me.

Our scientific world is our world of reasoning. It has its greatness and uses and attractions. We are ready to pay the homage due to it. But when it claims to have discovered this real world for us and laughs at the worlds of all simple-minded men, then we must say it is like a general grown intoxicated with his power, usurping the

throne of his king. For the reality of the world belongs to the
personality of man and not to reasoning, which, useful and great
though it be, is not the man himself.

If we could fully know what a piece of music was in Beethoven's
mind we could ourselves become so many Beethovens. But because
we cannot grasp its mystery we may altogether distrust the element
of Beethoven's personality in his sonata — though we are fully aware
that its true value lies in its power of touching the depth of our own
personality. But it is simpler to keep observation of the facts when
that sonata is played upon the piano. We can count the black and
white keys of the keyboard, measure the relative lengths of the
strings, the strength, velocity, and order of sequence in the movements of figures, and triumphantly assert that this is Beethoven's
sonata. Not only so, we can predict the accurate production of the
same sonata wherever and whenever our experiment is repeated
according to those observations. By constantly dealing with the
sonata from this point of view we may forget that both in its origin
and object dwells the personality of man, and however accurate and
orderly may be the facts of the interactions of the fingers and
strings, they do not comprehend the ultimate reality of the music.

A game is a game where there is a player to play it. Of course,
there is a law of the game which it is of use to us to analyze and to
master. But if it be asserted that in this law is its reality, then we
cannot accept it. For the game changes its aspects according to the
personality of its players: for some its end is the lust of gain, in
others that of applause; some find in it the means for whiling away
time and some the means for satisfying their social instinct, and
there are others who approach it in the spirit of disinterested curiosity to study its secrets. Yet all through its manifold aspects its law
remains the same. For the nature of Reality is the variedness of its
unity. And the world is like this game to us — it is the same and
yet not the same to us all.

Science deals with this element of sameness, the law of perspective and color combination, and not with the pictures — the pictures which are the creations of a personality and which appeal to the personality of those who see them. Science does this by eliminating from its field of research the personality of creation and fixing its attention only upon the medium of creation.

What is this medium? It is the medium which represents his self-imposed limitations — the law of space and time, of form and movement. This law is Reason, which is universal — Reason which guides the endless rhythm of the creative idea, perpetually manifesting itself in its ever-changing forms.

Our individual minds are the strings which catch the rhythmic vibrations of this universal mind and respond in music of space and time. The quality and number and pitch of our mind strings differ and their tuning has not yet come to its perfection, but their law is the law of the universal mind.

Because of the mind instruments which we possess we also have found our place as creators. We create not only art and social organizations but our inner nature and outer surroundings, the truth of which depends upon their harmony with the law of the universal mind. Of course, our creations are mere variations upon God's great theme of the universe. When we produce discords, they either have to end in a harmony or in silence. Our freedom as a creator finds its highest joy in contributing its own voice to the concert of the world-music.

Those who pursue the knowledge of finite for its own sake cannot find truth. For it is a dead wall obstructing the beyond. This knowledge merely accumulates but does not illuminate. It is like a lamp without its light, a violin without its music. You cannot know a book by measuring and weighing and counting its pages, by analyzing its paper. An inquisitive mouse may gnaw through the wooden frame of a piano, may cut all its strings to pieces, and yet travel farther and farther away from the music. This is the pursuit of the finite for its own sake.

We have seen that forms of things and their changes have no

absolute reality at all. Their truth dwells in our personality, and only there is it real and not abstract. We have seen that a mountain and a waterfall would become something else, or nothing at all to us, if our movement of mind changed in time and space.

We have also seen that this relational world of ours is not arbitrary. It is individual, yet it is universal. My world is mine, its element is my mind, yet it is not wholly unlike your world. Therefore it is not in my own individual personality that this reality is contained, but in an infinite personality.

When in its place we substitute law, then the whole world crumbles into abstractions; then it is elements and force, ions and electrons; it loses its appearance, its touch and taste; the world drama with its language of beauty is hushed, the music is silent, the stage mechanism becomes a ghost of itself in the dark, an unimaginable shadow of nothing, standing before no spectator.

In our crucible of reason the world of appearance vanishes and we call it illusion. This is the negative view. But our enjoyment is positive. A flower is nothing when we analyze it, but it is positively a flower when we enjoy it. This joy is real because it is personal. And perfect truth is only perfectly known by our personality.

Perpetual giving up is the truth of life. The perfection of this is our life's perfection. If we are to make this life our poem in all its expressions it must be fully suggestive of our soul which is infinite, not merely of our possessions which have no meaning in themselves. The consciousness of the infinite in us proves itself by our joy in giving ourselves out of our abundance. And then our work is the process of our renunciation, it is one with our life. It is like the flowing of the river, which is the river itself.

Let us live. Let us have the true joy of life, which is the joy of the poet in pouring himself out in his poem. Let us express our infinity in everything round us, in works we do, in things we use, in men with whom we deal, in the enjoyment of the world with which we are surrounded.

Only by living life fully can you outgrow it. When the fruit has served its full term, drawing its juice from the branch as it dances with the wind and matures in the sun, then it feels in its core the call of the beyond and becomes ready for its career of a wider life. But the wisdom of living is in that which gives you the power to give it up. For death is the gate of immortality. Therefore it is said, Do your work, but let not your work cling to you. For the work expresses your life so long as it flows with it, but when it clings then it impedes, and shows, not the life, but itself. Then like the sands carried by the stream it chokes the soul current. Activity of limbs is in the nature of physical life; but when limbs move in convulsion, then the movements are not in harmony with life but become a disease, like works that cling to a man and kill his soul.

We must not forget that life is here to express the eternal in us. If we smother our consciousness of the infinite either by slothfulness or by passionate pursuit of things that have no freedom of greatness in them, then like the fruit whose seed has become dead we go back into the primal gloom of the realm of the unformed. Life is perpetual creation; it has its truth when it outgrows itself in the infinite. But when it stops and accumulates and turns back to itself, when it has lost its outlook upon the beyond, then it must die. Then it is dismissed from the world of growth and with all its heaps of belongings crumbles into the dust of dissolution. Of them Isha Upanishad has said: "Those who slay their souls pass from hence to the gloom of the sunless world."

The question, "What is this soul," has thus been answered by the Isha Upanishad:

"It is one, and though unmoving is swifter than mind; organs of sense cannot reach it; while standing it progresses beyond others that run; in it the life inspiration maintains the fluid forces of life."

The mind has its limitations, the sense organs are severally occupied with things that are before them, but there is a spirit of oneness in us which goes beyond the thoughts of its mind, the movements of its bodily organs, which carries whole eternity in its present moment, while through its presence the life inspiration ever urges the life forces onward. Because we are conscious of this One in us which is more than all its belongings, which outlives the death of its moments, we cannot believe that it can die. Because it is one, because it is more than its parts, because it is continual survival, perpetual overflow, we feel it beyond all boundaries of death.

This consciousness of oneness beyond all boundaries is the consciousness of soul. And of this soul Isha Upanishad has said: "It moves. It moves not. It is in the distant. It is in the near. It is within all. It is outside all."

This is to know the soul across the boundaries of the near and the distance of the within and the without. I have known this wonder of wonders, this one in myself which is the center of all reality for me. But I cannot stop here. I cannot say that it exceeds all boundaries, and yet is bounded by myself. Therefore Isha Upanishad says:

"He who sees all things in the soul and the soul in all things is nevermore hidden."

We are hidden in ourselves, like a truth hidden in isolated facts. When we know that this One in us is one in all, then our truth is revealed.

But this knowledge of the unity of soul must not be an abstraction. It is not that negative kind of universalism which belongs neither to one nor to another. It is not an abstract soul, but it is my own soul which I must realize in others. I must know that if my soul were singularly mine then it could not be true; at the same time if it were not intimately mine it would not be real.

Through the help of logic we never could have arrived at the truth that the soul which is the unifying principle in me finds its perfection in its unity in others. We have known it through the joy of this truth. Our delight is in realizing ourselves outside us.

When I love, in other words, when I feel I am truer in someone else than myself, then I am glad, for the One in me realizes its truth of unity by uniting with others, and there is its joy.

Therefore the realization of our soul has its moral and its spiritual side. The moral side represents training of unselfishness, control of desires; the spiritual side represents sympathy and love. They should be taken together and never separated. The cultivation of the merely moral side of our nature leads us to the dark region of narrowness and hardness of heart, to the intolerant arrogance of goodness; and the cultivation of the merely spiritual side of nature leads us to a still darker region of revelry in intemperance of imagination.

By following the poet of Isha Upanishad we have come to the meaning of all reality, where the infinite is giving himself out through finitude. Reality is the expression of personality, like a poem, like a work of art. The Supreme Being is giving himself in his world and I am making it mine, like a poem which I realize by finding myself in it. If my own personality leaves the center of my world, then in a moment it loses all its attributes. From this I know that my world exists in relation to me, and I know that it has been given to the personal me by a personal being. The process of the giving can be classified and generalized by science, but not the gift. For the gift is the soul unto the soul, therefore it can only be realized by the soul in joy, not analyzed by the reason in logic.

Therefore the one cry of the personal man has been to know the Supreme Person. From the beginning of his history man has been feeling the touch of personality in all creation and trying to give it names and forms, weaving it in legends round his life and the life of his races, offering it worship and establishing relations with it through countless forms of ceremonial. This feeling of the touch of personality has given the centrifugal impulse in man's heart to break out in a ceaseless flow of reaction, in songs and pictures and poems, in images and temples and festivities. This has been the centripetal force which attracted men into groups and clans and communal organizations. And while man tills his soil and spins his cloths, mates and rears his children, toils for wealth and fights for power, he does not forget to proclaim in languages of solemn rhythm, in mysterious symbols, in structures of majestic stone, that in the heart of his world he has met the Immortal Person. In the sorrow of death and suffering of despair, when trust has been betrayed and love desecrated, when existence becomes tasteless and unmeaning, man standing upon the ruins of his hopes stretches his hands to the heavens to feel the touch of the Person across his darkened world.

VIII   THE PERSONALITY *

PRESCOTT LECKY

> The world hath many centers, one for each created being,
> and about each one it lieth in its own circle. Thou
> standest but half an ell from me, yet about thee lieth a
> universe whose center I am not but thou art.
> — THOMAS MANN, *Joseph in Egypt*

In this endeavor to give form and content to the concept of
the personality, it is important that the motive for the undertaking should not be misinterpreted. Let us therefore say at once
that this conception of the personality is not intended as a
contribution to knowledge of the sort which is verifiable by any
merely descriptive account of an organism's behavior. Its value for
scientific purposes is no less on that account. It is simply, as we
have said before, a means to an end, but a necessary means if
we are interested in the organization of behavior, and if we

* The present chapter is apparently the one upon which Lecky was laboring when
his work was cut short by his death. Its fragmentary character — the manuscript
represents only a tentative first draft — is the more regrettable since it is clear that
this was to have been one of the most exacting, as it was the culminating, task of
his life's work. The problem of composing his beliefs, of formulating the doctrine
in a way which might be adequate to express his ultimate intention is therefore
only partially solved. Unfortunately here least of all can any work of divination on
the part of an editor suffice to elaborate upon that intention which emerges, though
only incompletely, in the following pages. Paragraphs have been added from one of
Lecky's occasional papers, titled "The Theory of Self-Consistency." — EDITOR'S NOTE.

hope to achieve a scientific understanding of another individual. Until the end of the nineteenth century the physiological theory of stimulus-response, based on the analogy between the nervous system and a telegraph system, dominated all psychological thinking. But the theory, which substituted the analogy of a hydraulic system and endeavored to conceive of mental processes in terms of the behavior of liquids under pressure, proved inadequate for clinical purposes and was challenged by psychoanalysis. It was this analogy which gave rise to such concepts as repression, emotional outlets, sublimation, drainage, equilibrium, etc. Both theories attempt by the use of these analogies to maintain the appearance of consistency with the traditions of mechanistic science.

The hydraulic analogy seemed to offer an alternative to the telegraphic concept chiefly because of its greater flexibility for dealing with problems of motivation. Instead of relying on environmental forces acting as stimuli, it postulated a group of internal forces seeking external expression. But it has never been possible to explain all behavior as the expression of the same type of energy, which would be quite necessary, of course, if the hydraulic figure were followed literally. Freud attempted to confine his theory to the single instinct of love or sex, but he was forced to recognize the so-called ego motives, and later added the death instinct, which makes for aggression and hatred. Similarly, Adler began with the aggressive striving for power or superiority, but later was obliged to admit the existence of social feeling and cooperative tendencies. Other schools recognize much longer lists of instincts. But in all cases it has been observed that motives conflict and interfere with one another, which has led to the belief that each different motive must be treated independently. The result is that the hydraulic analogy leads to a number of dynamic units, just as the telegraphic concept, with its great variety of habits and reaction patterns, leads to a number of structural units. Both theories have thus succeeded in obscuring the integral character of the organism's activity: the organization has either been divided against itself or been reduced to a loose aggregate of elements.

These mechanistic figures of speech have been useful devices for preliminary organization of the data, but they have not produced a conception of man which disinterested students of the evidence are able to accept. After fifty years of research under mechanistic auspices, psychology is more disorganized in respect of its theoretical outlook than ever before in its history.

Instead of assuming beforehand, therefore, that man is a machine which is moved by forces, a lump whose future behavior is predictable from records of its past behavior, let us assume that as long as he remains alive he must be thought of as a unit in himself, a system which operates as a whole. His behavior must then be interpreted in terms of action rather than reaction, that is, in terms of purpose.

Mechanistic theories, since they assume that activity is only an effect of some antecedent cause, must attempt to explain activity itself, and must therefore seek to define or isolate the case of activity. The usual formulation is that the organism acts because it is stimulated. We assume, on the contrary, that every organism, as long as it remains alive, is continuously active, and hence continuously purposive. Life and activity are coexistent and inseparable. We do not have to explain why the organism acts, but only why it acts in one way rather than another. A stimulus does not initiate activity, but merely tends to modify in one or another way the activity already in progress.

Such a suggestion is by no means radical from a humanistic standpoint. Any theory which is erected on the basis of this principle of unified action, however, and any technique derived from the theory for clinical use, is automatically prohibited from assuming a plurality of purposes. One source of motivation only, the necessity to maintain the unity of the system, must serve as the universal dynamic principle. Not conflict but unity must be the fundamental postulate.

Practically all schools of psychotherapy aim at the elimination of conflict, in spite of the fact that conflict is postulated as fundamental. Hence it is clear that they too aim at unification as a goal, though the possibility of attaining the goal is inconsistent with their premises. It is obvious, then that conflict must be assumed to be a temporary disturbance only, a kind of illness in contrast to health rather than a permanent and necessary condition. Though conflict is usually present, it is not due to the structure of the personality itself. It is rather due to environmental changes which present a continuous series of new problems to be solved.

Although we assume a constant striving for unity, we do not assume that the outcome of the striving is necessarily successful. The environment sets the conditions of the problem which must be met, and in some instances an adequate solution may not be forthcoming. If the outcome could be guaranteed, as it is in classical physics, the mechanistic view would be reinstated and the postulate of purposive striving would be unnecessary.

We propose to apprehend all psychological phenomena as illustrations of the single principle of unity or self-consistency. We conceive of the personality as an organization of values which are felt to be consistent with one another. Behavior expresses the effort to maintain the integrity and unity of the organization.

The point is that all of an individual's values are organized into a single system, the preservation of whose integrity is essential. The nucleus of the system, around which the rest of the system revolves, is the individual's valuation of himself. The individual sees the world from his own viewpoint, with himself as the center. Any value entering the system which is inconsistent with the individual's valuation of himself cannot be assimilated; it meets with resistance and is likely, unless a general reorganization occurs, to be rejected. This resistance is a natural phenomenon; it is essential for the maintenance of individuality.

The changing situation presents continuous problems of adjustment, but the organization can make a unified movement only in one direction at a time, which explains why only a single tendency can be dominant at one time. In this way we avoid the assumption of a primitive reservoir of motives, represented in the Freudian scheme by the Id, or the need for a number of distinct and independent dynamic units or instincts such as McDougall postulates.

Freud clearly recognizes the unifying principle in his concept of the life instinct or love, though he regards it not as primary but as derived from the sexual instinct. The life instinct is contrasted, however, with the death instinct, hate, which divides the personality again and really sets up conflict as the fundamental principle. This contradiction is avoided when, in accordance with our view, the direction of derivation is reversed. The sex motive must be thought of as ultimately aimed at the achievement of unity in the same way as other motives. The striving for unity is constant, the striving for sex satisfaction variable, instead of the other way around.

The individual's organization of values makes itself evident in the regularity of his behavior. The organization not only defines his role in life but furnishes him with standards which he feels obliged to maintain. These standards become visible if we disregard the details of his physical movements, and apprehend his behavior as his standards translated into action.

The reliability of a child's behavior, as indicated either by tests or by general observation, is thus explained by the theory of self-consistency as the outward expression of relatively fixed internal standards. It is often argued that the reliability of a test proves that the test is measuring the child's ability. All that any test can measure, however, is the level of performance which is characteristic of the child at the time when the test is given. It is not the test which is reliable, but the child. We cannot interpret the score simply as a measure of ability unless we disregard the problem of resistance entirely, and assume not only the presence of specific abilities but also the motive to use them to the limit.

It is important not to confuse these internal psychological standards with any sort of external standards of how people in general *ought* to behave. There is nothing to prevent a person from accepting these external standards as his own and making them a part of his system. All members of a family, for instance, define themselves as members of the family and will act in consistency with that definition. We think of ourselves also as belonging to larger groups, for instance as all being workers in a science, as all being Americans, members of the human race, and so on. If we accept definitions of ourselves as members of groups, it is just as necessary to maintain these definitions as to maintain definitions of ourselves as isolated individuals.* Yet if a person does not accept them, he will not maintain them. The criminal is an obvious example.

Let us think of the individual, therefore, as a unified system with two sets of problems — one the problem of maintaining inner harmony within himself, and the other the problem of maintaining harmony with the environment, especially the social environment, in the midst of which he lives. In order to understand the environment he must keep his interpretations consistent with his experience, but in order to maintain his individuality he must organize his interpretations to form a system which is internally consistent. This consistency is not objective, of course, but subjective and wholly individual.

The personality develops as a result of actual contacts with the world, and incorporates into itself the meanings derived from external contacts. Essentially, it is the organization of experience into an integrated whole.

* This is the basis for reconciling the apparent contradiction between individual behavior and group behavior.

Only those situations which enter into individual experience, therefore, enter into the personality and need to be provided for. Ideally, then, we should begin by determining the nature of the individual's experience, especially during the first years of life, and observing the manner in which this experience is organized. But from a practical standpoint this is impossible; instead, we have to infer the organization from the way in which present situations are dealt with. That is why mechanistic explanations are useless. We must have some means of obtaining sufficient and relevant data to work with, but the real task is to create from the data a conception of the subject which will give us insight into his behavior and reveal its coherence and purpose.*

The most constant factor in the individual's experience, as we have said, is himself and the interpretation of his own meaning; the kind of person he is, the place which he occupies in the world, appear to represent the center or nucleus of the personality. . . .

We shall define the personality, then, as a unified scheme of experience, an organization of values that are consistent with one another. And we shall conceive the study of human beings as the study of personalities. The organization must be thought of, moreover, not merely as a figure of speech but as in some sense a reality. Whether the interpretations of behavior which are based on this conception should be regarded as true or not will depend to some extent on how one chooses to define truth. The mechanist also believes that his explanations are true. But so far as we are concerned,

---

* The only precedent which we have to guide us in this endeavor is Freud's attempt to conceptualize the personality from the standpoint of psychoanalysis. His scheme is a topographical arrangement of the mind into three main departments, the Id, the Ego, and the Super-ego, superimposed upon another three-way classification showing the parts which belong to the unconscious, preconscious, and conscious systems of ideas. The complexity of Freud's scheme to a large extent defeats his purpose. His effort to organize the interpretation of clinical observations has nevertheless been, we feel, an indispensable aid. The lack of simplicity in the scheme can be traced directly to a corresponding lack of simplicity in the theory itself, particularly with respect to the idea of a divided personality which is part conscious and part unconscious.

our search is simply for an explanation that will prove to be illuminating and fruitful.

We believe that all behavior must be explained in terms of this system. It is too early to attempt an exhaustive treatment, but some of the more familiar phenomena of psychology are interpreted as follows.

Identification represents the effort of the child to bring his ideas of himself and his parents into more unified relationship. He not only imitates his parents but adopts their views and opinions as his own. His parent's religion becomes his religion, their standards becomes his standards. In this way differences are eliminated, and the bonds of relationship strengthened by increasing the "consciousness of kind." Assimilation and identification go hand in hand; the child's weak ego, having originally no values of its own, is readily adaptable and takes on those values which aid in unifying the system as a whole.

An excellent illustration of the alteration of values which accompanies identification is found in the Book of Ruth, 1. 16–17, "For whither thou goest, I will go; and where thou lodgest, I will lodge; thy people shall be my people, and thy God my God: where thou diest will I die, and there will I be buried; the Lord do so to me, and more also, if aught but death part thee and me."

Most parents identify themselves with the child to some extent, and try as it were to make themselves more assimilable by taking over some of the child's standards. Such identification also occurs between lovers. When the process is carried to sentimental extremes, however, as when the parents talk baby-talk, it is obvious that the child will base its own values on unsound premises. There may be differences of opinion as to the desirability of some values, but it can hardly be of assistance to the child to derive its standards from the observation of childish behavior, whether on the part of its parents or other children.

This point, it seems to us, is overlooked by those modern theorists who would abolish the home altogether and segregate the children into child communities under scientific management where attachments to adults will not be formed. For it cannot be assumed that adult values are innate or instinctive in the child; and if they are not to be obtained by identification with adults, it is difficult to see from what other source they could be expected to arise. It is easy enough to construct Utopias where behavior is conceived as the automatic performance of mechanical habits, but the problem of establishing in the child a conception of life which will work to his benefit cannot be approached so optimistically.

Resistance is the opposite of assimilation and learning, and represents the refusal to reorganize the values, especially the ego values. With age, of course, the values become more firmly established, and adaptability decreases. To the psychiatrist, the striving of the patient to maintain his organization appears as a symptom of perversity. To the educator it appears as an obstacle to learning. But if we would really understand these resistances, we must see them not as neurotic or abnormal manifestations but as wholly natural devices for avoiding reorganization. If a person were able to adapt himself as readily as is sometimes expected, he would have no personality.

Whether resistance be thought of as desirable or undesirable, therefore, is wholly a matter of the point of view. The loyalty to individual values may interfere with efforts to change them, but this loyalty is also the source of honesty and integrity.

The following instance will illustrate that resistance to learning also has its favorable side. For years the deficiency of boys in reading, as compared with girls who receive the same instruction, has been widely recognized, particularly in elementary courses. We have discovered that this difference is due not to a lack of ability on the part of the boys but to a lack of reading material which is suitable for boys. The boy from six to eight years old, just beginning to learn to read, is mainly concerned with maintaining the conception of himself as manly. He likes to play cowboy, G-man, and Indian.

He tries not to cry when he gets a bump. Yet this boy, when the reading lesson begins, must stand up before his companions and read that, "the little red hen says 'Cluck! Cluck! Cluck!'" — or something equally inconsistent with his standards of how he should behave. To be obliged to read such material aloud, especially in the presence of others, is not consistent with his view of masculine values. If a boy is trying to maintain a standard of manliness on the playground, he does not abandon that standard merely because he walks from the playground into the classroom. When books on railroads and airplanes are provided, they serve to support these values and are assimilated eagerly. The point is, of course, that the assumed defect in reading never was a defect except from the standpoint of an unenlightened school system, but on the contrary was a manifestation of a wholesome, normal, and desirable resistance.

In the Freudian scheme, resistance is interpreted as the patient's desire to retain his neurosis, whereas we interpret it as the desire to maintain his personality. This enables us to point out that what the psychoanalyst calls a neurosis and what we call the personality are virtually identical. The patient is seeking to defend not a mental disease which the analyst is trying to remove but a scheme of life which the analyst is trying to change. Many analysts admit this freely. While we may think of a person's scheme of life as unconscious in the sense that it has not been consciously formulated as a whole, however, we could scarcely attribute the unconsciousness to the mechanism of repression.

The various so-called *emotional states* cannot be treated independently, but must be regarded as different aspects of a single motive, the striving for unity.

For example, love is the emotion subjectively experienced in reference to a person or object already assimilated and serving as a strong support to the idea of self. Grief is experienced when the personality must be reorganized due to the loss of one of its supports. Hatred and rage are impulses of rejection and destruction felt toward unassimilable objects. The emotion of horror appears when a situation arises suddenly which we are not prepared to assimilate, such as the sight of a ghastly accident.

Experiences which increase the sense of psychological unity and strength give rise to the emotion of joy and feelings of pleasure. Occasionally a person's own behavior may violate his conception of himself, producing feelings of remorse and guilt. In that case, the insult to himself, as it were, may be eliminated either by reinterpretation, or by seeking punishment sufficient to equalize the insult. Fear is felt when no adequate solution of a problem can be found; it is due to dynamic disorganization.

From our standpoint emotion is a concept which is necessary only when the problem of behavior is stated descriptively. A psychological theory which conceives of motivation as a phenomenon of organization has no need for the conception of emotion.

Thinking likewise has the aim of unifying the organization of ideas. Logic and emotion, so-called, therefore, are not in conflict, but work toward the same end. If most of our thinking appears to have the purpose of merely rationalizing our behavior to make it seem consistent, of defending conclusions already reached or justifying positions already taken, this is, indeed, what would be expected under the circumstances.

The Freudian theory of *repression,* which is regarded as the cornerstone of psychoanalytic theory, has undergone so many revisions that the exact present meaning of the concept is somewhat in doubt. The general idea seems to be, however, that emotions which are denied expression are suppressed into the unconscious, from which thereafter they continually seek some means of escape. There is no doubt that in certain cases this explanation seems quite plausible, but inasmuch as it presupposes the existence of emotion as a separate entity we are forced to reject the theory of repression and seek to reinterpret the phenomena from the standpoint of organization.

Let us take, for example, the psychological problem raised when a person feels insulted. This means that there has been thrust into his experience a value of himself or of someone with whom he is identified which he cannot assimilate. This inconsistency is a source of disturbance, and unless the person responsible "takes back" the insult the disturbance continues. If he refuses to "take it back," there is an impulse to retaliation. That is, the low value seems to be eliminated by hurling it back upon its author.

But suppose that, for reasons of expediency, it cannot be hurled back; what then? Shall we say with Freud that the energy (death instinct) has undergone repression into the reservoir of the Id, to seek expression later when the life instinct is less active, or shall we rather say that the organism continues to strive to remove the inconsistency and unify itself?

To answer this question, let us turn to the evidence of primitive behavior to which Freud himself so often appeals. How would the repression theory account for the exact balance between injury and reprisal provided for in primitive codes of vengeance, or the conception that justice has not been done unless the punishment inflicted is consistent with the crime?

Obviously, the motive is to correct the situation and make it more assimilable. We quote an illustration from the ancient Hebrew law as given in Leviticus, xxiv. 18–20; "And he that killeth a beast shall make it good; beast for beast. And if a man cause a blemish in his neighbor; as he hath done, so shall it be done to him; breach for breach, eye for eye, tooth for tooth; as he has caused a blemish in a man, so shall it be done to him again. And he that killeth a beast, he shall restore it; and he that killeth a man, he shall be put to death."

The impulse to retaliation aroused when a person has been insulted or treated unjustly is therefore not an accumulation of energy waiting to be discharged, but a purposive effort of the organization to rid itself of inconsistency.

IX TRUTH AND REALITY FROM TWO POINTS OF VIEW

DAVID SMILLIE

Metaphysics, among those who are unsophisticated in philosophy, is a subject bordering on the disreputable. It is presumably a subject which not only is abstruse but also has little bearing on the everyday facts of existence. Scientists in general have disclaimed any interest in metaphysics. In a world where science has pronounced status, it is not surprising that "reality" and "being" are topics to be avoided both at the dinner table and in serious professional circles.

As a member of this society, with training at least on the fringes of science, I realize that my own background in and knowledge of metaphysics are scant. However, I am not of the belief that "reality" and "being" are unworthy subjects of discussion. I have the profoundest belief that to understand human experience we cannot profitably ignore what people feel to be true and real, for it is upon their perception of what is real that people base their actions and decisions. The social scientist who blandly dismisses conceptions of reality different from his own as "distortion" and "failure to perceive reality" blinds himself to the possibility of understanding the creative thought of others.

My aim in this paper is to discuss two different approaches to the world and the resultant differences in the perception of what is real. In taking two points of view which differ significantly and in describing these two points of view as a dichotomy, I am not implying that my description is more than an abstraction of different kinds of human experience. I do claim, however, that these two points of view express significant aspects of our own culture, and that the exaggeration involved in my own abstractive description is a way of illustrating dramatically the differences which do occur, though perhaps less forcefully in the life experiences of others.

In discussing two attitudes toward reality I am describing the quality of experience rather than the mechanism of experiencing. In other words, I am not attempting here to outline a theory of the mechanism of perception and thought but rather to describe two sorts of experience that people have, called "perception" and "thought." These individual differences in the quality of experience have significance in understanding the things people feel to be real.

Each of us knows the world in which we live from two broad perspectives. The first is a personal point of view deriving from our own unique experiences and perceptions. From this orientation no experience can ever be fully shared or communicated, since it is inevitably imbedded in the unique and personal life of the experiencer. We may strive to awaken such an experience in others through the use of words or to share the experience in communion, but the experience is complete in itself. No categorization or translation or temporal manipulation can recreate the experience in public form.

The second orientation is established through a system of socially shared symbols and concepts. From this point of view the world has meaning only insofar as it can be shared and communicated. Symbols and abstractions are real in the sense that they create a world of order and stability. The world of unanalyzed experience is seen as a subjective, dreamlike state that represents only the shadows of truth and reality.

The first of these orientations I have called "immanent," referring to the indwelling quality of what is real. The second I have called "abstractive," denoting the abstraction *from* experience and the reification of these abstractions.

The immanent orientation is characterized by the desire to know the world through direct, personal experience. Analysis and categorization, which necessitate a withdrawal from the immediate experience in order to compare and contrast, have no place in such an orientation. One might *experience* a flower. It might be described as having exquisite coloring and fragrance, with various shades and textures blending to make a highly aesthetic pattern. This description, however, assumes that the flower is something discrete and separate from the individual viewing it, that the object has a number of qualities — color, fragrance, shading, and texture — and that these different qualities are combined by the individual into a pleasing pattern. From the immanent orientation, none of these things is true to the experience — none of these things is real. Analysis, comparison, and description are activities which are applied to the experience, but which are not a part of it. The object is not discrete and separate from the individual but is realized through experience. The flower does not have qualities, nor in any true sense does the experience. Qualities are attributes which when applied to the experience distort the nature of that experience by focusing on some points and eliminating others.

The experience of having direct knowledge through perception involves the elimination of boundaries between self and object. The perceiver does not feel that he exists as a distinct and disparate entity from what he perceives, but that he is at one with the world about him. As the world blends with him, so he too blends with the world, so that nothing is characterized as objective but the world is imbued with meaning and feeling by the experiencing individual. A dark sky is "lowering" rather than merely an indication of rain; creation has the quality of goodness rather than being the transposition of elements to form a new pattern.

The qualities of the world and the nature of existence are discovered through self-actualization and personal experience, rather than through objective and factual evidence, according to the immanent approach to reality. Since truth inheres in experience, rules governing the progress of thought are unimportant. In fact, the very conception of progress or the utilization of means to arrive at a given end is foreign to an immanent orientation. Activities or experiences have value in their own right and are not utilized to arrive at a given end. The young child, for instance, may walk for the joy of walking, enjoying the process of exploration and the use of his body. There need be no logic or formal rules followed to govern how he walks. In the same way an individual may approach life situations without awareness or concern for their logical coherence. What might seem like progress toward a goal when analyzed by a social scientist is not necessarily goal-oriented behavior on the part of the individual who is being observed.

Finally, the immanent orientation is characterized by receptiveness, in the sense of sensitivity to a wide variety of external and internal cues. This awareness is not so much a matter of attentiveness or focus of concentration upon many different features of the environment as a relaxation of concentration which allows awareness of many aspects of an experience. Thus, the person who is carefully focusing attention on a given part of the environment is much less conscious of other events than is the person who has a receptive attitude and is willing to lend himself to a wide variety of experiences.

The second approach to reality is that represented by a system of socially shared symbols and concepts. I have called this the "abstractive" orientation in reference to the use of common characteristics isolated from experience in the form of abstractions. Knowledge of the world from this point of view is derived from the manipulations of abstractions in logical ways to provide rational evidence. Personal experience taken by itself, without the benefit of objective verification, is treated with doubt, since it represents a subjective or biased view of the situation.

The self, from an abstractive point of view, is distinct and different from the environment. The mature individual is able to stand apart from what he observes and to report on an objective plane "that which exists." Of course, it is recognized from an abstractive orientation that the human perceiver is fallible in varying degrees, distorting or overemphasizing certain aspects of the situation. This distortion can, however, be overcome in one of two ways. The first is to provide a normative correction by bringing several individuals (of sufficient maturity) to view and report on the same situation, and then to take what is common to their descriptions or what can be arrived at through common agreement. The second method is to apply logical operations to the views one has obtained (or which have been reported by others), and through these abstract manipulations to arrive at a series of interconnected rational postulates. In neither case, however, is there a reliance upon the unanalyzed, personal experience of the subject.

One of the primary characteristics of the abstractive approach is the use of an explicitly defined set of mental operations, so constructed as to be applicable to a wide variety of different objects, events, and situations. In Western European society these operations have provided a stable set of accepted principles for two thousand years in the form of Aristotelian logic. It has been only in the last half century that there has been any serious criticism of traditional formal logic *from an abstractive point of view*. However, a reliance upon logic, either in Aristotelian or other forms, is foreign to an immanent approach, which relies upon the direct experience of the individual, without the application of any explicit set of mental operations. From the immanent point of view no logical manipulations can provide a true understanding of the world.

Finally there is the importance of conscious, deliberate intention in the adoption of the abstract orientation. The utilization of logic, the manipulation of images or abstractions in arriving at some pre-determined goal, requires effort and concentration. The focus of attention upon relevant detail and the elimination of extraneous impression are essential in following through a series of mental operations and arriving at a rational conclusion. This purposive direction of one's thinking requires a conception of self as a separate and free agent. The farther one can remove one's self from the immediate perception, the more one can divorce one's self from the experience of the moment, then the better can logical mental operations work unencumbered by extraneous, disturbing factors.

Although I have distinguished these two points of view on the basis of the above descriptions, using such terms as separation of self and the world, receptive and directed attitudes, etc., the fundamental distinction which underlies these characteristics is a difference in what is felt to be real. Each of these points of view incorporates different conceptions of the nature of ultimate reality. From the immanent point of view, reality is not something either "out there" or "in here," i.e., there is no distinction between internal and external reality. Reality is immanent in human experience, undissociated from the experiencer. Reality is, from this point of view, a process of being, or better of becoming, the becoming of the individual as an inherent participator in what is real. To communicate this attitude toward reality either one is forced into a language of mysticism, talking through analogy and metaphor, or one slips into language that is abstractive and carries the very denial of this point of view even as it describes it.

One can describe the perceptive reality as "inner" rather than "outer" reality or use some such phrase as Bridgman's "private mode" versus "public mode." * One may talk about a mystical versus a scientific approach to reality or an aesthetic versus an objective point of view. In each of these dichotomous labels there is an ele-

---

* P. W. Bridgman, "Some General Principles of Operational Analysis: Rejoinders and Second Thoughts," *Psychological Review*, 52, 281-284, (1945).

ment of what I have been trying to describe under the labels of immanent and abstractive orientations. However, a difficulty arises. Not only do the connotations of these terms span more or less what I have been discussing but also the terms and phrases represent a whole frame of reference which falls usually into an abstractive point of view. For the distinction between inner and outer reality uses the individual, distinct from the surround, as a frame of reference. A conception of reality which does not admit of such a distinction can hardly be elucidated by such terms. Bridgman's conception of "private" and "public" modes is a clarification of different ways in which an individual can know reality, but the reality which is known is essentially a derivation of abstractive knowing, not a distinction between two conceptions of reality. Abstractively, reality is existence distinct from the knower. The external world exists as a real world which is there to be explored and investigated by minds. Reality is something that has been and will continue to be, in the absence of experience.

I can illustrate the immanent approach to reality with a quotation from Aldous Huxley's *Doors of Perception,* in which he describes his experience under the drug mescalin. He has been describing his experience in his own home, perceiving the mundane objects of his environment in a new light, here talking about the legs of a bamboo chair:

I spent several minutes — or was it several centuries? — not merely gazing at those bamboo legs, but actually being them — or rather being myself in them; or, to be still more accurate (for "I" was not involved in the case, nor in any certain sense were "they") being my Not-self in the Not-self which was the chair.*

I should like to point out here that the self as a distinct and separately existing being is not a part of the experience, and Huxley is forced to use a negative phrase to account for the positive experi-

* Aldous Huxley, *Doors of Perception,* (New York: Harper & Brothers, 1954), p. 22.

ence. Also, there was no clear conception of time. Existence here is not a part of clearly defined objective reality, but is an aspect of experiencing, is indissociable from that experiencing. For the psychologist who operates primarily from an abstractive point of view one might say that Huxley was confused in his time orientation, that he was unable to make a distinction between self and other. While this is true from an abstractive point of view it fails to characterize the experience of Huxley, which contained neither confusion nor failure. In fact, for Huxley the experience was extremely clear and provided a kind of fulfillment which transcended the terms "failure" and "success."

These two orientations, the immanent and the abstractive, have been described here in opposition to one another, features of one being contrasted with the other. While these two orientations are to a certain extent mutually exclusive, they both represent human potentialities and are to a degree utilized by all men. In our own society young children are predominantly immanent in their orientation, although this characteristic is usually interpreted as a failure to adopt an abstractive orientation. Certain nonliterate peoples definitely rely upon an immanent rather than an abstractive approach to the world. On the other hand, all language represents the adoption to some extent of an abstractive orientation through the assumption of common referents. Foresight and planning, which are found among all peoples, depend also upon an abstractive point of view. It is only in general, then, that either one of these attitudes alone characterizes individuals, peoples, or situational responses.

Western culture has been predominantly abstractive in orientation, valuing the formal and the logical. This orientation has been epitomized by the development of Western science, with the emphasis upon an objective world, analytic methods, and a rational philosophy. While it may have seemed that science and reason have suffered at the hands of rigid orthodoxies devoid of reflective intelligence, it is just those orthodoxies that have relied most upon abstractive reasoning and outlook which have wielded the most power and survived the longest. George Bernard Shaw has demonstrated this point effectively in his play *Saint Joan,* in which the powers of reaction, in the persecution of Joan of Arc, rely upon logical formulations and reasoned argument rather than intuitive judgments.

In our culture a designation of "unreasonable" or "illogical" represents a derogation, an indication that the individual, either through deceit or inability, is not following the "rules of the game." However, so familiar is the game that we come to assume its immanence in all thought, its presence as a law of nature, discovered rather than created by man. Actually, logic represents a series of operations to be utilized in arriving at the validity or truth of a situation. The application of or appeal to any series of principles apart from an experienced personal situation represents the application of an abstractive rather than an immanent orientation. However, the use of logic does not insure for the individual a solution superior to an intuitive or immanent orientation. Western man in general, and in particular the contemporary cultural anthropologist, has looked with longing on a life existence which is infused with an immanent rather than abstractive view of life. More and more in recent years the domination of the abstractive outlook is being seriously questioned by those within Western culture.

The immanent orientation that is found most consistently in young children in our society is a quality which those who work with children can hardly fail to realize, yet it may be seen either as a positive orientation or as a deficit. The scientific observer who is himself using an abstractive orientation is apt to see children merely as immature adults, unable to reason properly and unable to view reality objectively. For the behavioristic psychologist, this view of children has probably accounted for the fact that children are so seldom utilized as subjects. The immanent orientation of the child is such that it operates to spoil the research designs which are the product of abstractive minds. Even a scientist like Piaget, who has spent a lifetime studying the thought and behavior of children, views the qualities of childhood thought as progressive steps toward an abstractive orientation.

The young child's immanent orientation, his approach to what is real, pervades his play and his relations to the world which he creates. Evidence, in the sense of objective facts, usually points only to what the child cannot do or does not believe. The usual intelligence test illustrates only whether the child is able to comprehend the abstractive reality of adults in our society, without showing what is true for the child. Growth of intelligence, from the point of view of these tests, represents the growing ability of the child to understand a world organized around principles which are foreign to the immanent orientation. Only through the "errors" which the child makes can such tests shed light upon the child's own world of reality, and even then the method is one of indirection not oriented toward his own experience.

The young child in his play shows that he does not make a distinction between the objective world of abstractive reality and his own personal experience. The blocks used for making a train are not means to an end goal "train" but *are* a train for the child. His constructions do not represent a finished object but are in constant process of becoming as his experiences transform them. Logical progress from one point to the next has no real meaning for him, since his reality unfolds through the process of experience. It is only as one bifurcates reality into objective existence and personal experience that it is necessary to justify or direct behavior according to principles which have a general applicability.

Recognition of these two orientations to reality, the immanent and the abstractive, is important because of the values that are inherent in our Western culture. Without consciously recognizing it, Western scientists and philosophers have imbued the abstractive with value and have relegated the immanent to inferior positions, with such terms as primitive, immature, and pathological. Such a valuation, ubiquitous and unrecognized in our own culture, has resulted in the imposition on others of standards and patterns of conformity which are quite foreign to their way of life. In assuming the importance of being realistic both for ourselves and others, we have seldom questioned the universality of our own reality.

X   HUMAN PERSONALITY

SARVEPALLI RADHAKRISHNAN

Man is not an altogether separate and peculiar being. He bears the marks of his origin in his organism, his fragile body, limited life, and bounded mind. He has grown out of the physical, vital, and animal life into the power of manhood. He is a part of universal nature, a whole carved out of nature's continuum. But man is not simply the animal gone up any more than an animal is a man gone down. Between the two there is a gulf. No amount of scientific observation can help us to explain the astonishing change.

Attempts are sometimes made to reduce man to the level of an animal. Behaviorist psychology assumes that human behavior can be observed like the phenomena studied by natural sciences. Psychology as a science should restrict itself to direct experimental observation. It has little to do with personal experiences, values, and purposes.

The inadequacy of behaviorism becomes more pointed at the human level. To reduce human behavior to reflex action is a travesty of the facts. The material provided by introspection is relevant to the science of psychology. The body as perceived from the inside is different from the body externally observed. The observation of the external manifestations of behavior does not tell us of the individual who is living through his experiences. The latter are immediate data and can be conveyed to others only mediately. Again, while every organism strives to preserve its health and wholeness of being and struggles to achieve a harmony of its essential parts in their full development, man alone has to do it with effort and will. What other objects of nature possess as a natural quality, man has to achieve through effort and endeavor. The theory of conditioned reflexes cannot account for intelligent behavior. If the behaviorist account were true, then man is a slave to his environment without any dignity or freedom. He will be automatically responding to the varying situations with reflexes conditioned and unconditioned. Deliberate attempts to lift himself by struggle and suffering, by self-discipline and self-development are futile. If a fount of type is shaken up in a bag, the text of Watson's Behaviorism would result if only the time allowed is indefinite. Such a view robs mentality of its meaning and stultifies its own truth. If a man thinks even as a stone runs downhill, his thought is absolutely determined and cannot be judged as either true or false.

In psychoanalysis, we seem to have an opposite story where mental phenomena are causal factors and physical behavior can be explained in terms of personal history. An objective treatment is not of much use and we have to cross-examine the individual about his dreams and associations. The greater part of our mind is hidden from us. It is buried or repressed and yet affects our waking consciousness. It is not possible to equate the "unconscious" of the psychologist with the "biological" of the behaviorist. It suggests that the unconscious and the conscious are parts of one whole.

While the behaviorist and the psychoanalyst treat of body and mind as distinct, the supporters of the *Gestalt-theorie* look upon mind-body as a whole. They lay stress on the importance of patterns or configurations in the psychophysical realm. Strictly speaking, there is only one whole, the totality of being. For practical convenience, we isolate wholes of varying degrees of completeness. If we take the process of walking, we can account for it only if we consider the nature of the organism and the nature of the world with which it is interacting. We cannot walk on water. Yet for practical purposes we distinguish the self as a system functioning in a larger whole. The psychological whole is distinguished into two elements of the self and the environment. Psychology studies the nature of the self which is also a whole in a relative sense. The human individual is not a corpse added to a ghost (Epictetus) or a soul plus an automaton (Descartes). It acts as a whole and not with its dissociated parts.

The atomistic psychology, which analyzes the stream of consciousness into separate units and accounts for the course of the stream by the interplay of these units, is now obsolete. The physiological evidence is against such a theory. The brain functions cannot be broken up into elementary units, occurring in distinct areas. The specific character of any brain process involved in any particular activity of the organism is a quality of the total process, a peculiarity of the total field and not a putting together of specific processes occurring in special areas. The *Gestalt* psychology holds that the stream of consciousness is not a sum of elements but a configuration in which every distinguishable part determines and is determined by the nature of the whole. Thoughts and their relations are unified wholes of subordinate parts and not mechanically added sums of independent units. The self is a unity which is more than a sum of its subordinate parts. It is an active living whole, a bodymind, the latest term in the evolutionary process.

The human self is an emergent aspect of the world process and not a substance different in kind from the process itself. Persistence of pattern constitutes unity of a thing or a self. Though every one of the constituents of the body is changing, the bodily system as an organized totality endures. It is the same with regard to the human self which is a unity of diverse parts with an enduring structure. Transient as many of its elements are, the plan of organization, however, is preserved.

Reality is everywhere complex. It is so even in the atom. The self as real need not be simple. Locke confesses that a simple substance distinct from its manifestations could be "a hidden something, I know not what, in behind." Hume's arguments against the theory of self as a being or a substance which in some inexplicable way transcends the totality of its content still hold good. Such a substance is not observable and there is no evidence that it exists. Kant urges that the notion is self-contradictory, for all we know is an object of the self and never the self itself. If the soul were of the indestructible, atomic character, its existence would be of no value at all, much less its continuance. The self has no element which is self-identical throughout. The body is continuously changing. It is a scene of unending waste made good by repair. Thoughts and emotions are constantly changing. There is nothing concrete in the individual which is not produced and which will not pass away, nothing from which there is no escape, or change. The distinctiveness of selfhood does not lie in its simplicity but in the specific organization of its contents.

Often, the self is confused with a series of mental states. Buddha opposed the two extreme views that the self is an unchanging essence and that it is absolutely different each moment. He held to the middle position that the self arises through the past as its cause.* It is a system of responses to environmental situations. It is a connected whole, whose parts work together. Even the most primitive individual faces the world as a unity. The self is not a collection of mental states but is characterized by organization. It is an organization which is active as a whole. Its activity is not as Gentile thinks, within a world of its own, where the mind creates its own environment and is uncontrolled by external facts. The self is not encased in a hard shell. It is constantly interacting with the environment.

The organization of the self, however, is a matter of degree. The lower animals which are tied to immediate situations do not have the unity and organization characteristics of the human self, though

* Samyukta Nikaya ii. 20; see Visuddhinagga, ch. xvii.

they also have an instinctive unity. By the ability to use symbols and reflect on experience, a higher synthesis is rendered possible at the human level, where the organization is not simply external. The instinctive control of animal behavior yields to the rational determination of the self. The human self is able to save the past, bind it with the present, and face the future. The self is a teleological unity, which is the only thing constant in the concrete, busy, active, dynamic self. Each soul has its life's star, its main purpose, "Man is altogether formed of his desires." * In all his transformations, certain persistent and distinguishable characters remain. As the unity of a single melody is realized in the passage of time, the unity of self is realized in the series of stages toward the attainment of ends.

What we call a person at any stage is the cross-section of the growing entity. We speak of the person as the same so long as certain determinable characteristics are found for a definite period of time. The organization of the contents has a specific character which constitutes the individual's uniqueness. As the whole is more than the sum of its parts, it determines the nature of the parts and their functioning. The individual carries his uniqueness even unto his thumb prints, as criminals know to their cost.

In a true sense therefore, personality is a mask. It is the part we play in the drama of life, an imperfect expression of the groundswell of our nature. Each looks at the world from a characteristic point of view. The mental data can be systematized in different ways and so long as they are fused into a single whole, we have a single self. The phenomena of multiple personality point out that for the same period or different periods we may have different conceptions of our self due to loss of consciousness or discontinuity. If the experiences are not sufficiently integrated, selfhood becomes loose and is often broken up into a series of relatively unconnected systems of behavior and we have cases of many selves.

The self as an organized whole is to be distinguished from the

* Kamamayaevayam purusah (Brh. Up. iv. 4-5).

self as subject. The former is the problem for psychology, the latter for metaphysics. In all experience we have the duality between the subject experiencing and the object experienced. The subject of experience is said to be distinct from every moment of the experience. It is the persistent substratum which makes all knowledge, recognition, and retention possible. However much such a substratum may be essential as a principle of explanation, psychology does not tell us of it.

It is sometimes argued that the series of experience is aware of itself as a series. The whole series is involved in the knowledge of each item, which is difficult to understand. Hume reduces the subject to the object and makes the self a bundle of conscious happenings, for he could not find the "I" among his mental states. But the impressions cannot be made into a whole without the activity of the self. There is no explanation as to why the rapidly passing experiences hang together as the experiences of one and the same individual. The laws of association cannot account for this fact. Kant rightly contends that the laws of association mean a self which is more than a mere haphazard bundle of experiences.

William James looks upon the passing thought as the subject of the experience. It gathers up into itself all that has previously occurred and grows on by assimilating the new. The thought is the thinker. But we cannot understand how one state can absorb another.

James Ward believes that William James confuses process and content, subject and object. He argues that every moment of experience has the three aspects of attention, feeling, and presentation. While the first two are subjective, presentation is the object of experience. For Ward, the successive acts of attention manifest the subject's existence. Ward is correct in making out that the nature of self is constituted more by the acts of remembering, thinking, and willing than by the materials or contents remembered, thought, or willed. The activities rather than the contents with which they deal form the self, though the two are inseparable. The active self is held to be more persistent than the contents which are ever changing. Ward's "subject" is far too abstract and is postulated for the purpose of explaining experience.

Ward's view reminds us of Kant's "I think," which must accompany all experiences. The "I think" of Kant is often represented as a mere logical form which accompanies all objects of consciousness. Though the relation of such a changeless passive entity, which remains the same yesterday, today, and forever, to the constantly changing experiences is not easy to conceive, such a subject is assumed to account for the synthesis involved in experience. It is said to be the ground of all categories, that which makes possible the empirical unity of consciousness. The deeper strand of Kant's teaching does not favor the view of the self as an abstraction.

The subject and object of consciousness are elements which are distinguishable but not separable in experience, which is one. The distinction between the two comes before us as a distinction within a whole. If the two were independent of each other, knowledge would become a mystery. They are ideal factors in the whole of experience and not opposite divisions or separate parts of it. We cannot build knowledge from out of them, for it is the ultimate fact behind which we cannot go. The true subject or the self is not an object which we can find in knowledge for it is the very condition of knowledge. It is different from all objects, the body, the senses, the empirical self itself. We cannot make the subject the property of any substance or the effect of any cause, for it is the basis of all such relations. It is not the empirical self but the reality without which there could be no such thing as an empirical self. The individuals are able to have common experience, know a real world as identical for all because there is an ideal self operative in all. The individual who is aware of himself as limited has the direct consciousness of something which limits him and his purposes. The consciousness of limit involves the action of the greater unlimited self in us. In order to assign a limit to our thought, we must in some sense be beyond that limit. To confuse the subject with the mind immersed in bodily experience prevents us from attaining complete comprehension of the object that appears to confront us. The true subject is the simple, self-subsistent, universal spirit which cannot be directly presented as the object. When Plato says that the mind in man is the offspring of the eternal world-mind, when Aristotle speaks of an "active reason" at the apex of the soul which is divine and creative, when Kant distinguishes the synthetic principle from the merely empirical self, they are referring to the self as subject. The deeper unity is what Kant refers to as the transcendental self. Only in calling it the self he is applying to noumenal reality a category of the phenomenal world. It is not an abstract form of selfhood, for it is that which manifests itself in the organization of the empirical self. It is within this universal spirit that the distinction of subject and object arises. While the empirical self is always correlated with a not-self, the universal self includes all and has nothing outside to limit it. The Hindu thinkers call it the atman as distinguished from the empirical self of the jivatman.

When we raise the question about the unifying agency in selfhood we are raising the more general question of the principle of unity in all existents, physical and biological included. Their unity is of the same character as the unity of selfhood, though less complex and less personal, but in principle it is the same.

The integral relationship between the organism and its environment which we found to be true of the subhuman grades of reality is also true of the human world. Human individuals are not unchanging substrata of change with accidental qualities and related to one another externally but are elements in an interrelated system. They are centers of experience or processes of becoming through a creative synthesis of their relations. They possess a certain relative independence though the general nature of the system conditions them all. Instead of being a self-contained individual, each empirical self is the expression or focussing of something beyond itself. The real whole or individual is that which includes persons and their environment and these exist in themselves by a process of abstraction. However self-conscious or self-determining, the human being is not absolutely individual. From the first his world is equally real with himself and his interactions with it influence the growth of his individuality. The individual and the world coexist and subsist together.

At the biological level, there is no such thing as an individual center of life. The cells in an organism are unintelligible apart from the whole. Their life is centered in the life of the whole. While plants and animals lead "whole" lives harmoniously, human beings set up discords between themselves and their environment. The unity between the organism and the environment which is a striking point in the subhuman world becomes sundered in the human. While the human being belongs to a larger world which penetrates him at every pore and lives through his interactions with it, his self-consciousness sets up a dualism which is untrue to fact and opposed to his whole nature. He forgets that his interests are not private to himself and believes himself to be distinct with his own form and individuality. While this strong sense of individuality is necessary for action, it is confused with individualism. He is in a state of unstable equilibrium. His conscience is the sign of a divided life. He is a flame of unrest full of uncertain seeking and disorder. So long as the individual suffers from separateness he is restive and homesick. He is always striving to get beyond his separateness.

Human progress lies in an increasing awareness of the universal working in man. Through the exploring of nature, the striving after wisdom, and the seeking of God, the individual struggles to achieve a harmony between himself and his environment. He finds his goodness in what is more than himself. He realizes that his fragmentariness will be cured only if he is devoted to the whole. Fullness of life means service to the whole. So he strives after values, frames ideals, and struggles to build up a world of unity and harmony. He forms associations, develops common interests by organizing families, tribes, churches, and countries. Knowledge, art, morality, and religion are the devices employed by man to realize his destiny as a member of a spiritual fellowship, a kingdom in which each is in the whole and the whole is in some measure in each. "That they all may be one as Thou Father art in me and I in Thee that they also may be one in us." Such a union based on knowledge, love, and service is closer and more intimate than any represented by the lower orders of existence.

The peculiar privilege of the human self is that he can consciously join and work for the whole and embody in his own life the purpose of the whole. This embodiment differs vastly in degree from individual to individual. It is the source of the difference between superior and inferior souls. The two elements of selfhood, uniqueness (each-ness) and universality (all-ness) grow together until at last the most unique becomes the most universal. While every individual fulfills his real function in the whole and obtains value and dignity, no one individual is as wide as the whole itself. It is limited because it is only one individual element in what is much greater than itself.

There is a tendency, especially in the West, to overestimate the place of the human self. Descartes attempts to derive everything from the certainty of his own isolated selfhood. It is not realized that the thought of the self which wants to explain everything, the will of the self which wants to subjugate everything, are themselves the expression of a deeper whole, which includes the self and its object. If the self is not widened into the universal spirit, the values themselves become merely subjective and the self itself will collapse into nothing. Man's continual striving for perfection in spite of all error and misunderstanding, defeat and disappointment, his perpetual attempt to transform all occurrences into harmony, to make the external express the inward, and the partial success which has attended his efforts, show that the task he is attempting is one in line with the genius of reality. The values we strive for are organic to existence. The whole course of nature is an expression of meaning to be understood by man. Interaction with individuals, knowledge of one another and social relations with one another are possible because we all form parts of one system.

XI BEING AND VALUE IN A PRIMITIVE CULTURE *

DOROTHY LEE

Anthropologists have realized in recent years that people of other cultures than our own not only act differently but have a different basis for their behavior. They act upon different premises; they perceive reality differently, and codify it differently. In this codification, language is largely instrumental. It incorporates the premises of the culture, and codifies reality in such a way that it presents it as absolute to the members of each culture. Other aspects of behavior also express, if not as clearly, the specific phrasing of reality which each culture makes for itself. Therefore, through an intensive analysis of language, ceremonial and everyday behavior, myths and magical formulas, it is possible to arrive at the philosophic basis of a culture, and to see to some extent how reality appears to its members.

I present in the following pages such an analysis: a study of being and value in the culture of the Trobriand Islanders of the Archipelago stretching between New Guinea and the Solomon Islands. This society has been described at length by Bronislaw Malinowski, whose works have furnished the data for this study.

The Trobrianders are concerned with being, and being alone. Change and becoming are foreign to their thinking. An object or

* This study was originally undertaken in an attempt to answer the questions of my husband, Otis Lee.

event is grasped and evaluated in terms of itself alone, that is, irrespective of other beings. The Trobriander can describe being for the benefit of the ethnographer; otherwise, he usually refers to it by a word, one word only. All being, to be significant, must be Trobriand being, and therefore experienced at the appropriate time as a matter of course by the members of each Trobriand community; to describe it would be redundant. Being is never defined, in our sense of the word. Definition presents an object in terms of *what it is like* and *what it is unlike,* that is, in terms of its distinguishing characteristics. The Trobriander is interested only in *what it is*. And each event or being is grasped timelessly; in our terms it contains its past, present, and future, but these distinctions are nonexistent for the Trobriander. There is, however, one sense in which being is not self-contained. To be, it must be part of an ordained pattern; this aspect will be elaborated below.

Being is discrete and self-contained; it has no attributes outside of itself. Its qualities are identical with it and without them it is not itself. It has no predicate; it is itself. To say a word representing an object or act is to imply the existence of this, and all the qualities it incorporates. If I were to go with a Trobriander to a garden where the *taytu,* a species of yam, had just been harvested, I would come back and tell you: "There are good taytu there; just the right degree of ripeness, large and perfectly shaped; not a blight to be seen, not one rotten spot; nicely rounded at the tips, with no spiky points; all first-run harvesting, no second gleanings." The Trobriander would come back and say "taytu"; and he would have said all that I did and more. Even the phrase "There are taytu" would represent a tautology, since existence is implied in being, is in fact an ingredient of being to the Trobriander. And all the attributes, even if he could find words for them at hand in his own language, would have been tautological, since the concept of taytu contains them all. In fact, if one of these were absent, the object would not have been a taytu. Such a tuber, if it is not at the proper harvesting ripeness, is not a taytu. If it is unripe, it is a *bwanawa;* if overripe, spent, it is not a spent taytu but something else, a *yowana.* If it is blighted it is a *nukunokuna.* If it has a rotten patch, it is a *taboula;* if misshapen, it is an *usasu;* if perfect in shape but small, it is a *yagogu.* If the tuber, whatever its shape or condition, is a post-harvest gleaning, it is an *ulumadala.* When the spent tuber, the yowana, sends its shoots underground, as we would put it, it is not a yowana with shoots, but a *silisata.* When new tubers have formed on these shoots, it is not a silisata, but a *gadena.* An object can not change an attribute and retain its identity. Some range of growth or modification within being is probably allowed, otherwise speech would be impossible; but I doubt whether they are conscious of it. As soon as such change, if we may introduce one of our concepts here, is officially recognized, the object ceases to be itself.

As being is identical with the object, there is no word for "to be"; as being is changeless, there is no word meaning "to become." Becoming involves temporality, but Trobriand being has no reference to time. With us change in time is a value, and place in a developmental sequence is necessary for evaluation. We can not respond with approval or disapproval unless we know that a thing is getting bigger or better or surer. If I am told that Robert Smith is an instructor at $3000, I can not respond to this adequately, unless I know that he is just out of graduate school, or that he used to be a professor at the age of forty, but now, at sixty, he has been demoted to this position. Our language is full of terms such as the one I have just used — demotion — giving us tools for the evaluation of being in terms of place in a climactic historical sequence. By dint of constant vigilance, we can refrain from using these terms; but we have no choice when it comes to placing events in time. Our language codifies reality in such a way as to predispose us to view events in terms of temporality. Even if I decide to use such expressions as "it be" or "it flow," I have achieved nothing, since you who hear me automatically make these acceptable to yourself by translating them into "it is" and "it flows," merely putting me down as uneducated. Whenever I make an assertion, I have to give it temporal limits in reference to past, present, or future, or at any rate I have to imply temporality. Trobriand verbs are timeless, making no temporal distinctions. A Trobriander can, if he chooses, refer to an act as completed, but that, it seems to me, is an aspect of the act, not a temporal reference. History and mythical reality are not "the past" to the Trobriander. They are forever present, participating in all current being, giving meaning to all his activities and all existence. A Trobriander will speak of the garden which his mother's brother planted, or the one which the mythical Tudava planted, in exactly the same terms with which he will refer to the garden which he himself is planting now; and it will give him satisfaction to do so.

Being is apprehended as a whole, not in terms of attributes. This is something difficult for members of our culture to achieve; we rarely value sheer being in itself, except perhaps when we are "blindly" in love. Even mothers are often incapable of valuing their children in this way, demanding instead attributes and achievements before they will respond with love. I watched a college student once in a predicament created by this inability to react to being itself. Faced with a vivid, gurgling infant in the presence of its mother, she felt it necessary to react but had no basis for doing so. She tried hard to discover attributes to guide her, asking "Does she talk?" "Does she creep?" hoping for something on which to base approval; and finally, having received a negative answer to all her questions, she remained dumb and immobilized. The Trobriander does not say "how bright" or "how big"; his equivalent in this situation would have been "how baby."

Being is evaluated discretely, in terms of itself alone, not in comparison with others. This, again, is foreign to our thinking, except perhaps in the sphere of art. To return to Robert Smith, if you tell me that he is an instructor at $3000 a year, I can respond to this with approbation, commiseration, etc., only if I know what the rank and pay of other men instructors are apt to be. To evaluate, I have to compare this being with other beings of its kind. To be good, being has to be as good as, if not better than. For the Trobriander, being is good only as itself.

Now our own language makes it easy, though not imperative, to compare beings at every turn. It provides us with a large number of comparatives, through morphology and vocabulary. Our speech is studded with terms such as "better," "bigger," "inferior," "average," "compared to," "normal," "equal," "in relation to," etc., showing that we constantly are passing judgment according to a comparative standard. The Trobriander has no such means, unless we accept his rarely used words "it-sames" and "it-differents" as comparative. The magic formulas given by Malinowski are full of similes, as only in this way can they be made comprehensible to his readers. But in Trobriand, these are all metaphors. Where Malinowski's translation reads, for example, "thy shoots are as quick as the eyes of the black ant," the Trobriand text reads, "no thine eye, thine eye black-ant." When Malinowski says, "I am your senior," the Trobriand text reads, "old man I."

We can see this emphasis on *being* alone when we analyze the Trobriand sentence. Here we find that the words are presented discretely, without elements to show the relation of one word to the other. A verb contains its subject, a noun contains its predicate as well as its other attributes. The few words which Malinowski translated as adjectives are either nouns — a big-one, or verbs — it-goods. The language does not even express an object-to-object relationship, as ours does for example when it relates grammatical subject to the object which is acted upon. In English, we express this relationship through word order; when we say, for example,

"Mary ate the pie," or "John kicked Mary," * we clearly distinguish the actor from the one acted upon, by order of precedence, and we cannot avoid making the distinction. The Trobriander, on the other hand, merely expresses act and participants; *i-wo-ye tau* (it-beat-man) means either that the man is beating someone or that someone is beating the man. Such a phrase usually refers either to a known situation, which needs no elucidation, or is told within a context which makes its meaning clear. If, however, the Trobriander for some reason feels that he must specify, he can do so; but he does not do so as a matter of course, as we do, since his language does not predispose or constrain him to do so.

To be, an object must be true to itself, not in terms of its relationship with other beings. To be good, it must be the same always. Sameness is a value to the Trobrianders. Trobriand being never came into existence; it has always been, exactly as now, above ground in "historic" ** times, below ground in mythical times. At some time the ancestress of each group emerged from a specific hole, bringing with her all the customs, skills, and beliefs of that group, their patterns of behavior, the details of their magic, their pedigreed yams. This "past" is immanent in all Trobriand being. Instead of description in terms of attributes, the Trobriander gives an account of historical or mythical past, presenting essence. In all his undertakings, this "past" is present, giving to them validity and value. Wherever he goes, his surroundings have meaning for him; every

* That it is word order, not the rarely present morphology, on which we depend, is evident from the fact that when we hear "John kicked she," we automatically change this to "John kicked her." We correct the morphology, understanding the statement according to order. If we depended on morphology for the expression of relationship, we would have understood it according to the morphology, and corrected the statement into "She kicked John." In American English at present, we use morphological distinction in this connection for purposes of aesthetics, or even snobbery, not for clarity.

** I use quotation marks for terms which we, from the point of view of our own culture, would apply; terms which would otherwise require cumbersome qualification whenever they appear.

waterhole, rock, or cleft is imbued with mythical significance. Myth
and history, as intrinsic to being, enhance value. For example, the
Trobrianders have certain important valuables which constitute the
gifts in the *kula,* an endless circular series of ceremonial gift-givings
which occupies, with the preparation involved, perhaps half the life
of Trobriand men. These objects have value, but no "utility"; they
are "ornaments" which can not be used to adorn the "owner"; and
they can be possessed only a few months by each recipient. Giving-
in-itself, that is, nonpurposive giving, is good; through participation
in this gift-giving pattern the kula valuables are good. Each valuable
is named and its personal history known. In this lies much of its
value; giver and recipient, and even the village of the "owner," get
satisfaction out of the recounting of the specific kula acts of which
the article was a part, going from named giver to named recipient.
Chronology and historical sequence are irrelevant; the history is
important not as development but as the ingredient of being.

The Trobriander has no word for history. When he wants to distinguish between different kinds of occasions, he will say, for
example, "Molubabeba in-child-his," that is, "in the childhood of
Molubabeba," not a previous phase of *this* time, but a different kind
of time. For him, history is an unordered repository of anecdote;
he is not interested in chronological sequence. For example, Malinowski recorded an account of a famine which was given with complete disregard to chronology, an effect which is achieved only
deliberately by our sophisticated writers. If we rearrange the clusters
of statements so that they represent for us a historical sequence, we
have to give them in the following order: one, four, three, two, five.

For us, chronological sequence is of vital importance, largely
because we are interested not so much in the event itself, but rather
in its place within a *related* series of events; we look for its ante-
cedents and its consequences. We are concerned with the causal or
telic relationship between events or acts. To the Trobriander, events
do not fall of themselves into a pattern of causal relationships, as

they do for us. I am not here concerned with the question of whether causality is given, or is read into existence. Whichever may be the case, we in our culture automatically see and seek relationships, not essence, and express relationship mainly in terms of cause or purpose. The maddeningly persistent question of our young children is "why," because this is the question implicit in most of our ordinary statements and other behavior,* to be answered either in causal or telic terms, since cause and purpose are equally dynamic for us, and are identified in our use of "why." Aesthetically, as well as practically, cause and purpose are both important to us; cause gives us a satisfying explanation and purpose ennobles or gives meaning to the act. We teach the importance of purposive action to infants, directly and indirectly by act and speech. We teach it in the schoolroom, in sports, in politics, in moral precept. The unreflective scientist takes causation for granted, the orthodox historian studies history to discover the causes for events. To the Trobriander, on the other hand, being or event remains discrete, sufficient unto itself, true and of value as itself, judged and motivated and understood in terms of itself alone. In the face of this apprehension of being, concepts such as causation and purpose appear irrelevant; I have introduced them here only because they are so basic to our thinking that we accept them as given in experience, and their presence is assumed by us in all cultures, as a matter of course.** In the language of the Trobrianders, there are no terms such as "because,"

* This does not mean that Trobriand parents are relieved from such questions; they are probably constantly asked "what." According to Margaret Mead this is what the Manus children are continually asking adults.

** This absence of causal concepts, as well as of a comparative standard, seemed at first so striking to me that I wrote a paper describing Trobriand thought in terms of what it was not, as noncausal and noncomparative. It now seems to me that I was viewing the Trobrianders then through the eyes of my own culture, relationally, seeing them according to what they were unlike, and so stressing the absence of concepts which have no relevance to their thought. I am indebted to my student Beatrice Thorsch for helping me to arrive at the positive view presented in this paper. The paper in question is: "A Primitive System of Values," *Philosophy of Science*, Vol. VII (1940), pp. 355-378.

"so as to," "cause," "reason," "effect," "purpose," "to this end," "so that," "why." This does not mean that the Trobrianders are incapable of explaining a sequence in terms of cause and effect, but rather that this relationship is of no significance. In the texts given by Malinowski, "for" (*pela*) occurs occasionally, in such a context that it is possible to translate it as "because," as Malinowski does, and it sounds natural that one should do so; and, once or twice, "what-thing-for" is used in such a position that we can take it to mean "for what purpose." It is significant that "pela" is verbal, meaning "to jump," not a connecting link but a leap to an other. I shall not go here into a discussion of the meaning of the doubtful "pela"; I do not think it is an expression of causality, but even if it is, it occurs extremely rarely and does not contradict the conclusion that, for the Trobriander, events do not automatically fall into the mold of causality or teleology. Malinowski's frequent "why" evoked from the Trobrianders either confused and self-contradictory answers, or the usual "It was ordained of old" — not an explanation but a description of value, tautological but necessary for the ignorant ethnographer.

We ask here, how is influence or motivation or effect phrased among the Trobrianders? How is magical action understood, for example? The answer is, it is understood in exactly these terms, as action, not cause. The magician does not *cause* certain things to be; he *does* them. As the gardener with his material implements burns the brush, breaks the clods, etc., so the garden magician with his various formulas "awakens the sprout," "drives up the shoot over-ground," "throws the headgear of the taytu," "makes several branches," "pushes the taytu tubers into the soil," according to Trobriand account. This is not influence, nor the force of magic; rather it is "to magic." Malinowski, in presenting accounts of magic, uses purposive phraseology, since in this way only can his readers understand magic. But where he gives in translation, "The *okwala* rite is made so that taytu might really grow, so that it might ripen," the Trobriand has actually said, "Okwala, it-grow truly, it ripen"; just a number of events. It so happens, in the example, that the sequence in the account corresponds to the actual order of fact; but quite often there is not even such correspondence. And in the acts themselves there is often not even the sequence into which we could at least read causality. For example, when the Trobriander wants to fell a tree he first exorcises the *tokway,* the tree-dwelling spirit, reciting a spell which gets the tokway down. After that he gives the tokway some food. If the food was offered first, on the ground, or at least promised, we could see this as a causal inducement. Actually, the tokway has no alternative and no freedom of choice at all; he is brought down by the spell. The offering of the food itself is merely part of the established procedure, and is not causally related to the exorcism.

It follows that the Trobriander performs acts because of the activity itself, not for its effects; that he values objects because they are good, not good for; in fact, objects and activities that are good for, are of no value to him. Take, for example, his yams and his yam gardening, and food meant yams. It was only after he had occupied himself with his Trobriander material for about fifteen years and written several books on the subject, that Malinowski realized that taro was an ancient and substantial item of food, much easier to grow than yams, less demanding of care and good soil, perhaps almost as important as yams from the point of view of sheer material nourishment. But taro is only good for; it is only good for food, or, less than that, for stopping hunger; and it is grown for such use. Therefore it was of no value or importance to the Trobriander, and escaped Malinowski's notice. Yams, on the other hand, incorporate the social good. They are good in themselves, and participate daily in good situations, as free, non-utile gifts.

A man gardens yams with the expenditure of much care and effort, with physical and magical skills, putting in long, hot hours of work. He gardens as many plots as he is capable of — not as many as his neighbors, or as many as he "needs." About half of these he sets aside as the *urigubu* plots. These he harvests with pride, exhibiting beautiful heaps of taytu. Then he sends this harvest, by festively arrayed youths and maidens, not to his yam house, but to the hamlet of his sister's husband. In this man's garden the taytu are heaped again, and it is this man now who exhibits them with pride as the gift. Finally, his yam house is put in order, and magic is performed in it. Ideally, the magic makes the taytu rot uneaten in the yam house; it fills the owners with nausea at the thought of eating the taytu; it gives them, instead, an urge to go to the bush and eat what grows there. This keeps the taytu free of purpose; ideally, they are not food. Taytu are constantly being given and received as gifts, in a system of free giving without what we call ulterior motives; not for altruism, not in barter or exchange for. Most of the gift taytu are usually eaten eventually, but only incidentally. In the urigubu gardens of the man who grew them have remained all the tubers which are not taytu; the ones which are misshapen, or unduly small, or blighted in some way. These go to the gardener's not-good yam house. They are merely to be eaten, and we do not hear of them again. The taytu, however, have a very important place in the everyday, as well as the ceremonial, life of the people. Taytu are not, like the taro, good for. Taytu have value, not use; value lies in being, not in relationship.

The pariahs among the Trobrianders are the people who barter. There is one such unfortunate district of highly skilled manufacturers who have no adequate soil for the growing of taytu. They barter manufactured articles, spending their time in this not-good occupation, but more than that, they are lacking in the growing of taytu and in pure gift-giving, that is, in good. They are greatly despised by the agricultural villages. The coastal villages also cannot grow many yams, and acquire more through what seems to us an exchange of fish for yams. However, this has been patterned along gift-giving lines, and escapes the purposiveness of barter. A man of a specific interior village will have a life-long gift-partner in a fishing village. Whenever he wants to, he arrives at the fishing village with some baskets of yams, and leaves them as a gift at a specific spot. This precipitates a pattern of events which ends in his returning home with a gift of fish. He can not go to *any* village with his taytu, or to *any* man within this village; the gift to anyone else would have no meaning, neither would it induce anyone else to go fishing. His taytu were not pay or inducement, but the opening step in a specific patterned procedure involving a specific individual.

Here another aspect of Trobriand being is involved. I have spoken of being as discrete, and apprehended as itself alone. I must now qualify this statement. Being has no independent existence. It is itself only as part of an established pattern. To members of our culture, being is defined by its attributes, relationships, and functions; temporarily in terms of becoming, spatially in terms of its relationships. For the Trobrianders, being is defined by a fixed place in an established pattern. It is perhaps too much to ask my readers to believe that one element in a pattern can be and is perceived only in terms of its specific position within the pattern itself, and without reference to any other element; that in fact a pattern is conceived as something other than a system of relationships. Nevertheless, I believe such to be the case among the Trobrianders. Being is not seen in terms of its relationships to a plurality of elements in the pattern, but rather as a fixed point in a single, changeless whole. Only in this place can being be itself; only as it fills its place is it desired or valued. Being is good and true in terms of pattern. Gift-giving, for example, is good only within a patterned Trobriand situation. It is neither virtuous nor altruistic; both these terms involve meaningless relational concepts. In Trobriand gift-giving, the need of the recipient, or the effect upon him, is not involved. I doubt whether the Trobrianders could be persuaded to send yams to the starving Bikinians; and even if they did send yams, their act would not have value. The harvest gift to the sister's husband is not an act of altruism. The giver is concerned only with fulfilling his role, his place in a specific Trobriand pattern. If he gave taro to his sister's husband, the gift would not have been good; if he gave the yams to his own brother, his act would not have been good. What is good in this situation is the urigubu. To be good, this gift must be urigubu; to be true, that is, to be urigubu, it must be (a) a gift of taytu; (b) from man to sister's husband; (c) at harvest time. Both the good and the true are defined by place in pattern. Taytu figure as gifts upon different occasions, between different individuals. In each case the gift is named and valued differently. When taytu are given to a friend at the launching of a canoe, they follow a different procedure, and are *kabigodoya;* when they are a harvest gift to a specialist, they are a *karibudaboda.* Taytu, then, are urigubu, kabigodoya, karibudaboda, according to their place in different patterns; and each gift derives different being and different value in accordance to the pattern in which it has place. I should explain here that in each case the taytu remain taytu though they participate in different situations; it is the gift which is different according to its place in a different pattern.

This conception of being and value gave the early pearl traders much trouble. They found out soon that money or the things they offered were no inducement to work. They noticed, however, that the Trobrianders set great store by certain large blades made of stone. At first, they had these imitated carelessly, but found that the natives did not want them; then they had them made of slate in Europe, but these also were rejected by the Trobrianders. Finally they had the native stone quarried and sent to Parisian craftsmen; but these beautiful blades also were rejected. These things, of course, could not be valued, since they were not truly Trobriand, had not been made "as ordained of old"; but more than that, they could not be an inducement, and could have no meaning, since they were external to the pattern. When the Trobrianders were finally persuaded to dive for pay, it was only the natives of those villages

which had always dived for oysters who were persuaded; those of
the other coastal villages, where diving had not been ordained of
old, would not dive. And the natives of the appropriate villages did
so grudgingly. To the disgust of the pearl traders, they would leave
their diving and go off fishing for the day, as soon as a number of
baskets of yams made their appearance on the beach, even though
the traders offered them twenty times as many yams. The natives
would work for extraneous inducement as long as there was no good
undertaking to indulge in; but when their gift-partners arrived with
yams, they initiated a patterned situation which had meaning for
the natives.

You will say, "But is not this an inducement or cause?" I think it
is not. By themselves, the few baskets of yams on the beach are just
a few baskets of yams. Offered by the trader they would have had
no meaning. Brought from a different Trobriand village, they
would have effected nothing; and when they come from the appropriate village, it is only the partners of the specific givers who go
off fishing as a matter of course. Given from anyone to anyone, the
taytu are of no value. I think the yams are not an inducement to
action. The giving of them, however, starts a pattern; once the gift
has taken place, the pattern becomes evident and the recipient is
presented with a role which holds value for him; to get satisfaction
from it, to be a good Trobriander, he must fill it. By us, the two
acts, the receiving of the yams and the procuring of the fish, are
seen in relationship; and this relationship is seen as dynamic; one
act influences the other, or causes the other. To the Trobriander,
what is dynamic is the validity and value derived from the pattern.
The coastal villager goes fishing because (this is my own word) he
gets satisfaction from fulfilling his role in the pattern.

The appearance of the baskets of yams is not a cause, but it does
precipitate a pattern. The Trobrianders have their own equivalent
for cause, in terms of their concept of pattern. For this they use the
term *u'ula,* a word very commonly used, for what we would call a

variety of meanings. It stands for the trunk of a tree below the branches; for the base of a pole, or the bottom of a structure; it means the organizer of an expedition or the initiator of any undertaking; it refers to the first part of a magical formula. The u'ula is sometimes contemporaneous with the rest of the object or pattern, sometimes not. To the Trobriander, I think, it indicates place, not temporality. Realized or not, the pattern is always there; the pole has a bottom, the spell a beginning; and this pattern is known as a whole, not as a temporal process. Once made evident through the u'ula, the total must be realized. To this extent, and in our terms only, can we understand u'ula to be the equivalent of "cause"; the u'ula is dynamic but only in reference to the pattern, not toward the next event. The u'ula precipitates the next event, but only incidentally, because it precipitates the patterned procedure through its place in the pattern; it so happens that the next event is a part of this pattern.

This is how we can understand the "actual" and mythical behavior of the Trobrianders. For example, when an *uvalaku,* a kula expedition of a special kind, has been organized to sail to distant tribes where the Trobrianders will receive as gifts certain necklaces from specific partners, the chief gives a *kayguya'u,* a great ceremonial distribution of food. This is an act very serious in its implications, and performed after much consultation and deliberation; because, once this kayguya'u is given, the expedition must be carried out to its end, however unfavorable the winds, or the conditions within the village. Once the pattern has been initiated, has been given evidence, the whole must be realized, or, to put it differently, the whole is inevitably there; I am floundering here because my language can not reproduce the Trobriand identity of the concepts underlying *has been, must be,* and *is.* Knowing the pattern, the Trobriander knows how to act to the end of the pattern. Conversely, the kayguya'u is an u'ula, has meaning, and can even be said to be itself only by virtue of its place in the uvalaku pattern. Outside of it, it is just another food-distribution, initiating nothing, unless it is something else as part of another pattern.

For us, not only purpose but previous action is used as a basis or guide for determining what to do next. For the Trobriander, who does not see acts in relation, pattern is the "guide"; though actually it does not "lead" him to a decision, since his act is predetermined by the pattern. There is a sequence in one of the myths which exemplifies this. Toweyre kills his brother who has been acting in an un-Trobriand fashion, working for individual ends. This act of Toweyre is not part of a Trobriand pattern; however, this does not mean that he now has to come to an independent decision on how to act on the basis of murdering his brother. A brother's death itself initiates a pattern. As the next of kin,* Toweyre goes back to the village and instructs his dead brother's children to prepare the body for the funeral, and he himself arranges for the appropriate food distribution, the *sagali*.

Within the pattern the Trobriander feels safe and acts with assurance. Away from home, he likes to reproduce known previous order, even physically. When a food distribution, a sagali, is given, to which many different hamlets from a distance are invited, the geographic location of these hamlets is reproduced on the beach. (I am afraid it is impossible for me to show conclusively that this is not an interest in relative position.) Again, in one of the myths is given a description of a shipwreck, a dreadful event since it plunges the sailors into witch-infested waters. The crew of the large canoe drift ashore clinging to the outrigger, onto which they have jumped from their places in the canoe. As they reach shore they are in great danger from the flying witches; in the face of it, they walk in exactly the order in which they have drifted ashore; when they sit waiting for night to come and hide them from the witches, they maintain this order; in this order they finally march to their village where they are medicated magically to free them from danger. Now

* In Trobriand society, a man's children and his father are not his kin.

they are safe again and the order need not be maintained. Again, it is impossible for us not to see here the order of lineal relationship; but I do not think that it appears as relational to the Trobrianders.

For members of our culture, value lies ideally in change, in moving away from the established pattern; and safety is ensured through scientific prediction, not exact experience. We hopefully expect next year to be better, brighter, different; if, as we hope, it brings change, we can safely meet it with the use of logic and science. Our advertisers thrive on this value of the different, the not-experienced; our industries have long depended on our love for new models. The Trobriander, on the contrary, expects and wants next year to be the same as this year and as the year before his culture emerged from underground. Advertising is nonsense for the Trobriander, because the new is not good and the old is known and valued, so to talk about it persuasively is nonsense. In repetition of the experienced, in sameness, he finds not boredom but satisfaction as well as safety. Members of our culture go into unchartered seas fearlessly, depending on compass and the science of navigation; they explore new lands eagerly. The Trobrianders go into *known* waters; they recount the kula myths, and then go from known landmark to known landmark, myth-imbued and full of history; they do not even set their course by the stars or the sun. They repeat old journeyings, their own or those of mythical or historical kula figures.

Something must be said here about individual and pattern; how does an individual Trobriander enter a pattern? There are various ways in which he does so and we in our culture would distinguish them according to the principle of whether he enters automatically or whether he does so by act of will. By virtue of being born, an individual enters certain patterns of behavior in terms of certain people, those, for example, who are his relatives by blood or affinity. Here he has no choice; the pattern happens to him through the accident of his birth. Again, when his sister marries, or his wife dies, or his kula partner arrives, this precipitates a pattern of activities involving his participation, where he has no choice unless, of course, he is ready to be un-Trobriand. There are certain patterns, however, where he does have freedom of choice: here, whether the pattern is to be precipitated or not devolves on an act of will of his own. This is the only point where he does have freedom; once he initiates the pattern, he must follow an established procedure. However, I think the concept of freedom of choice is incommensurate with Trobriand value or behavior and, in fact, a false measure. For us, to act as we want to act necessarily involves freedom of choice, but for the Trobriander the concept is meaningless. I think the Trobriander has no more and no less freedom when he initiates than when he continues an ordained pattern. In each case, he acts as he wants to because the act, and the pattern which validates it, holds satisfaction for him; he acts in this way because he is Trobriand, and the pattern is Trobriand. To be Trobriand is to be good. "Act of will" and "freedom of choice" are irrelevant as principles of classification or evaluation.

Then comes the question of whether all beings are part of a pattern, and its corollary: is all being good? Is any being good apart from pattern? I do not think that all being is good; rather, that the good, or value, is found in being, but not in all being. There is much giving going on daily, but it is not good giving; it may be merely desultory giving from husband to wife or a man to his brother — gift situations which are not part of any gift pattern. Much of the unpatterned everyday behavior is not good; eating is not good, nor is love-magic, or love-making. On the other hand, some being is good apart from the pattern in which it participates. Such are the *vaygu'a* with which the pearl traders failed so miserably; such also is the taytu. In each case, the history of these is a pattern in itself. The taytu, for example, is planted and grown according to an ordained pattern. Each part of the procedure is inaugurated by a garden magician, and no member of the gardening group can act independently, can choose to leave his scrub not burned or have it burned at a different time, or set fire to it himself rather than wait for the magician to do the initial firing. At one time the resident magistrate ignorantly set fire to the scrub himself and thus initiated a year of drought. On the other hand, taro is not good; but none of the activities concerned with it are patterned. The gardener in this case proceeds as he likes, and incorporates whatever magic he chooses into the process. Ultimately, then, it is pattern that bestows value; but good being may incorporate its own pattern. Whether this is a difference between good being (taytu or kula givings) and not-good being (taro and gifts to one's brother) or whether it is rather a difference between being and mere existence, I am not qualified to say.

Is the Trobriander truly blind to relationship? Does he never respond to external motivation? The gardening of the Trobriander certainly can be seen as work toward the end of growing yams. Obviously — to us — when a man gives the harvest gift, this act brings giver and receiver into relation; how can the Trobriander fail to see this relation? We would say that it is impossible to have pattern without having elements in relation to one another. These objections are inherent to our own codification of reality. We make them because it is impossible for members of our culture to apprehend being without relationships. We can see motivation only as coming from outside, in relationship, and would therefore say that where we have acts there must be motivation, and where there is motivation relationships must be recognized. Again, we are accustomed to equate change with the dynamic, sameness with the static; and to put these pairs in opposition. So it is hard for us to see that sameness itself can be dynamic, as it is for the Trobriander, who does not need "motivation" for his acts, since their very sameness holds value so that they "motivate" themselves.

These objections raise a further and a more basic question: is the Trobriander blind to relationships, or are there no relationships? Do we who base our behavior on relationships read these relationships into reality, or are they given? Which codification is true to reality? I would say that the two are not mutually exclusive. They represent different facets of reality and different meaningful phrasings for each culture. The fact that each culture has chosen to base itself on only one aspect does not mean that the other is false. Our peculiar codification makes us blind to other aspects of reality, or makes these meaningless when presented. But one codification does not exhaust reality; neither, if it were false, would a society, I believe, be able to survive with it at its base. The Trobrianders, according to our view of life, should be bored automatons. Actually they act as they want to act, poised and sure, in activities which hold meaning and satisfaction. Whether they are given or read into reality by us, temporality, causation, teleology, and relationship in general have neither meaning nor relevance for Trobriand behavior; but Trobriand behavior is nevertheless good because it is concerned with being; and being, in its appropriate pattern, incorporates value and truth.

XII THE MEANING OF "TO MAKE" AND "TO HAVE": POSSESSION

JEAN-PAUL SARTRE

If I consider the object which I possess, I see that the quality of *being possessed* does not indicate a purely external denomination marking the object's external relation to me; on the contrary, this quality affects its very depths; it appears to me and it appears to others as making a part of the object's being. This is why primitive societies say of certain individuals that they are "possessed"; the "possessed" are thought of as *belonging to*. This is also the significance of primitive funeral ceremonies where the dead are buried with the objects which belong to them. The rational explanation, "so that they can use the objects," is evidently after the event. It is more probable that at the period when this kind of custom appeared spontaneously, no explanation seemed to be required. The objects had the specific quality *belonging to the deceased*. They formed a whole with him; there was no more question of burying the dead man without his usual objects than of burying him without one of his legs. The corpse, the cup from which the dead man drank, the knife which he used *make a single dead person*. The custom of burning widows in Malabar can very well be included under this principle; the woman has been possessed; the dead man takes her along with him in his death. In the eyes of the community, by rights she is dead; the burning is only to help her pass from this death by right to death in fact. Objects which cannot be put in the grave are haunted. A ghost is only the concrete materialization of the idea that the house and furnishings "are possessed." To say that a house is haunted means that neither money nor effort will efface the metaphysical, absolute fact of *its possession* by a former occupant. It is true that the ghosts which haunt ancestral castles are degraded Lares. But what are these Lares if not layers of possession which have been deposited one by one on the walls and furnishings of the house? The very expression which designates the relation of the object to its owner indicates sufficiently the deep penetration of the appropriation; to be possessed means *to be for someone (être à)*. This means that the possessed object is touched *in its being*. We have seen moreover that the destruction of the possessor involves the destruction of the right of the possessed and inversely the survival of the possessed involves the survival of the right of the possessor. The bond of possession is an internal bond of *being*. I meet the possessor in and through the object which he possesses. This is evidently the explanation of the importance of *relics;* and we mean by this not only religious relics but also and especially the totality of the property of a famous man in which we try to rediscover him, the souvenirs of the beloved dead which seem to "perpetuate" his memory. (Consider, for example, the Victor Hugo Museum, or the "objects which belonged" to Balzac, to Flaubert.)

This internal, ontological bond between the possessed and the possessor (which customs like branding have often attempted to materialize) cannot be explained by a "realistic" theory of appropriation. If we are right in defining realism as a doctrine which makes subject and object two independent substances possessing existence for themselves, and by themselves, then a realistic theory can no more account for appropriation than it can for knowledge, which is one of the forms of appropriation; both remain external relations uniting temporarily subject and object. But we have seen that a substantial existence must be attributed to the object known. It is the same with ownership in general: the possessed object exists in itself, is defined by permanence, nontemporality, a sufficiency of being, in a word by substantiality. Therefore we must put *unselbständigkeit* * on the side of the possessing subject. A substance cannot appropriate another substance, and if we apprehend in things a certain quality of "being possessed," it is because originally the internal relation of the for-itself ** to the in-itself,† which is ownership, derives its origin from the insufficiency of being in the for-itself. It is obvious that the object possessed is not *really* affected by the act of appropriation, any more than the object known is affected by knowledge. It remains untouched (except in cases where the possessed is a human being, like a slave or a prostitute). But this quality on the part of the possessed does not affect its meaning ideally in the least; in a word, its meaning is to reflect this possession to the for-itself.

If the possessor and the possessed are united by an internal relation based on the insufficiency of being in the for-itself, we must try to determine the nature and the meaning of the *dyad* which they form. In fact the internal relation is synthetic and effects the unification of the possessor and the possessed. This means that the possessor and the possessed constitute ideally a unique reality. To possess is to be united with the object possessed in the form of appropriation; to wish to possess is to wish to be united to an object in this relation. Thus the desire of a particular object is not the simple desire *of* this object; it is the desire to be united with the object in an internal relation, in the mode of constituting with it the unity "possessor-possessed." The desire *to have* is at bottom reducible to the desire to be related to a certain object in a certain *relation of being*.

In the project of possession we meet a for-itself which is *un*-

* Lack of independence.
** Being–for–itself refers to man, a nature involving purpose and change, never to be but always about to be.
† Being–in–itself refers to the nature of objects, complete and unchanging.

selbständig, separated by a nothingness from the possibility which it is. This possibility is the possibility of appropriating the *object.* We meet in addition a *value* which haunts the for-itself and which stands as the ideal indication of the total being which would be realized by the union in identity of the possibility; I mean here the being which would be realized if I were in the indissoluble unity of identity — myself and my property. Thus appropriation would be a relation of being between a for-itself and a concrete in-itself, and this relation would be pervaded by the ideal indication of an identification between this for-itself and the in-itself which is possessed.

To possess means *to have for myself;* that is, to be the proper end of the existence of the object. If possession is entirely and concretely given, the possessor is the reason for being (*raison d'être*) of the possessed object. I possess this pen; that means this pen exists *for me,* has been made *for me.* Moreover originally it is I who make for myself the object which I want to possess. My bow and arrows — that means the objects which I have made for myself. Division of labor can dim this original relation but cannot make it disappear. *Luxury* is a degradation of it; in the primitive form of luxury I possess an object which I *have had made* for myself by people belonging to *me* (slaves, servants born in the house). Luxury then is the form of ownership closest to primitive ownership; it is this which next to ownership itself throws the most light on the relation of *creation* which originally constitutes appropriation. This relation in a society where the division of labor is pushed to the limit is hidden but not suppressed. The object which I possess is one which I *have bought.* Money represents my strength; it is less a possession in itself than an instrument for possessing. That is why, except in most unusual cases of avarice, money is effaced before its possibility for purchase; it is evanescent, it is made to unveil the object, the concrete thing; money has only a transitive being. But *to me* it appears as a creative force: to buy an object is a symbolic act which amounts to creating the object. That is why money is synonymous with power; not only because it is in fact capable of procuring for us what we desire but especially because it represents the effectiveness of my desire as such. Precisely because it is transcended toward the thing, surpassed, and simply *implied,* it represents my magical bond with the object. Money suppresses the *technical* connection of subject and object and renders the desire immediately operative, like the magic wishes of fairy tales. Stop before a showcase with money in your pocket; the objects displayed are already more than half yours. Thus money establishes a bond of appropriation between the for-itself and the total collection of objects in the world. By means of money desire as such is already informer and creator.

Thus through a continuous degradation, the bond of creation is maintained between subject and object. To have is first to create. And the bond of ownership which is established then is a bond of continuous creation; the object possessed is inserted by me into the total form of *my* environment; its existence is determined by my situation and by its integration in that same situation. *My* lamp is not only that electric bulb, that shade, that wrought iron stand; it is a certain power of lighting *this* desk, these books, this table; it is a certain luminous nuance of my work at night in connection with my habits of reading or writing late; it is animated, colored, defined by the use which I make of it; it *is* that use and exists only through it. If isolated from my desk, from my work, and placed in a lot of objects on the floor of a salesroom, my lamp is radically extinguished; it is no longer *my* lamp; it has returned to its original matter. Thus I am responsible for the existence of my possessions in the human order. Through ownership I raise them up to a certain type of functional being; and my simple *life* appears to me as creative exactly because by its continuity it perpetuates the quality of *being possessed* in each of the objects in my possession. I draw the collection of my surroundings into being along with myself. If they are taken from me, they die as my arm would die if it were severed from me.

But the original, radical relation of creation is a relation of emanation, and the difficulties encountered by the Cartesian theory of substance are there to help us discover this relation. What I create is mine—if by creating we mean to bring matter and form to existence. The tragedy of the absolute Creator, if he existed, would be the impossibility of getting out of himself, for whatever he created could be only himself. Where could my creation derive any objectivity and independence since its form and its matter are from me? Only a sort of inertia could close it off from my presence, but in order for this same inertia to function, I must sustain it in existence by a continuous creation. Thus to the extent that I appear to myself as *creating* objects by the sole relation of appropriation, these objects are *myself*. The totality of my possessions reflects the totality of my being. I *am* what I have. It is I myself which I touch in this cup, in this trinket. This mountain which I climb is myself to the extent that I conquer it; and when I am at its summit, which I have "achieved" at the cost of this same effort, when I attain this magnificent view of the valley and the surrounding peaks, then I *am* the view, the panorama is myself dilated to the horizon, for it exists only through me, only for me. But creation is an evanescent concept which can exist only through its movement. If we stop it, it disappears. At the extreme limits of its acceptance, it is annihilated; either I find only my pure subjectivity or else I encounter a naked, indifferent materiality which no longer has any relation to me. *Creation* can be conceived and maintained only as a continued transition from one term to the other. As the object rises up in my world, it must simultaneously be wholly me and wholly independent of me. This is what we believe that we are realizing in possession. The possessed object as possessed is a continuous creation; but still it remains there, it exists by itself; it is in-itself; if I turn away from it, it does not thereby cease to exist; if I go away, it *represents* me in my desk, in my room, in *this* place in the world. From the start it is impenetrable. This pen is entirely myself, at the very point at which I no longer even distinguish it from the act of writing, which is *my* act. And yet, on the other hand, it is intact; my ownership does not change it; there is only an ideal relation between it and me. In a sense I enjoy my ownership if I surpass it toward use, but if I wish to contemplate it, the bond of possession is effaced, I no longer understand what it means to possess. The pipe there on the table is independent, indifferent. I pick it up, I feel it, I contemplate it so as to realize this appropriation; but just because these gestures are meant to give me the *enjoyment* of this appropriation, they miss their mark. I have merely an inert, wooden stem between my fingers. It is only when I pass beyond *my* objects toward a goal, when I utilize them, that I can enjoy their possession.

Thus the relation of continuous creation incloses within it as its implicit contradiction the absolute independence, the in-itself of the object created. Possession is a magical relation; I *am* these objects which I possess, but outside, so-to-speak, facing myself; I create them as independent of me; what I possess is mine outside of me, outside all subjectivity, as an in-itself which escapes me at each instant and whose creation at each instant I perpetuate.

XIII THE DEVELOPMENT OF PERSONALITY

CARL G. JUNG

The achievement of personality means nothing less than the best possible development of all that lies in a particular, single being. It is impossible to foresee what an infinite number of conditions must be fufilled to bring this about. A whole human life span in all its biological, social, and spiritual aspects is needed. Personality is the highest realization of the inborn distinctiveness of the particular living being. Personality is an act of the greatest courage in the face of life, and means unconditional affirmation of all that constitutes the individual, the most successful adaptation to the universal conditions of human existence, with the greatest possible freedom of personal decision.

To educate someone to *this* seems to me to be no small matter. It is surely the heaviest task that the spiritual world of today has set itself. And, indeed, it is a dangerous task, as dangerous as the bold and unconsiderate undertaking of nature to let women bear children. Would it not be a sacrilegious, Promethean, or even Luciferian enterprise if a superman should venture in his alchemistic retort to give rise to a homunculus, who would then grow into a golem? And yet he would only be doing what nature does every day. There is no human horror or abnormity that did not lie in the womb of a loving mother. As the sun shines upon the just and the unjust, and as women who bear and give suck protect the children

147

of God and of the devil with equal love, unconcerned about the possible results, so we, too, are parts of this singular nature, and like it, carry within us the unpredictable.

Personality develops itself in the course of life from germs that are hard or impossible to discern, and it is only our actions that reveal who we are. We are like the sun that nourishes the life of the earth and brings forth every kind of lovely, strange, and evil thing; we are like the mothers who bear in their wombs unknown happiness and suffering. At first we do not know what deeds or misdeeds, what destiny, what good or evil we contain, and only the autumn can show what the spring has engendered; only in the evening will it be seen what the morning began.

Personality as a complete realization of the fullness of our being is an unattainable ideal. But unattainability is no counterargument against an ideal, for ideals are only signposts, never goals.

As the child must develop in order to be brought up, so the personality must first unfold before it can be subjected to education. And here the danger already begins. We are dealing with something unpredictable; we do not know how and in what direction the budding personality will develop, and we have learned enough of nature and the reality of the world to be rightly somewhat distrustful. We have been brought up in the Christian teaching of belief in the original evil of human nature. But even persons who no longer hold to the Christian teaching are naturally distrustful and anxious with regard to the possibilities that lie in the underground chambers of their being. Even enlightened, materialistic psychologists like Freud give us a very unpleasant picture of the things that slumber in the background and in the depths of human nature. It is, therefore, something of a hazard to put in a good word for the unfolding of personality. But the human spirit is full of the strangest contradictions. We praise "sacred motherhood" and never think of holding it responsible for all such human monsters as criminals, the dangerously insane, epileptics, idiots, and cripples of every kind who yet are born. But we are beset by the most serious doubts when it comes to granting a free development to human personality. "But then anything would be possible," people say. Or they warm up the feeble objection of "individualism." Yet individualism has never been a natural development, but only an unnatural usurpation, an unadapted, impertinent pose that often proves its hollowness with collapse before the slightest obstacle. Here we are dealing with something else.

Now, no one develops his personality because someone told him it would be useful or advisable for him to do so. Nature has never yet allowed herself to be imposed upon by well-meaning advice. Only coercion working through causal connections moves nature, and human nature also. Nothing changes itself without need, and human personality least of all. It is immensely conservative, not to say inert. Only the sharpest need is able to rouse it. The development of personality obeys no wish, no command, and no insight, but only need; it wants the motivating coercion of inner or outer necessities. Any other development would be individualism. This is why the accusation of individualism is a cheap insult when it is raised against the natural development of personality.

The saying "For many are called, but few are chosen" applies here as nowhere else; for the development of personality from its germinal state to full consciousness is at once a charism and a curse. Its first result is the conscious and unavoidable separation of the single being from the undifferentiated and unconscious herd. This means isolation, and there is no more comforting word for it. Neither family, nor society, nor position can save him from it, nor the most successful adaptation to actual surroundings, nor yet the most frictionless fitting in with them. The development of personality is a favor that must be paid for dearly. But people who talk the most about the development of personality are those who least consider the results, which are such as to frighten away all weaker spirits.

Yet the development of personality means more than the mere fear of bringing monsters into the world, or the fear of isolation. It also means fidelity to the law of one's being.

For the word "fidelity" I should prefer, in this connection, to use the Greek word of the New Testament, κίστις, which is mistakenly translated as "faith." It really means trust, trustful loyalty. Fidelity to the law of one's being is a trust in this law, a loyal perseverance and trustful hope; in short, such an attitude as a religious man should have to God. And now it becomes apparent that a dilemma heavily weighted with consequences emerges from behind our problem: personality can never develop itself unless the individual chooses his own way consciously and with conscious, moral decision. Not only the causal motive, the need, but a conscious, moral decision must lend its strength to the process of the development of personality. If the first, that is, need, is lacking, then the so-called development would be mere acrobatics of the will; if the latter is missing, that is, the conscious decision, then the development will come to rest in a stupefying, unconscious automatism. But a man can make a moral choice of his own way only when he holds it to be the best. If any other way were held to be better, then he would live and develop that other personality in place of his own. The other ways are the conventions of a moral, social, political, philosophic, or religious nature. The fact that the conventions always flourish in one form or another proves that the overwhelming majority of mankind chooses not its own way but the conventions, and so does not develop itself but a method and a collectivity at the cost of its own fullness.

Just as the psychic and social life of mankind at a primitive level is exclusively a group life with a high degree of unconsciousness in the individual, so the later historical process of development is also a collective matter and will, no doubt, remain so. This is why I believe in convention as a collective necessity. It is a makeshift and not an ideal, whether in respect to morals or religion, for subjection to it always means repudiation of wholeness and a flight from the final consequences of one's own being.

What, in the last analysis, induces a man to choose his own way and so to climb out of unconscious identity with the mass as out of a fog bank? It cannot be necessity, for necessity comes to many and they all save themselves in convention. It cannot be moral choice, for as a rule a man decides for convention. What is it, then, that inexorably tilts the beam in favor of the *extraordinary?*

It is what is called vocation: an irrational factor that fatefully forces a man to emancipate himself from the herd and its trodden paths. True personality always has vocation and believes in it, has fidelity to it as to God, in spite of the fact that, as the ordinary man would say, it is only a feeling of individual vocation. But this vocation acts like a law of God from which there is no escape. That many go to ruin upon their own ways means nothing to him who has vocation. He must obey his own law, as if it were a demon that whisperingly indicated to him new and strange ways. Who has vocation hears the voice of the inner man; he is *called.*

Now, vocation, or the feeling of vocation, is not perchance the prerogative of great personalities, but also belongs to the small ones all the way down to the duodecimo format; only, with the decrease of proportions, it becomes more veiled and unconscious. It is as if the voice of the inner demon moved further and further off and spoke more rarely and indistinctly. The smaller the personality is, so much the more unclear and unconscious it becomes, till it finally merges into one with society, surrendering its own wholeness and dissolving instead into the wholeness of the group. In the place of the inner voice appears the voice of the social group and its conventions, and in the place of vocation, the collective necessities.

But it happens to not a few, even in this unconscious social state, to be summoned by the individual voice, whereupon they are at once differentiated from the others and feel themselves confronted by a problem that the others do not know about. It is generally impossible for a man to explain to his fellow beings what has happened, for understanding is cut off by a wall of the strongest prejudices. "I am just like everyone else"; there is "no such thing," or if there is, then, of course, it is "morbid" and moreover quite inexpedient; it is "a monstrous presumption to suppose that anything of that sort could have any significance"; indeed, it is "nothing but psychology."

This last objection is highly popular today. It arises from a singular undervaluation of psychic life, which people apparently regard as something personal, arbitrary, and therefore completely futile. And this, paradoxically enough, along with the present-day enthusiasm for psychology. After all, the unconscious is "nothing but fantasy"! He "merely thought" so and so, etc. People take themselves for magicians who conjure the psychic hither and yon and mold it to suit their needs. They deny what is uncomfortable, sublimate the unwished for, explain away anything that causes anxiety, correct faults, and suppose in the end that they have finally arranged everything beautifully. In the meanwhile they have forgotten the main point, which is that psychic life is only to the smallest extent identical with consciousness and its sleight-of-hand tricks, while for much the greater part it is unconscious fact that lies there hard and heavy as granite, immovable and inaccessible, yet ready, whenever unknown laws shall dictate, to plunge down upon us. The gigantic catastrophes that threaten *us* are not elemental happenings of a physical or biological kind, but are psychic events. We are threatened in a fearful way by wars and revolutions that are nothing else than psychic epidemics. At any moment a few million people may be seized by a madness, and then we have another world war or a devastating revolution. Instead of being exposed to wild beasts, tumbling rocks, and inundating waters, man is exposed today to the elemental forces of his own psyche. Psychic life is a world-power that exceeds by many times all the powers of the earth. The enlightenment which stripped nature and human institutions of gods overlooked the one god of fear who dwells in the psyche. Fear of God is in place, if anywhere, before the dominating power of psychic life.

But these are all mere abstractions. Everyone knows that the intellect — that handyman — can put it this way and in quite a different way too. It is wholly a different matter when this objective, psychic fact, hard as granite and heavy as lead, confronts the individual as an inner experience and says to him in an audible voice, "This is what will and must happen." Then he feels himself called, just as do the social groups when a war is on, or a revolution, or any other madness. Not for nothing is it just our own epoch that calls for the liberating personality, for the one who distinguishes himself from the inescapable power of collectivity, thus freeing himself at least in a psychic way, and who lights a hopeful watchfire announcing to others that at least *one* man has succeeded in escaping from the fateful identity with the group soul. The fact is that the group, because of its unconsciousness, has no freedom of choice, so that, within it, psychic life works itself out like an uncontrolled law of nature. There is set going a causally connected process that comes to rest only in catastrophe. The people always long for a hero, a slayer of dragons, when it feels the danger of psychic forces; hence the cry for personality.

But what has the single personality to do with the need of the many? First of all, he is a part of the people as a whole and as exposed to the force that moves the whole as are all the others. The only thing that distinguishes this person from all the others is his vocation. He has been called away from the all-powerful, all-oppressing psychic life that is his own and his people's affliction. If he listens to the voice then he is different and isolated, for he has decided to follow the law that confronts him from within. His "own" law, everyone will cry. He alone knows better — has to know better: it is *the* law, *the* vocation, as little his "own" as the lion that fells him, although it is undoubtedly this particular lion that kills him, and not any other lion. Only in this sense can he speak of "his" vocation, "his" law.

With the very decision to put his own way above all other ways he has already in large part fulfilled his liberating vocation. He has canceled the validity of all other ways for himself. He has placed *his* law above all conventions, and so has shoved aside, as far as he is concerned, all those things that not only failed to prevent the great danger but actually brought it on. For conventions are in themselves soulless mechanisms that can never do more than grasp the routine of life. Creative life is always on the yonder side of convention. This is how it comes about that, when the mere routine of life in the form of traditional conventions predominates, a destructive outbreak of the creative forces *must* follow. But such an outbreak is only catastrophic as a *mass phenomenon,* and never in the individual who consciously subordinates himself to these higher powers and places his abilities at their service. The mechanism of convention keeps people *unconscious,* and then, like wild game, they can follow their customary runways without the necessity of conscious choice. This unintentional effect of even the best conventions is unavoidable, and it is also a terrible danger. For when new conditions not provided for by the old conventions arise, then panic seizes the human being who has been held unconscious by routine, much as it seizes an animal, and with equally unpredictable results.

Certainly, all human beings resemble one another, for otherwise they could not succumb to the same delusion; and the foundation of the psyche, upon which individual consciousness rests, is universally the same, beyond a doubt, for otherwise people could never reach a common understanding. In this sense, personality with its peculiar psychic make-up is itself not something absolutely unique and happening but once. The uniqueness holds only for the *individuality* of the personality, as it does for each and every individuality. To become a personality is not the absolute prerogative of the man of genius. He may even have genius without either having personality or being a personality. Insofar as every individual has his own inborn law of life, it is theoretically possible for every man to follow this law before all others and so to become a personality — that is, to achieve completeness. But since life can only exist in the form of living units, which is to say of individuals, the law of life in the last analysis always tends towards a *life that is individually lived*. Although, at bottom, one cannot conceive the objective-psychic in any other way than as an actuality that is universal and uniform, and although this means that all men share the same primary, psychic condition, still the objective-psychic must individuate itself as soon as it manifests itself, for there is no way in which it can express itself except through the single individual. The only exception to this is when it seizes upon the group; but in that case it leads by rules of nature to a catastrophe, and for the simple reason that it acts only through unconscious channels and is not assimilated by any consciousness so as to be assigned its place among all the other conditions of life.

Only the man who is able *consciously* to affirm the power of the vocation confronting him from within becomes a personality; he who succumbs to it falls a prey to the blind flux of happening and is destroyed. The greatness and the liberating effect of all genuine personality consists in this, that it subjects itself of free choice to its vocation and consciously translates into its own individual reality what would lead only to ruin if it were lived unconsciously by the group.

Yes, what is called personality is a great and mysterious question. All that can be said about it is curiously unsatisfactory and inadequate, and there is always the threatening danger that the discussion will lose itself in mere talk that is as redundant as it is hollow. All the usual little remedies and medicaments of psychology fall somewhat short in this connection, just as they do with the man of genius or the creative human being. Derivation from ancestral heredity and from the milieu does not quite succeed; inventing fictions about childhood, which is so popular today, ends — to put it mildly — in the inappropriate; the explanation from necessity — "he had no money, was ill," and so forth — remains caught in mere externalities. Something irrational, that cannot be rationalized, must always supervene, a *deus ex machina* or an *asylum ignorantiæ* — that well-known superscription standing for God. Here the problem seems to extend into an extrahuman realm, and this, from the beginning, has been covered by some one of the names of God.

As can be seen, I also have had to refer to the inner voice, the vocation, and to designate it as a powerful objective-psychic element in order to characterize the way in which it acts in the developing personality and appears subjectively in any given case.

Just as great personality acts upon society to alleviate, liberate, transform, and heal, so the birth of personality has a restoring effect upon the individual. It is as if a stream that was losing itself in marshy tributaries suddenly discovered its proper bed, or as if a stone that lay upon a germinating seed were lifted away so that the sprout could begin its natural growth.

The inner voice is the voice of a fuller life, of a wider, more comprehensive consciousness. That is why in mythology the birth of the hero or the symbolic rebirth coincides with sunrise: the development of personality is synonymous with an increase of awareness. For the same reason most heroes are characterized by solar attributes, and the moment of the birth of their great personalities is called illumination.

The fear that the majority of natural human beings feels before the inner voice is not so childish as one might suppose. The contents that confront a limited consciousness are in no sense harmless, as is shown by the classic example of the life of Christ, or the equally significant experience of Mara in the legend of Buddha; as a rule, they spell the very danger that is specific to the individual concerned. What the inner voice brings close to us is generally something that is not good, but evil. This must be so, first of all, for the reason that we are generally not as unconscious of our virtues as of our vices, and then because we suffer less from the good than from the bad.

As I have explained above, the inner voice brings to consciousness whatever the whole — whether the nation to which we belong or the humanity of which we are a part — suffers from. But it presents this evil in individual form, so that at first we would suppose all this evil to be only a trait of individual character. The inner voice brings forward what is evil in a temptingly convincing way, so as to make us succumb to it. If we do not succumb to it in part, then nothing of this apparent evil goes into us, and then also no renewal and no healing can take place. (I call the evil of the inner voice "apparent," and this sounds too optimistic.) If the "I" completely succumbs to the inner voice, then its contents act as if they were so many devils, and a catastrophe follows. But if the "I" succumbs only in part, and if by self-assertion it can save itself from being completely swallowed, then it can assimilate the voice, and it is seen that the evil was only an evil semblance, while in reality it brought healing and illumination. The character of the inner voice is "Luciferian" in the most proper and unequivocal sense of the word, and that is why it places a man face to face with final moral decisions, without which he could never attain consciousness and become a personality. In a most unaccountable way the lowest and the highest, the best and the most atrocious, the truest and the falsest are mingled together in the inner voice, which thus opens up an abyss of confusion, deception, and despair.

It is, of course, ridiculous to accuse the voice of nature, the all-good and the all-destroying, of evil. If it appears to us preeminently bad, this is at bottom a matter of the old truth that the good is always an enemy of the better. We would be foolish if we did not cling to the traditional good as long as ever possible. But as Faust says:

> When we attain the good the world present us,
> We call the better lie and sham!

Something good is unfortunately not eternally good, for otherwise there would be nothing better. If the better is to come, then the good must stand aside. This is why Meister Eckhart said, "God is not good, or else he could be better."

There are times in the history of the world (our own may be one of them) when something that is good must make way; what is destined to be better thus appears at first to be evil. This last sentence shows how dangerous it is even to touch upon these problems, for how easy it would be, according to this, for evil to smuggle itself in by simply explaining that it is the potentially better! The problems of the inner voice are full of hidden pits and snares. It is a most dangerous and slippery region, just as dangerous and devious as life itself when it rejects the aid of handrails. But whoever is unable to lose his life by the same token will never gain it. The birth of the hero and the heroic life are always threatened. Typical examples are the serpents of Hera that threaten the infant Heracles; Python, who wishes to destroy the light god Apollo at birth; and the slaying of the first-born in Bethlehem. The development of personality is a wager, and it is tragic that the demon of the inner voice should spell greatest danger and indispensable help at the same time. It is tragic, but logical. It is artlessly so.

May we, therefore, be thankful to humanity, to all the well-meaning shepherds of the flock, and to all the anxious fathers of the hosts of children, when they erect protective walls, set up efficacious pictures, and recommend passable roads that sinuously wind around the abysses?

When all is said and done, the hero, leader, and savior is also the one who discovers a new way to greater certainty. Everything could be left as it was if this new way did not absolutely demand to be discovered, and did not visit humanity with all the plagues of Egypt until it is found. The undiscovered way in us is like something of the psyche that is alive. The classic Chinese philosophy calls it "Tao," and compares it to a watercourse that resistlessly moves toward its goal. To be in Tao means fulfillment, wholeness, a vocation performed, beginning and end and complete realization of the meaning of existence innate in things. Personality is Tao.

XIV SELF-ACTUALIZING PEOPLE: A STUDY OF PSYCHOLOGICAL HEALTH

A. H. MASLOW

PERSONAL FOREWORD

The study to be reported here is unusual in various ways. It was not planned as an ordinary research; it was not a social venture but a private one, motivated by my own curiosity and pointed toward the solution of various personal moral, ethical, and scientific problems. I sought only to convince and to teach myself (as is quite proper in a personal quest) rather than to prove or to demonstrate to others. For this reason, it has no "design."

Quite unexpectedly, however, these studies have proved to be so enlightening, and even startling to me (and a few others), that it seems fair that some sort of report should be made to others in spite of this and other shortcomings.

At first I had thought that I could present the lessons I had learned, without reference to their technically questionable source, simply by a series of discrete and independent "theoretical" papers. Some of these have appeared [23-27] and more will in the future. But even these papers suggested that it would be more honest to indicate the "data" from which they sprang, for in actuality I considered them empirical reports rather than theoretical constructions.

Finally, I consider the problem of psychological health to be so

160

pressing, that *any* leads, *any* suggestions, *any* bits of data, however moot, are endowed with a certain temporary value. This kind of research is in principle so difficult — involving as it does a kind of lifting oneself by one's axiological bootstraps — that if we were to wait for conventionally reliable data we should have to wait forever. It seems that the only manly thing to do is not to fear mistakes, to plunge in, to do the best that one can, hoping to learn enough from blunders to correct them eventually. At present the only alternative is simply to refuse to work with the problem. Accordingly, for whatever use can be made of it, the following report is presented with due apologies to those who insist upon conventional reliability, validity, sampling, etc.

Subjects and Methods

The subjects were selected from among personal acquaintances and friends, and from among public and historical figures. In addition three thousand college students were screened, but yielded only one immediately usable subject and a dozen or so possible future subjects. It was hoped that figures created by novelists or dramatists could be used for demonstration purposes, but none was found that was usable in our culture and our time (in itself a thought-provoking finding).

The "first clinical definition," on the basis of which subjects were finally chosen or rejected, had a positive as well as a merely negative side. The negative criterion was an absence of neurosis, psychopathic personality, psychosis, or strong tendencies in these directions. Possibly psychosomatic illness called forth closer scrutiny and screening. Wherever possible Rorschach tests were given, but turned out to be far more useful in revealing concealed psychopathology than in selecting healthy people. The positive criterion for selection was positive evidence of self-actualization (SA), as yet a difficult syndrome to describe accurately. For the purposes of this discussion, it may be loosely described as the full use and exploitation of talents, capacities, potentialities, etc. Such people seem to be fulfilling themselves and to be doing the best that they are capable of doing. They are people who have developed or are developing to the full stature of which they are capable.[11, 21, 24, 25, 27]

This connotes also either gratification past or present of the basic emotional needs for safety, belongingness love, respect, and self-respect, and of the cognitive needs for knowledge and for understanding or, in a few cases, "conquest" of these needs. This is to say that all subjects felt safe and unanxious, accepted, loved and loving, respectworthy and respected, and that they had worked out their philosophical, religious, or axiological bearings. It is still an open question as to whether this "basic gratification" is a sufficient or only a prerequisite condition of self-actualization. It may be that self-actualization means basic gratification plus at least minimum talent, capacity, or "richness."

In general, the technique of selection used was that of *iteration*, previously used in studies of the personality syndromes of self-esteem and of security.[22] This consists briefly in starting with the personal or cultural nontechnical state of belief, collating the various extant usages and definitions of the syndrome and then defining it more carefully, still in terms of actual usage (what might be called the "lexicographical stage"), with, however, the elimination of the logical and factual inconsistencies customarily found in folk definitions.

On the basis of the "corrected folk definition," the first groups of subjects are selected, a group who are high in the quality and a group who are low in it. These people are studied as carefully as possible in the clinical style, and on the basis of this empirical study the original "corrected folk definition" is further changed and corrected as required by the data now in hand. This gives the "first clinical definition." On the basis of this new definition, the original group of subjects is reselected, some being retained, some being dropped, and some new ones being added. This second level group of subjects is then, in its turn, clinically and if possible experimentally and statistically studied, which in turn causes modification, correction, and enrichment of the first clinical definition, with which in turn a new group of subjects is selected and so on. In this way an originally vague and unscientific folk-concept can become more and more exact, more and more operational in character, and therefore more scientific.

Of course, external, theoretical, and practical considerations may intrude into this spiral-like process of self-correction. For instance, early in this study, it was found that folk usage was so unrealistically demanding that no living human being could possibly fit the definition. We had to stop excluding a possible subject on the basis of single foibles, mistakes, or foolishness; or to put it in another way, we could not use perfection as a basis for selection since no subject was perfect.

Another such problem was presented by the fact that in all cases it was impossible to get full and satisfactory information of the kind usually demanded in clinical work. Possible subjects, when informed of the purpose of the research, became self-conscious, froze up, laughed off the whole effort, or broke off the relationship. As a result, since this early experience all subjects have been studied indirectly, indeed almost surreptitiously.

Since living people were studied whose names could not be divulged, two desiderata or even requirements of ordinary scientific work became impossible to achieve: namely, repeatability of the investigation and public availability of the data upon which conclusions were made. These difficulties are partly overcome by the inclusion of public and historical figures, and by the supplementary study of young people and children who could conceivably be used publicly.

The subjects have been divided into the following categories:

Cases:

Three fairly sure and one probable contemporary.

Two fairly sure historical figures (Lincoln in his last years and Thomas Jefferson).

Six highly probably public and historical figures (Einstein, Eleanor Roosevelt, Jane Addams, William James, and Spinoza).

Partial Cases:

Five contemporaries who fairly certainly fall short somewhat but who can yet be used for study.

Seven historical figures who probably or certainly fall short, but who can yet be used for study: Walt Whitman, Henry Thoreau, Beethoven, F. D. Roosevelt, Freud.

Potential or Possible Cases:

Sixteen younger people who seem to be developing in the direction of self-actualization, G. W. Carver, Eugene V. Debbs, Albert Schweitzer, Thomas Eakins, Fritz Kreisler, Goethe.

GATHERING AND PRESENTATION OF THE DATA

"Data" here consist not so much of the usual gathering of specific and discrete facts as in the slow development of a global or holistic impression of the sort that we form of our friends and acquaintances. It was rarely possible to "set up" a situation, to ask pointed questions, or to do any testing with my older subjects (although this *was* possible and was done with younger subjects). Contacts were fortuitous and of the ordinary social sort. Friends and relations were questioned where this was possible.

Because of this and also because of the small number of subjects as well as the incompleteness of the data for many subjects, any quantitative presentation is impossible: only composite "impressions" can be offered for whatever they may be worth (and of course they are worth much less than controlled objective observation since the investigator is never *quite* certain about what is description and what is projection).

The holistic analysis of these total impressions yields, as the most important and useful whole-characteristics of self-actualizing people for further clinical and experimental study, the following:

1. More Efficient Perception of Reality and More Comfortable Relations With It

The first form in which this capacity was noticed was as an unusual ability to detect the spurious, the fake, and the dishonest in personality and, in general, to judge people correctly and efficiently. In an informal check experiment with a group of college students, a clear tendency was discerned for the more secure (the more healthy) to judge their professors more accurately than did the less secure students.

As the study progressed, it slowly became apparent that this efficiency extended to many other areas of life — indeed *all* areas that were tested. In art and music, in things of the intellect, in scientific matters, in politics and public affairs, they seemed as a group to be able to see concealed or confused realities more swiftly and more correctly than others. Thus, an informal experiment indicated that their predictions of the future from whatever facts were in hand at the time seemed to be more often correct, because less based upon wish, desire, anxiety, fear, or upon generalized, character-determined optimism or pessimism.

At first this was phrased as good taste or good judgment, the implication being relative and not absolute. But for many reasons (some to be detailed below), it has become progressively more clear that this had better be called perception (not taste) of something that was absolutely "there" (reality, not a set of opinions).[30, 32] It is hoped that this conclusion — or hypothesis — can soon be put to the experimental test.

If this is so it would be impossible to overstress the importance of the implications of this phenomenon. Recently Money-Kyrle,[28, 29,] an English psychoanalyst, has indicated that he believes it possible to call a neurotic person not only *relatively* but *absolutely* inefficient, simply because he does not perceive the real world as accurately or as efficiently as does the healthy person. The neurotic is not only emotionally sick — he is cognitively *wrong*. If health and neurosis are respectively correct and incorrect perceptions of reality, propositions of fact and propositions of value merge in this area, and in principle, value-propositions should then be empirically demonstrable rather than merely matters of taste or exhortation. For those who have wrestled with this problem it will be clear that we may have here a partial basis for a true science of values, and consequently of ethics, social relations, politics, religion, etc.

It is doubtful that maladjustment or even extreme neurosis would disturb perception enough to affect acuity of perception of light or touch or odor. But it is probable that this effect can be demonstrated in spheres of perception removed from the merely physiological, e.g., Einstellung Experiment,[34,] etc. It should also follow that the effects of wish, desire, prejudice, upon perception as in many recent experiments should be very much less in healthy people than in sick. A priori considerations encourage the hypothesis that this superiority in the perception of reality eventuates in a superior ability to reason, to perceive the truth, to come to conclusions to be logical and to be cognitively efficient, in general.[17, 36]

One particularly impressive and instructive aspect of this better relationship with reality has been described in another place.[23] It was found that self-actualizing people distinguished far more easily than most the fresh, concrete, and idiosyncratic from the generic, abstract, and "rubricized." The consequence is that they live more in the "real" world of nature than in the man-made set of concepts, expectations, beliefs, and stereotypes which most people confuse with the world. They are therefore far more apt to perceive what is "there" rather than their own wishes, hopes, fears, anxieties, their own theories and beliefs, or those of their cultural group.

The relationship with the unknown seems to be of exceptional promise as another bridge between academic and clinical psychology. Our healthy subjects are uniformly unthreatened and unfrightened by the unknown, being therein quite different from average men. They accept it, are comfortable with it, and, often are even *more* attracted by it than by the known. To use Frenkel-Brunswik's phrase, they can tolerate the ambiguous.[7]

These latter, it is true, are the intellectuals, the researchers, and the scientists so that perhaps the major determinant here is intellectual power. And yet we all know how many scientists with high IQ, through timidity, conventionality, anxiety, or other character defects, occupy themselves exclusively with what is known, with polishing it, arranging and rearranging it, classifying it, and otherwise puttering with it instead of discovering, as they are supposed to do.[5, 31, 32]

Since for healthy people the unknown is not frightening, they do not have to spend any time laying the ghost, whistling past the cemetery, or otherwise protecting themselves against imagined dangers. They do not neglect the unknown, or deny it, or run away from it, or try to make believe it is really known, nor do they organize, dichotomize, or rubricize it prematurely. They do not cling to the familiar, nor is their quest for truth a catastrophic need for certainty, safety, definiteness, and order, such as we see in an exaggerated form in Goldstein's brain-injured,[11] or in the compulsive-obsessive neurotic. They can be, when the objective total situation calls for it, comfortably disorderly, anarchic, chaotic, vague, doubtful, uncertain, ambiguous, indefinite, approximate, inexact, or inaccurate (all, at certain moments in science, art, or life in general, quite desirable).

Thus it comes about that doubt, tentativeness, uncertainty with the consequent necessity for abeyance of decision, which is for most a torture, can be for some a pleasantly stimulating challenge, a high spot in life rather than a low.

2. *Acceptance (Self, Others, Nature)*

A good many personal qualities which can be perceived on the surface and which seem at first to be various and unconnected, may be understood as manifestations or derivatives of a more fundamental single attitude, namely of a relative lack of overriding guilt, of crippling shame, and of extreme or severe anxiety. This is in direct contrast with the neurotic person who in every instance may be described as crippled by guilt and/or shame and/or anxiety. Even the normal member of our culture feels unnecessarily guilty or ashamed about too many things and has anxieties in too many unnecessary situations. Our healthy individuals find it possible to accept themselves and their own nature without chagrin or complaint or, for that matter, even without thinking about the matter very much.

They can accept their own human nature with all its shortcomings, with all its discrepancies from the ideal image, without feeling real concern. It would convey the wrong impression to say that they are self-satisfied. What we must say rather is that they can take the frailties and sins, weaknesses and evils of human nature in the same unquestioning spirit that one takes or accepts the characteristics of nature. One does not complain about water because it is wet, or about rocks because they are hard, or about trees because they are green. As the child looks out upon the world with wide, uncritical, innocent eyes, simply noting and observing what is the case, without either arguing the matter or demanding that it be otherwise, so does the self-actualizing person look upon human nature in himself and in others. This is of course not the same as resignation in the Eastern sense, but resignation too can be observed in our subjects especially in the face of illness and death.

Be it observed that this amounts to saying in another form what we have already described; namely, that the self-actualized person sees reality more clearly: our subjects see human nature as it *is* and not as they would prefer it to be. Their eyes see what is before them without being strained through spectacles of various sorts to distort or shape or color the reality.[5, 23]

The first and most obvious level of acceptance is at the so-called animal level. These self-actualizing people tend to be good and lusty animals, hearty in their appetites and enjoying themselves mightily without regret or shame or apology. They seem to have a uniformly good appetite for food; they seem to sleep well; they seem to enjoy their sexual lives without unnecessary inhibition and so on for all the relatively physiological impulses. They are able to "accept" themselves not only on these low levels, but at all levels as well; e.g., love, safety, belongingness, honor, self-respect. All of these are accepted without question as worth while simply because they are part of human nature, and because these people are inclined to accept the work of nature rather than to argue with her for not having constructed things to a different pattern. This shows itself in a relative lack of the disgusts and aversions seen in average people and especially in neurotics, e.g., food annoyances, disgust with body products, body odors, and body functions.

Closely related to self-acceptance and to acceptance of others is (a) their lack of defensiveness, protective coloration, or pose, and (b) their distaste for such artificialities in others. Cant, guile, hypocrisy' "front," "face," playing a game, trying to impress in conventional ways: these are all absent in themselves to an unusual degree. Since they can live comfortably even with their own shortcomings, these finally come to be perceived, especially in later life, as not shortcomings at all but simply as neutral personal characteristics.

This is not an absolute lack of guilt, shame, sadness, anxiety, defensiveness; it is a lack of unnecessary (because unrealistic) guilt, etc. The animal processes, e.g., sex, urination, pregnancy, menstruation, growing old, etc., are part of reality and so must be accepted. Thus, no healthy woman feels guilty or defensive about being female or about any of the female processes.

What healthy people do feel guilty about (or ashamed, anxious, sad, or defensive) are (a) improvable shortcomings, e.g., laziness, thoughtlessness, loss of temper, hurting others; (b) stubborn remnants of psychological ill health e.g., prejudice, jealousy, envy; (c) habit, which, though relatively independent of character structure, may yet be very strong, or (d) shortcomings of the species or of the culture or of the group with which they have identified. The general formula seems to be that healthy people will feel bad about discrepancies between what is and what might very well be or ought to be.[1, 10, 12]

3. Spontaneity

Self-actualizing people can all be described as relatively spontaneous in behavior and far more spontaneous than that in their inner life, thoughts, impulses, etc. Their behavior is marked by simplicity and naturalness, and by lack of artificiality or straining for effect. This does not necessarily mean consistently unconventional behavior. If we were to take an actual count of the number of times that the self-actualizing person behaved in an unconventional manner the tally would not be high. His unconventionality is not superficial but essential or internal. It is his impulses, thought, consciousness that are so unusually unconventional, spontaneous, and natural. Apparently recognizing that the world of people in which he lives could not understand or accept this, and since he has no wish to hurt them or to fight with them over every triviality, he will go through the ceremonies and rituals of convention with a good-humored shrug and with the best possible grace. Thus I have seen a man accept an "honor" he laughed at and even despised in private, rather than make an issue of it and hurt the people who thought they were pleasing him.

That this "conventionality" is a cloak which rests very lightly upon his shoulders and is easily cast aside can be seen from the fact that the self-actualizing person practically never allows convention to hamper him or inhibit him from doing anything that he considers very important or basic. It is at such moments that his essential lack of conventionality appears and not as with the average Bohemian or authority-rebel who makes great issues of trivial things and who will fight against some unimportant regulation as if it were a world issue.

This same inner attitude can also be seen in those moments when the person becomes keenly absorbed in something that is close to one of his main interests. He can then be seen quite casually to drop off all sorts of rules of behavior to which at other times he conforms; it is as if he has to make a conscious effort to be conventional; as if he were conventional voluntarily and by design.

Finally this external habit of behavior can be voluntarily dropped in the company of people who do not demand or expect routine behavior. That this relative control of behavior is felt as something of a burden is seen by our subjects' preference for such company as allows them to be more free, natural, and spontaneous and which relieves them of what they find sometimes to be effortful conduct.

One consequence or correlate of this characteristic is that these people have codes of ethics which are relatively autonomous and individual rather than conventional. The unthinking observer might sometimes believe them to be "unethical" since they can break not only conventions but laws when the situation seems to demand it. But the very opposite is the case. They are the most ethical of people even though their ethics are not necessarily the same as those of the people around them. It is this kind of observation which leads us to understand very assuredly that the ordinary "ethical" behavior of the average person is largely conventional behavior rather than truly ethical behavior, e.g., behavior based on fundamentally accepted principles.

Because of this alienation from ordinary conventions and from the ordinarily accepted hypocrisies, lies, and inconsistencies of social life they sometimes feel like spies or aliens in a foreign land and sometimes behave so.

I should not give the impression that they try to hide what they are like. Sometimes they let themselves go deliberately, out of momentary irritation with customary rigidity or with conventional blindness. They may for instance be trying to teach someone, or they may be trying to protect someone from hurt or injustice, or they may sometimes find emotions bubbling up from within them which are so pleasant or even ecstatic that it seems almost sacrilegious to suppress them. In such instances I have observed that they are not anxious or guilty or ashamed of the impression that they make on the onlooker. It is their claim that they usually behave in a conventional fashion simply because no great issues are involved or because they know people will be hurt or embarrassed by any other kind of behavior.

Their ease of penetration to reality, their closer approach to an animallike or childlike acceptance and spontaneity imply a superior awareness of their own impulses, desires, opinions, and subjective reactions in general.[9, 27, 31, 32] Clinical study of this capacity confirms beyond a doubt the opinion, e.g., of Fromm,[9, 10] that the average "normal," "well-adjusted" person often hasn't even the slightest idea of what he is, of what he wants, of what his own opinions are.

It was such findings as these that led ultimately to the discovery of a most profound difference between self-actualizing people and others; namely that the motivational life of self-actualizing people is not only quantitatively different but also qualitatively different from that of ordinary people.[25, 27] It seems probable that we must construct a profoundly different psychology of motivation for self-actualizing people, i.e., expression-or growth-motivation, rather than deficiency-motivation. Indeed, it may turn out to be more fruitful to consider the concept of "motivation" to apply *only* to non-self-actualizers. Our subjects no longer "strive" in the ordinary sense but rather "develop." They attempt to grow to perfection and to develop more and more fully in their own style. The motivation of ordinary men is a striving for the basic need gratification which they lack. But self-actualizing people in fact lack none of these gratifications; and yet they have impulses. They work, they try, and they are ambitious even though in an unusual sense. For them motivation is just character-growth, character-expression, maturation, and development; in a word, self-actualization. Could these self-actualizing people be more human, more revealing of the "original nature" of the species, closer to the "species-type" in the taxonomical sense? Ought a biological species to be judged by its crippled, warped, only partially developed specimens, or by examples that have been overdomesticated, caged, and trained?

4. Problem-Centering

Our subjects are in general strongly focussed on problems outside themselves. In current terminology they are problem-centered rather than ego-centered. They generally are not problems for themselves and are not generally much concerned about themselves; i.e., as contrasted with the ordinary introspectiveness that one finds in insecure people. These individuals customarily have some mission in life, some task to fulfill, some problem outside of themselves which enlists much of their energies.[2]

This is not necessarily a task that they would prefer or choose for themselves; it may be a task that they feel is their responsibility, duty, or obligation. This is why we use the phrase "a task that they must do" rather than the phrase "a task that they want to do." In general these tasks are nonpersonal or "unselfish," concerned rather with the good of mankind in general, or of a nation in general, or of a few individuals in the subject's family.

With a few exceptions we can say that our subjects are ordinarily concerned with basic issues and eternal questions of the type that we have learned to call by the names philosophical or ethical. Such people live customarily in the widest possible frame of reference. They seem never to get so close to the trees that they fail to see the forest. They work within a framework of values which are broad and not petty, universal and not local, and in terms of a century rather than the moment. In a word these people are all in one sense or another philosophers, however homely.

Of course, such an attitude carries with it dozens of implications for every area of daily living. For instance, one of the main "presenting symptoms" originally worked with ("bigness"—lack of smallness, triviality, pettiness) can be subsumed under this more general heading. This impression of being above small things, of having a larger horizon, a wider breadth of vision, of living in the widest frame of reference, *sub specie aeternitatis,* is of the utmost social and interpersonal importance, it seems to impart a certain serenity and lack of worry over immediate concerns which makes life easier not only for themselves but for all who are associated with them.

5. The Quality of Detachment; The Need for Privacy

For all my subjects it is true that they can be solitary, without harm to themselves and without discomfort. Furthermore it is true for almost all of them that they positively like solitude and privacy to a definitely greater degree than the average person. The dichotomy "introvert-extrovert" applies hardly at all to these people and will not be used here. The term that seems to be most useful is "detachment."

It is often possible for them to remain above the battle, to remain unruffled, undisturbed by that which produces turmoil in others. They find it easy to be aloof, reserved, and also calm and serene; thus it becomes possible for them to take personal misfortunes without reacting violently as the ordinary person does. They seem to be able to retain their dignity even in undignified surroundings and situations. Perhaps this comes in part from their tendency to stick by their own interpretation of a situation rather than to rely upon what other people feel or think about the matter.

This quality of detachment may have some connection with certain other qualities as well. For one thing it is possible to call my subjects more objective (in all senses of that word) than average people. We have seen that they are more problem-centered than ego-centered. This is true even when the problem concerns themselves, their own wishes, motives, hopes, or aspirations. Consequently they have the ability to concentrate to a degree not usual for ordinary men. Intense concentration produces as a by-product such phenomena as "absent-mindedness," the ability to forget and to be oblivious of other surroundings. An example is the ability to sleep soundly, to have undisturbed appetite, to be able to smile and laugh through a period of problems, worry, and responsibility.

In social relations with most people, detachment creates certain troubles and problems. It is easily interpreted by "normal" people as coldness, snobbishness, lack of affection, unfriendliness, or even hostility. By contrast the ordinary friendship relationship is more clinging, more demanding, more desirous of reassurance, compliment, support, warmth, and exclusiveness. It is true that self-actualizing people do not "need" others in the ordinary sense. But since this being needed or being missed is the usual earnest of friendship, it is evident that detachment will not easily be accepted by average people.

6. Autonomy, Independence of Culture and Environment

One characteristic of self-actualizing people which to a certain extent crosscuts much of what we have already described is their relative independence of the physical and social environment. Since they are propelled by growth motivation rather than deficiency motivation, self-actualizing people are not dependent for their main satisfactions on the real world, or other people or culture or means-to-ends or, in general, on extrinsic satisfactions. Rather they are dependent for their own development and continued growth upon their own potentialities and latent resources. Just as the tree needs sunshine and water and food, so do most people need love, safety, and the other basic need gratifications which can come only from without. But once these external satisfiers are obtained, once these inner deficiencies are satiated by outside satisfiers, the true problem of individual human development begins, i.e., self-actualization.

This independence of environment means a relative stability in the face of hard knocks, blows, deprivations, frustrations, and the like. These people can maintain a relative serenity and happiness in the midst of circumstances that would drive other people to suicide. They have also been described as "self-contained."

Deficiency-motivated people *must* have other people available since most of their main need-gratifications (love, safety, respect, prestige, belongingness) can come only from other human beings. But growth-motivated people may actually be *hampered* by others. The determinants of satisfaction and of the good life are for them now inner-individual and not social. They have become strong enough to be independent of the good opinion of other people, or even of their affection. The honors, the status, the rewards, the prestige, and the love they can bestow must have become less important than self-development and inner growth.[13, 30, 31, 33, 35, 38] We must remember that the best technique we know even though not the only one, for getting to this point of independence from love and respect, is to have been given plenty of this very same love and respect in the past.[25]

7. Continued Freshness of Appreciation

Self-actualized people have the wonderful capacity to appreciate again and again, freshly and naïvely, the basic goods of life — with awe, pleasure, wonder, and even ecstasy, however stale these experiences may have become to others. Thus, for such people every sunset is as beautiful as the first one, any flower may be of breathtaking loveliness even after he has seen a million flowers. The thousandth baby he sees is just as miraculous a product as the first one he saw. He remains as convinced of his luck in marriage thirty years after his marriage and is as surprised by his wife's beauty when she is sixty as he was forty years before. For such people even the casual workaday, moment-to-moment business of living can be thrilling, exciting, and ecstatic. These intense feelings do not come all the time; they come occasionally rather than usually, but at the most unexpected moments. The person may cross the river on the ferry ten times and at the eleventh crossing have a strong recurrence of the same feelings, the same reaction of beauty and excitement, as when he crossed the ferry for the first time.[6]

There are some differences in choice of beautiful objects. Some subjects go primarily to nature. For others it is primarily children, and for a few subjects it has been primarily great music; but it may certainly be said that they derive ecstasy, inspiration, and strength from the basic experiences of life. No one of them, for instance, will get this same sort of reaction from going to a night club or getting a lot of money or having a good time at a party.

Perhaps one special experience may be added. For several of my subjects the sexual pleasures and particularly the orgasm provided not passing pleasure alone, but some kind of basic strengthening and revivifying that some people derive from music or nature. I shall say more about this in the section on the mystic experience.

It is probable that this acute richness of subjective experience is an aspect of closeness of relationship to the concrete and fresh, *per se* reality discussed above. Perhaps what we call staleness in experience is a consequence of ticketing off a rich perception into one or another category or rubric as it proves to be no longer advantageous or useful, or threatening or otherwise ego-involved.[23]

8. The "Mystic Experience," the "Oceanic Feeling"

Those subjective expressions which have been called the mystic experience and described so well by William James [14] are a fairly common experience for our subjects. The strong emotions described in the previous section sometimes get strong enough, chaotic and widespread enough, to be called mystic experiences. My interest and attention in this subject was first enlisted by several of my subjects who described their sexual orgasms in vaguely familiar terms which later I remembered had been used by various writers to describe what *they* called the mystic experience. There were the same feelings of limitless horizons opening up to the vision, of the feeling of being simultaneously more powerful and also more helpless than one ever was before, the feeling of great ecstasy and wonder and awe, the loss of placing in time and space with, finally, the conviction that something extremely important and valuable had happened so that the subject is to some extent transformed and strengthened even in his daily life by such experiences.[13, 30, 35]

It is quite important to dissociate this experience from any theological or supernatural reference even though for thousands of years they have been linked. None of our subjects spontaneously made any such tieup, although in later conversations some semireligious conclusions were drawn by a few, e.g., "life must have a meaning," etc. Because this experience is a natural experience, well within the jurisdiction of science, it is probably better to use Freud's term for it, i.e., the oceanic feeling.

We may also learn from our subjects that such experiences can occur in a lesser degree of intensity. The theological literature had generally assumed an absolute, qualitative difference between the mystic experience and all others. As soon as it is divorced from supernatural reference and studied as a natural phenomenon, it becomes possible to place the mystic experience on a quantitative continuum from intense to mild. We discover then that the *mild* mystic experience occurs in many, perhaps even most, individuals, and that in the favored individual it occurs dozens of times a day.

Apparently the acute mystic experience is a tremendous intensification of *any* of the experiences in which there is loss of self or transcendence of it, e.g., problem-centering, intense concentration, "muga" behavior, as described by Benedict,[4] intense sensuous experience, self-forgetful and intense enjoyment of music or art.

9. Gemeinschaftsgefühl

This word, invented by Alfred Adler,[1] is the only one available which describes well the "flavor" of the feelings for mankind expressed by self-actualizing subjects. They have for human beings in general a deep feeling of identification, sympathy, and affection, in spite of the occasional anger, impatience, or disgust described below. Because of this they have a genuine desire to help the human race. It is as if they were all members of a single family. One's feelings toward his brothers would be on the whole affectionate even if these brothers were foolish, weak or even if they were sometimes nasty. They would still be more easily forgiven than strangers.

If one's view is not general enough and if it is not spread over a long enough period of time, then one may not see this feeling of identification with mankind. The self-actualizing person is after all **very** different from other people in thought, impulse, behavior, emotion. When it comes down to it, in certain basic ways he is like an alien in a strange land. Very few really understand him, however much they may like him. He is often saddened, exasperated, and even enraged by the shortcomings of the average person, and, while they are to him ordinarily no more than a nuisance, they sometimes become bitter tragedy. However far apart he is from them at times he nevertheless feels a basic underlying kinship with these creatures whom he must regard with, if not condescension, at least the knowledge that he can do many things better than they can, that he can see things that they cannot see, that the truth which is so clear to him is for most people veiled and hidden. This is what Adler called the "older-brotherly" attitude.

10. Interpersonal Relations — SA

Self-actualizing people have deeper and more profound interpersonal relations than any other adults (although not necessarily deeper than those of children). They are capable of more fusion, greater love, more perfect identification, more obliteration of the ego boundaries than other people would consider possible. There are however certain special characteristics of these relationships. In the first place it is my observation that the opposite members in these relationships are ordinarily (in about two-thirds of the cases) also self-actualizing persons. There is high selectiveness here, considering the small proportion of such people in the general population.

One consequence of this phenomenon and of certain others as well is that self-actualizing people have these especially deep ties with rather few individuals. Their circle of friends is rather small. The ones they love profoundly are few in number. Partly this is for the reason that being very close to someone in this self-actualizing style seems to require a good deal of time. Devotion is not a matter of a moment. One subject expressed it so: "I haven't got time for many friends. Nobody has, that is, if they are to be real friends." The only possible exception in my group was one woman who seemed to be especially equipped socially. It was almost as if her appointed task in life was to have close and warm and beautiful relations with all the members of her family and their families as well as all her friends and theirs. Perhaps this was because she was an uneducated woman who had no formal "task" or "career." This exclusiveness of devotion can and does exist side by side with a wide-spreading *gemeinschaftsgefühl,* benevolence, affection, and friendliness (as qualified above). These people *tend* to be kind or at least patient to almost everyone. They have an especially tender love for children and are easily touched by them. In a very real even though special sense, they love, or rather, have compassion for all mankind.

This "love" does not imply lack of discrimination. The fact is that they can speak realistically and harshly of those who deserve it, and especially of the hypocritical, the pretentious, the pompous, or the self-inflated. But the face-to-face relationship even with these people does not show signs of realistically low evaluations. One explanatory statement was about as follows: "Most people after all do not amount to much but they *could* have. They make all sorts of foolish mistakes and wind up being miserable and not knowing how they got that way when their intentions were good. Those who are not nice are usually paying for it in deep unhappiness. They should be pitied rather than attacked."

Perhaps the briefest possible description is to say that their hostile reactions to others are (a) deserved, (b) for the good of the person attacked or for someone else's good. This is to say, with Fromm, that their hostility is not character-based but is reactive or situational.

All the subjects for whom I have data show in common another characteristic which is appropriate to mention here, namely, that they attract at least some admirers, "friends," or even disciples or worshippers. The relation between the individual and his train of admirers is apt to be rather one-sided. The admirers are apt to demand more than our individual is willing to give. And furthermore these devotions are apt to be rather embarrassing, distressing, and even distasteful to the self-actualizing person, since they often go beyond ordinary bounds. The usual picture reveals our subject being kind and pleasant when forced into these relationships but ordinarily trying to avoid them as gracefully as possible.

11. The Democratic Character Structure

All my subjects without exception may be said to be democratic people in the deepest possible sense. I say this on the basis of a previous analysis of authoritarian and democratic character structures [20] which is too elaborate to present here; it is possible only to describe some aspects of this behavior in short space. These people have all the obvious or superficial democratic characteristics. They can be and are friendly with anyone of suitable character regardless of class, education, political belief, race, or color. As a matter of fact it often seems as if they are not even aware of these differences which are for the average person so obvious and so important.

They have not only this most obvious quality but their democratic feeling goes deeper as well. For instance they find it possible to learn from anybody who has something to teach them — no matter what other characteristics he may have. In such a learning relationship they do not try to maintain any outward "dignity" or to maintain status or age prestige or the like. It should even be said that my subjects share a quality that could be called "humility" of a certain type. They are all quite well aware of their own worth, so that there is no humbleness of the cringing or of the designing and calculating type. They are equally aware of how little they know in comparison with what *could* be known and what *is* known by others. Because of this it is possible for them without pose to be honestly respectful and even humble before people who can teach them something which they do not know or who have a skill they do not possess. They give this honest respect to a carpenter who is a good carpenter; or for that matter to anybody who is a master of his own tools or his own craft.

The careful distinction must be made between this democratic feeling and a lack of discrimination in taste, of an undiscriminating equality of any one human being with any other. These individuals, themselves elite, select for their friends elite, but this is an elite of character, capacity, and talent, rather than of birth, race, blood, name, family, age, youth, fame, or power.

Most profound but also most vague is the hard-to-get-at tendency to give a certain quantum of respect to *any* human being just because he is a human individual; our subjects seem not to wish to go beyond a certain minimum point, even with scoundrels, of demeaning, of derogating, of robbing of dignity.

12. Means and Ends

I have found none of my subjects to be chronically unsure about the difference between right and wrong in his actual living. Whether or not they could verbalize the matter they rarely showed in their day-to-day living the chaos, the confusion, the inconsistency, or the conflict that is so common in the average person's ethical dealings. This may be phrased also in such terms as: these individuals are strongly ethical, they have definite moral standards, they do right and do not do wrong. Needless to say, their notions of right and wrong are often not the conventional ones.

One way of expressing the quality I am trying to describe was suggested by Dr. David Levy who pointed out that a few centuries ago these would all have been described as "men who walk in the path of God" or as the "Godly man." So far as religion is concerned, none of my subjects are orthodoxly religious, but on the other hand I know of only one who describes himself as an atheist (as against four of the *total* group studied). All the others for whom I have information hesitate to call themselves atheists. They say that they believe in a God but describe this God more as a metaphysical concept than as a personal figure. Whether or not they could be called religious people as a group must then depend entirely on the concept or definition of religion that we choose to use. If religion is defined only in social-behavioral terms, then these are all "religious" people, the atheists included. But if more conservatively we use the term religion so as to include and stress the supernatural element (certainly the more common usage) then our answer must be quite different, for then almost none of them are religious.

Self-actualizing people most of the time behave as though, for them, means and ends are clearly distinguishable. In general, they are fixed on ends rather than on means, and means are quite definitely subordinated to these ends. This however is an over-simple statement. Our subjects make the situation more complex by often regarding as ends-in-themselves many experiences and activities which are, for other people, only means-to-ends. Our subjects are somewhat more likely to appreciate for its own sake, and in an absolute way, the "doing itself"; they can often enjoy for its own sake the getting-to-someplace as well as the arriving. It is occasionally possible for them to make out of the most trivial and routine activity an intrinsically enjoyable game or dance or play. Wertheimer pointed out that some children are so creative that they can transform hackneyed routine, mechanical, and rote experiences — e.g., as in one of his experiments, transporting books from one set of shelves to another — into a structured and amusing game of a sort by doing this according to a certain system or with a certain rhythm.

13. Philosophical, Unhostile Sense of Humor

One very early finding that was quite easy to make, because it was common to all my subjects, was that their sense of humor is not of the ordinary type. They do not consider funny what the average man considers to be funny. Thus they do not laugh at hostile humor (making people laugh by hurting someone) or superiority humor (laughing at someone else's inferiority) or authority-rebellion humor (the unfunny smutty joke). Characteristically what they consider humor is more closely allied to philosophy than to anything else. It may also be called the humor of the real because it consists in large part in poking fun at human beings in general when they are foolish, or forget their place in the universe, or try to be big when they are actually small. This can take the form of poking fun at themselves but this is not done in any masochistic or clown-like way. Lincoln's humor can serve as a suitable example. Probably Lincoln never made a joke which hurt anybody else; it is also likely that many or even most of his jokes had something to say, had a function beyond just producing a laugh. They often seemed to be education in a more palatable form, akin to parables or fables.

On a simple quantitative basis, our subjects may be said to be humorous less often than the average of the population. Punning, joking, witty remarks, gay repartee, persiflage of the ordinary sort is much less often seen than the rather thoughtful, philosophical humor which elicits a smile more usually than a laugh, which is intrinsic to the situation rather than added to it, which is spontaneous rather than planned, and which very often can never be repeated. It should not be surprising that the average man, accustomed as he is to joke books and belly laughs, considers our subjects to be rather on the sober and serious side.

14. Creativeness — SA

This is a universal characteristic of all the people studied or observed. There is no exception. Each one shows in one way or another a special kind of creativeness or originality or inventiveness which has certain peculiar characteristics. These special characteristics can be understood more fully in the light of discussion later in this paper. For one thing, it is different from "special-talent creativeness" of the Mozart type. We may as well face the fact that the so-called "geniuses" display ability which we do not understand. All we can say of them is that they seem to be specially endowed with a drive and a capacity which may have rather little relationship to the rest of the personality and with which, from all evidence, the individuals seem to be born. Such talent we have no concern with here since it does not rest upon psychic health or basic satisfaction. The creativeness of the self-actualized man seems rather to be kin to the naïve and universal creativeness of unspoiled children. It seems to be more a fundamental characteristic of common human nature — a potentiality given to all human beings at birth. Most human beings lose this as they become acculturated, but some few individuals seem either to retain this fresh and naïve direct way of looking at life, or else, if they have lost it as most people do, then they later in life recover it.

This creativeness appears in some of our subjects not in the usual forms of writing books, composing music, or producing artistic objects, but rather may be much more humble. It is as if this special type of creativeness, being an expression of healthy personality, is projected out upon the world or touches whatever activity the person is engaged in. In this sense there can be creative shoemakers or carpenters or clerks. Whatever one does can be done with a certain attitude, a certain spirit which arises out of the nature of the character of the person performing the act. One can even *see* creatively as the child does.

This quality is differentiated here for the sake of discussion, as if it were something separate from the characteristics which precede it and follow it; but this is not actually the case. Perhaps when we speak of creativeness here we are simply describing from another point of view, namely, from the point of view of consequences, what we have described above as a greater freshness, penetration, and efficiency of perception. These people seem to see the true and the real more easily. It is because of this that they seem to other more limited men creative.

Furthermore, as we have seen, these individuals are less inhibited, less constricted, less bound — in a word, less acculturated. In more positive terms, they are more spontaneous, more natural, "more human." This too would have as one of its consequences what would seem to other people to be creativeness. If we assume, as we may from our study of children, that all people were once spontaneous and perhaps in their deepest roots still are, but that these people have in addition to their deep spontaneity a superficial but powerful set of inhibitions, then this spontaneity must be checked so as not to appear very often. If there were no choking-off forces, then we might expect that every human being would show this special type of creativeness.

THE IMPERFECTIONS OF SELF-ACTUALIZING PEOPLE

The ordinary mistake that is made by novelists, poets, and essayists about the good human being is to make him so good that he is a caricature, so that nobody would like to be like him. The individual's own wishes for perfection and his guilt and shame about shortcomings are projected upon various kinds of people from whom the average man demands much more than he himself gives. Thus teachers and ministers are ordinarily conceived to be rather joyless people who have no mundane desires and who have no weaknesses. It is my belief that most of the novelists who have attempted to portray good (healthy) people did this sort of thing, making them into stuffed shirts or marionettes or unreal projections of unreal ideals, rather than into the robust, hearty, lusty individuals they really are. Our subjects show many of the lesser human failings — if they are in fact failings. They too are equipped with silly, wasteful, or thoughtless habits. They can be boring, stubborn, irritating. They are by no means free from a rather superficial vanity, pride, partiality to their own productions, family, friends, and children.

Our subjects are occasionally capable of an extraordinary and unexpected ruthlessness. It must be remembered that they are very strong people. This makes it possible for them to display a surgical coldness when this is called for, beyond the power of the average man. The man who found that a long-trusted acquaintance was dishonest cut himself off from this friendship sharply and abruptly and without any pangs whatsoever. Another woman who was married to someone she did not love, when she decided on divorce, did it with a decisiveness that looked almost like ruthlessness. Some of them recover so quickly from the death of people close to them as to seem heartless.

Not only are these people strong but also they are independent of the opinions of other people. One woman, extremely irritated by the stuffy conventionalism of some individuals she was introduced to at a gathering, went far out of her way to shock these people by her language and behavior. One might say that it was all right for her to react to irritation in this way, but another result was that these people were completely hostile not only to the woman but to the friends in whose home this meeting took place. While our subject *wanted* to alienate these people, the host and hostess did not.

We may mention one more example which arises primarily from the absorption of our subjects in an impersonal world. In their concentration, in their fascinated interest, in their intense concentration on some phenomenon or question, they may become absent-minded or humorless and forget their ordinary social politeness. In such circumstances, they are apt to show themselves more clearly as essentially not interested in chatting, gay conversation, party-going or the like, they may use language or behavior which may be distressing, shocking, insulting, or hurtful to others. Other undesirable (at least from the point of view of others) consequences of detachment have been listed above.

Even their kindness can lead them into mistakes, e.g., marrying out of pity, getting too closely involved with neurotics, bores, unhappy people, and then being sorry for it, allowing scoundrels to impose on them for a while, giving more than they demand so that occasionally they encourage parasites and psychopaths, etc.

Finally, it has already been pointed out that these people are *not* free of guilt, anxiety, sadness, self-castigation, internal strife, and conflict. The fact that these arise out of nonneurotic sources is of little consequence to most people today (even to most psychologists) who are therefore apt to think them *un*healthy for this reason.

THE VALUES OF SELF-ACTUALIZATION

A firm foundation for a value-system is automatically furnished to the self-actualizer by his philosophic acceptance of the nature of his self, of human nature, of much of social life, and of nature and physical reality. These "acceptance-values" account for a high percentage of the total of his individual value-judgments from day to day. What he approves of, disapproves of, is loyal to, opposes, or proposes, what pleases him or displeases him can often be understood as surface derivations of this source trait of acceptance.

Not only is this foundation automatically (and universally) supplied to *all* SA's by their intrinsic dynamics (so that in at least this respect fully developed human nature may be universal and cross-cultural); other determiners are supplied as well by these same dynamics. Among these are (a) his peculiarly comfortable relationships with reality, (b) his *gemeinschaftsgefühl,* (c) his basically satisfied condition from which flow, as epiphenomena, various consequences of surplus, of wealth, of overflowing abundance, (d) his characteristic relations to means and ends, etc. (see above).

One most important consequence of this attitude toward the world — as well as a validation of it — is the fact that conflict and struggle, ambivalence and uncertainty over choices lessen or disappear in many areas of life. Apparently morality is largely an epiphenomenon of nonacceptance or dissatisfaction. Many "problems" are seen to be gratuitous and fade out of existence in the atmosphere of pagan acceptance. It is not so much that the problem is solved as that it becomes clearly seen that it never was an intrinsic problem in the first place, but only a sick-man-created one, e.g., card-playing, dancing, wearing short dresses, exposing the head (in some churches) or *not* exposing the head (in others), drinking wine, or eating some meats and not others, or eating them on some days but not on others. Not only are such trivialities deflated; the process also goes on at a more important level, e.g., the relations between the sexes, attitudes toward the structure of the body and toward its functioning, and toward death itself.

The pursuit of this finding to more profound levels has suggested to the writer that much else of what passes for morals, ethics, and values may be the gratuitous epiphenomena of the pervasive psychopathology of the "average." Many conflicts, frustrations, and threats (which force the kind of choice in which value is expressed) evaporate or resolve for the self-actualizing person in the same way as do, let us say, conflicts over dancing. For him the seemingly irreconcilable battle of the sexes becomes no conflict at all but rather a delightful collaboration. The "antagonistic" interests of adults and children turn out to be not so antagonistic after all. Just as with sex and age differences, so also is it with natural differences, class and caste differences, political differences, role differences, religious differences, etc. As we know, these are each fertile breeding grounds for anxiety, fear, hostility, aggression, defensiveness, and jealousy. But it begins to appear that they *need not be,* for our subject's reaction to differences is much less often of this undesirable type.

To take the teacher-student relationship as a specific paradigm, our teacher-subjects behaved in a very unneurotic way simply by interpreting the whole situation differently, i.e., as a pleasant collaboration rather than as a clash of wills, of authority, of dignity, etc. the replacement of artificial dignity — which is easily and inevitably threatened — with the natural simplicity which is *not* easily threatened; the giving up of the attempt to be omniscient and omnipotent; the absence of student-threatening authoritarianism; the refusal to regard the students as competing with each other or with the teacher; the refusal to assume the "professor" stereotype and the insistence on remaining as realistically human as, say, a plumber or a carpenter; all of these created a classroom atmosphere in which suspicion, wariness, defensiveness, hostility, and anxiety disappeared. So also do similar threat-responses tend to disappear in marriages, in families, and in other interpersonal situations when threat itself is reduced.

It is possible to generalize even further for it seems possible that most or perhaps even all value dichotomies or polarities tend to disappear or resolve in self-actualizing people. These people are neither selfish nor unselfish in the ordinary sense; they are both (or neither).

They are neither rationalists nor intuitionalists, neither classical nor romantic, neither self-interested nor other-interested, neither introverts nor extroverts, etc. Rather they are both. Or to be accurate, in them these dichotomies simply do not apply.

The principles and the values of the desperate man and of the psychologically healthy man must be different in at least some ways. They have profoundly different perceptions (interpretations) of the physical world, the social world, and the private psychological world, whose organization and economy is in part the responsibility of the person's value system. For the basically deprived man the world is a dangerous place, a jungle, and enemy territory populated by (a) those whom he can dominate and (b) those who can dominate him. His value system is of necessity, like that of any jungle denizen, dominated and organized by the "lower" needs, especially the creature needs and the safety needs. The basically satisfied person is in a different case. He can afford out of his abundance to take these needs and their satisfaction for granted and can devote himself to higher gratifications. This is to say that their value systems are different, in fact, *must* be different.

The topmost portion of the value system of the SA person is entirely unique and idiosyncratic-character-structure-expressive. This must be true by definition, for self-actualization is actualization of a self, and no two selves are altogether alike. There is only one Renoir, one Brahms, one Spinoza. Our subjects had very much in common, as we have seen, and yet at the same time were more completely individualized, more unmistakably themselves, less easily confounded with others than any average control group could possibly be. That is to say, they are simultaneously very much like and very much unlike each other. They are more completely "individual" than any group that has ever been described and yet are also more completely socialized, more identified with humanity, than any other group yet described.

BIBLIOGRAPHY

1. Adler, A. *Social Interest.* New York: G. P. Putnam's Sons, 1939.
2. Angyal, A. *Foundations for a Science of Personality.* New York: Commonwealth Fund, 1941.
3. Benedict, R. *Synergy in Society.* (Unpublished Lectures) Bryn Mawr: *c.* 1942.
4. ———. *The Chrysanthemum and the Sword.* Boston: Houghton Mifflin Company, 1946.
5. Bergson, H. *Creative Evolution.* New York: The Modern Library, 1944.
6. Eastman, M. *The Enjoyment of Poetry.* New York: Charles Scribner's Sons, 1928.
7. Frenkel-Brunswik, E. "Intolerance of Ambiguities." *Journal of Personality,* (in press).
8. Freud, S. *Collected Papers.* Vol. 11. London: Hogarth Press, 1924.
9. Fromm E. *Escape from Freedom.* New York: Farrar & Rinehart, Inc., 1941.
10. ———. *Man for Himself.* New York: Rinehart & Co., Inc., 1947.

11. Goldstein, K. *The Organism*. New York: American Book Co., 1939.
12. Horney, K. *Our Inner Conflicts*. New York: W. W. Norton & Company, Inc., 1945.
13. Huxley, A. *The Perennial Philosophy*. New York: Harper & Brothers, 1944.
14. James, W. *The Varieties of Religious Experience*. New York: The Modern Library, 1943.
15. Johnson, W. *People in Quandaries*. New York: Harper & Brothers, 1946.
16. King, C. D. "The Meaning of Normal." *Journal of Biology and Medicine*, 17:493-501 (1945).
17. Kohler, W. *The Place of Values in a World of Facts*. New York: Liverright Publishing Corporation, 1938.
18. Korzybski, A. *Science and Sanity*. 3rd ed. Lakeville, Conn: International Non-Aristotelian Library Publishing Co., 1948.
19. Maier, N. R. F. "The Role of Frustration in Social Movements." *Psychological Review*, 49:586-599 (1942).
20. Maslow, A. H. "The Authoritarian Character Structure." *Journal of Social Psychology*, 18:401-411 (1943).
21. ———. "A Theory of Human Motivation." *Psychological Review*, 50:370-396 (1943).
22. ———. "Dynamics of Personality Organization I and II. *Psychological Review*, 50:514-539, 541-558 (1943).
23. ———. "Cognition of the Particular and of the Generic." *Psychological Review*, 55:20-40 (1948).
24. ———. "Higher and Lower Needs." *Journal of Psychology*, 25:433-436 (1948).
25. ———. "Some Theoretical Consequences of Basic Need-Gratification." *Journal of Personality*, 16:402-416 (1948).
26. ———. "Our Maligned Animal Nature." *Journal of Psychology*, 28:273-278 (1949).
27. ———. "The Expressive Component of Behavior." *Psychological Review*, 56:26-272 (1949).
28. Money-Kyrle, R. E. "Towards a Common Aim — A Psycho-Analytical Contribution to Ethics." *British Journal of Medical Psychology*, 20:105-117 (1944).
29. ———. "Some Aspects of Political Ethics from the Psycho-Analytical Point of View." *International Journal of Psychoanalysis*, 25:166-171 (1944).

30. Northrop, F. S. C. *The Meeting of East and West.* New York: The Macmillan Company, 1946.
31. Rand, A. *The Fountainhead.* Indianapolis: The Bobbs-Merrill Company, 1943.
32. Reik, T. *Listening With the Third Ear.* New York: Farrar, Strauss & Co., 1948.
33. Rogers, C. R. *Counseling and Psychotherapy.* New York: Houghton Mifflin Company, 1942.
34. Rokeach, M. "Generalized Mental Rigidity as a Factor in Ethocentrism." *Journal of Abnormal and Social Psychology,* 43:259-278 (1948).
35. Taylor, E. *Richer by Asia.* Boston: Houghton Mifflin Company, 1947.
36. Wertheimer, M. "Some Problems in the Theory of Ethics." *Social Research,* 2:353-367 (1935).
37. Whitehead, A. N. *The Aims of Education.* New York: Mentor Books, 1949.
38. Wolfe, T. *You Can't Go Home Again.* New York: Harper & Brothers, 1949.

XV WHAT IT MEANS TO BECOME A PERSON

CARL R. ROGERS

A frequently raised question is: "What problems do people bring to you and other counselors at the Counseling Center?" I always feel baffled by this question. One reply is that they bring every kind of problem one can imagine, and quite a number that I believe no one would imagine. There is the student concerned about failing in college; the housewife disturbed about her marriage; the individual who feels he is teetering on the edge of a complete breakdown or psychosis; the responsible professional man who spends much of his time in sexual fantasies and functions inefficiently in his work; the brilliant student, at the top of his class, who is paralyzed by the conviction that he is hopelessly and helplessly inadequate; the parent who is distressed by his child's behavior; the popular girl who finds herself unaccountably overtaken by sharp spells of black depression; the woman who fears that life and love are passing her by, and that her good graduate record is a poor recompense; the man who has become convinced that powerful and sinister forces are plotting against him — I could go on and on with the many different and unique problems which people bring to us. They run the gamut of life's experiences. Yet there is no satisfaction in giving this type of catalog, for, as counselor, I know that the problem as stated in the first interview will not be the problem as seen in the second or third hour, and by the tenth interview it will be a still different problem

195

or series of problems. You can see why I feel baffled as to how to answer this simple question.

I have however come to believe that, in spite of this bewildering horizontal multiplicity, there is a simple answer. As I follow the experience of many clients in the therapeutic relationship which we endeavor to create for them, it seems to me that each one has the same problem. Below the level of the problem situation about which the individual is complaining — behind the trouble with studies, or wife, or employer, or with his own uncontrollable or bizarre behavior, or with his frightening feelings, lies one central search. It seems to me that at bottom each person is asking: "Who am I, really? How can I get in touch with this real self, underlying all my surface behavior? How can I become myself?"

THE PROCESS OF BECOMING

Getting Behind the Mask

Let me try to explain what I mean when I say that it appears that the goal the individual most wishes to achieve, the end which he knowingly and unknowingly pursues, is to become himself.

When a person comes to me, troubled by his unique combination of difficulties, I have found it most worth while to try to create a relationship with him in which he is safe and free. It is my purpose to understand the way he feels in his own inner world, to accept him as he is, to create an atmosphere of freedom in which he can move in his thinking and feeling and being, in any direction he desires. How does he use this freedom?

It is my experience that he uses it to become more and more himself. He begins to drop the false fronts, or the masks, or the roles, with which he has faced life. He appears to be trying to discover something more basic, something more truly himself. At first he lays aside masks which he is to some degree aware of using. One young woman describes in a counseling interview one of the masks she has been using, and how uncertain she is whether underneath this appeasing, ingratiating front there is any real self with convictions.

I was thinking about this business of standards. I somehow developed a sort of knack, I guess, of — well — a habit — of trying to make people feel at ease around me, or to make things go along smoothly. There always had to be some appeaser around, being sorta the oil that soothed the waters. At a small meeting, or a little party, or something — I could help things go along nicely and appear to be having a good time. And sometimes I'd surprise myself by arguing against what I really thought when I saw that the person in charge would be quite unhappy about it if I didn't. In other words I just wasn't ever — I mean, I didn't find myself ever being set and definite about things. Now the reason why I did it probably was I'd been doing it around home so much. I just didn't stand up for my own convictions, until I don't know whether I have any convictions to stand up for. I haven't been really honestly being myself, or actually knowing what my real self is, and I've been just playing a sort of false role.

You can, in this excerpt, see her examining the mask she has been using, recognizing her dissatisfaction with it, and wondering how to get to the real self underneath, if such a self exists.

In this attempt to discover his own self, the client typically uses the therapeutic relationship to explore, to examine the various aspects of his own experience, to recognize and face up to the deep contradictions which he often discovers. He learns how much of his behavior, even how much of the feeling he experiences, is not real, is not something which flows from the genuine reactions of his organism, but is a façade, a front behind which he has been hiding. He discovers how much of his life is guided by what he thinks he *should* be, not by what he is. Often he discovers that he exists only in response to the demands of others, that he seems to have no self of his own, that he is only trying to think, and feel, and behave in the way that others believe he *ought* to think and feel and behave.

In this connection I have been astonished to find how accurately the Danish philosopher Soren Kierkegaard pictured the dilemma of the individual more than a century ago with keen psychological insight. He points out that the most common despair is to be in despair at not choosing, or willing, to be one's self; but that the deepest form of despair is to choose "to be another than himself." On the other hand "to will to be that self which one truly is, is indeed the opposite of despair," and this choice is the deepest responsibility of man. As I read some of his writings I almost feel that he must have listened in on the statements made by our clients as they search and explore for the reality of self — often a painful and troubling search.

This exploration becomes even more disturbing when they find themselves involved in removing the false faces which they had not known were false faces. They begin to engage in the frightening task of exploring the turbulent and sometimes violent feelings within themselves. To remove a mask which you had thought was part of your real self can be a deeply disturbing experience, yet when there is freedom to think and feel and be, the individual moves toward such a goal. A few statements from a person who had completed a series of psychotherapeutic interviews will illustrate this. She uses many metaphors as she tells how she struggled to get to the core of herself.

As I look at it now, I was peeling off layer after layer of defenses, I'd build them up, try them, and then discard them when you remained the same. I didn't know what was at the bottom and I was very much afraid to find out, but I *had* to keep on trying. At first I felt there was *nothing* within me — just a great emptiness where I needed and wanted a solid core. Then I began to feel that I was facing a solid brick wall, too high to get over and too thick to go through. One day the wall became translucent, rather than solid. After this, the wall seemed to disappear but beyond it I discovered a dam holding back violent, churning waters. I felt as if I were holding back the force of these waters and if I opened even a tiny hole I and all about me would be destroyed in the ensuing torrent of feelings represented by the water. Finally I could stand the strain no longer and I let go. All I did, actually, was to succumb to complete and utter self-pity, then hate, then love. After this experience, I felt as if I had leaped a brink and was safely on the other side, though still tottering a bit on the edge. I don't know what I was searching for or where I was going, but I felt then as I have always felt whenever I really lived, that I was moving forward.

I believe this represents rather well the feelings of many an individual that if the false front, the wall, the dam, is not maintained, then everything will be swept away in the violence of the feelings that he discovers pent up in his private world. Yet it also illustrates the compelling necessity which the individual feels to search for and become himself. It also begins to indicate the way in which the individual determines the reality in himself — that when he fully experiences the feelings which at an organic level he *is,* as this client experienced her self-pity, hatred, and love, then he feels an assurance that he is being a part of his real self.

The Experiencing of Feeling

I would like to say something more about this experiencing of feeling. It is truly the discovery of unknown elements of self. The phenomenon I am trying to describe is something which I think is quite difficult to get across in any meaningful way. In our daily lives there are a thousand and one reasons for not letting ourselves experience our attitudes fully, reasons from our past and from the present, reasons that reside within the social situation. It seems too dangerous, too potentially damaging, to experience them freely and fully. But in the safety and freedom of the therapeutic relationship they can be experienced fully, clear to the limit of what they are. They can be and are experienced in a fashion that I like to think of as a "pure culture," so that for the moment the person *is* his fear, or he *is* his anger, or he *is* his tenderness, or whatever.

Perhaps again I can indicate this somewhat better by giving an example from a client that will convey something of what I mean. This comes from the recording of the thirty-first interview with this woman. She has talked several times of a recurrent feeling which troubles her and which she cannot quite pin down and define. Is it a feeling that developed because she had practically no relationship with her parents? Is it a guilty feeling? She is not quite sure, and she ends this kind of talk with this statement:

CLIENT.   And I have the feeling that it isn't guilt (*pause, she weeps*). So . . . course I mean, I can't verbalize it yet. It's just being *terribly hurt!*

THERAPIST.,   M–hm. It isn't guilt except in the sense of being very much wounded somehow.

C.   (*weeping*). It's . . . you know, often I've been guilty of it myself, but in later years, when I've heard parents . . . say to their children "stop crying," I've had a feeling, as though, well, why should they tell them to stop crying? They feel sorry for themselves, and who can feel more adequately sorry for himself than a child. Well, that is sort of what . . . I mean, as — as though I thought that they should let him cry. And . . . feel sorry for him too, maybe. In a . . . rather objective kind of way. Well, that's . . . that's something of the kind of thing I've been experiencing. I mean, now . . . just right now.

T.   That catches a little more of the flavor of the feeling, that it's almost as if you're really weeping for yourself. . . .

C.   And then of course, I've come to . . . to see and to feel that over this . . . see, I've covered it up (*weeps*). I've covered it up with so much *bitterness*, which in turn I had to cover up (*weeps*). *That's* what I want to get rid of! I almost don't *care* if I hurt.

T.   (*gently*). You feel that here at the basis of it, as you experienced it, is a feeling of real tears for yourself. But that you *can't* show, mustn't show, so that's been covered by bitterness that you don't like, that you'd like to be rid of. You almost feel you'd rather absorb the hurt than to . . . than to feel the bitterness (*pause*). And what you seem to be saying quite strongly is, I do *hurt*, and I've tried to cover it up.

C.   I didn't *know* it.

T.   M–hm. Like a new discovery really.

C. (*speaking at the same time*). I never really did know. It's almost
a physical thing. It's . . . it's sort of as though I were looking within
myself at all kinds of . . . nerve endings and — and bits of — of . . .
things that have been sort of mashed (*weeping*).

T. As though some of the most delicate aspects of you — physically
almost — have been crushed or hurt.

C. Yes. And you know, I do get the feeling, oh, you poor thing
(*pause*).

T. Just can't help but feel very deeply sorry for the person that is
you.

I hope that perhaps this excerpt conveys a little of the thing I have
been talking about, the experiencing of a feeling all the way to the
limit. She was feeling herself as though she were nothing but hurt
at that moment, nothing but sorrow for her crushed self. It is not
only hurt and sorrow that are experienced in this all-out kind of
fashion. It may be jealousy, or destructive anger, or deep desire, or
confidence and pride, or sensitive tenderness, or shuddering fear, or
outgoing love. It may be any of the emotions of which man is
capable.

What I have gradually learned from experiences such as this is
that the individual in such a moment is coming to *be* what he *is*.
When a person has, throughout therapy, experienced in this fashion
all the emotions which organismically arise in him, and has experienced them in this knowing and open manner, then he has experienced *himself,* in all the richness that exists within himself. He has
become what he is.

The Discovery of Self in Experience

Let us pursue a bit further this question of what it means to
become one's self. It is a most perplexing question and again I will
try to take from a statement by a client, written between interviews,
a suggestion of an answer. She tells how the various façades by
which she has been living have somehow crumpled and collapsed,

bringing a feeling of confusion, but also a feeling of relief. She continues:

You know, it seems as if all the energy that went into holding the arbitrary pattern together was quite unnecessary — a waste. You think you have to make the pattern yourself; but there are so many pieces, and it's so hard to see where they fit. Sometimes you put them in the wrong place, and the more pieces misfitted, the more effort it takes to hold them in place, until at last you are so tired that even that awful confusion is better than holding on any longer. Then you discover that left to themselves the jumbled pieces fall quite naturally into their own places, and a living pattern emerges without any effort at all on your part. Your job is just to discover it, and in the course of that, you will find yourself. You must even let your own experience tell you its own meaning; the minute *you* tell it what it means, you are at war with yourself.

Let me see if I can take her poetic expression and translate it into the meaning it has for me. I believe she is saying that to be herself means to find the pattern, the underlying order, which exists in the ceaselessly changing flow of her experience. Rather than to try to hold her experience into the form of a mask, or to make it be a form or structure that it is not, being herself means to discover the unity and harmony which exists in her own actual feelings and reactions. It means that the real self is something which is comfortably discovered *in* one's experience, not something imposed *upon* it.

Through these excerpts from the statements of clients, I have been trying to suggest what happens in the warmth and understanding of a facilitating relationship with a therapist. It seems that gradually, painfully, the individual explores what is behind the masks he presents to the world, and even behind the masks with which he has been deceiving himself. Deeply and often vividly he experiences the various elements of himself which have been hidden within. Thus to an increasing degree he becomes himself — not a façade of conformity to others, nor a cynical denial of all feeling, nor a front of intellectual rationality, but a living, breathing, feeling, fluctuating process — in short, he becomes a person.

The Person Who Emerges

I imagine that some of you are asking: "But what *kind* of a person does he become? It isn't enough to say that he drops the façades. What kind of person lies underneath?" Since one of the most obvious facts is that each individual tends to become a separate and distinct and unique person, the answer is not easy. However I would like to point out some of the characteristic trends which I see. No one person would fully exemplify these characteristics, no one person fully achieves the description I will give, but I do see certain generalizations which can be drawn, based upon living a therapeutic relationship with many clients.

Openness to Experience

First of all I would say that in this process the individual becomes more open to his experience. This is a phrase which has come to have a great deal of meaning to me. It is the opposite of defensiveness. Psychological research has shown the way in which sensory evidence, if it runs contrary to the pattern of organization of the self, tends to be distorted in awareness. In other words we cannot see all that our senses report, but only the things which fit the picture we have.

Now in a safe relationship of the sort I have described, this defensiveness, or rigidity, tends to be replaced by an increasing openness to experience. The individual becomes more openly aware of his own feelings and attitudes as they exist in him at an organic level. He also becomes more aware of reality as it exists outside of himself, instead of perceiving it in preconceived categories. He sees that not all trees are green, not all men are stern fathers, not all women are rejecting, not all failure experiences prove that he is no good, and the like. He is able to take in the evidence in a new situation *as it is,* rather than distorting it to fit a pattern which he already holds. As you might expect, this increasing ability to be open to experience makes him far more realistic in dealing with new people, new situations, new problems. It means that his beliefs are not rigid, that he can tolerate ambiguity. He can receive much conflicting evidence without forcing closure upon the situation. This openness of awareness to what exists at *this moment* in *this situation* is, I believe, an important element in the description of the person who emerges from therapy.

Perhaps I can give this concept a more vivid meaning if I illustrate it from a recorded interview. A young professional man reports in the forty-eighth interview the way in which he has become more open to some of his bodily sensations, as well as other feelings.

CLIENT. It doesn't seem to me that it would be possible for anybody to relate all the changes that I feel. But I certainly have felt recently that I have more respect for, more objectivity toward, my physical makeup. I mean I don't expect too much of myself. This is how it works out: It feels to me that in the past I used to fight a certain tiredness that I felt after supper. Well, now I feel pretty sure that I really *am* tired — that I am not making myself tired — that I am just physiologically lower. It seemed that I was just constantly criticizing my tiredness.

THERAPIST. So you can let yourself *be* tired, instead of feeling along with it a kind of criticism of it.

C. Yes, that I shouldn't be tired or something. And it seems in a way to be pretty profound that I can just not fight this tiredness, and along with it goes a real feeling that being tired isn't such an awful thing. I think I can also kind of pick up a thread here of why I should be that way in the way my father is and the way he looks at some of these things. For instance, say that I was sick, and I would report this, and it would seem that overtly he would want to do something about it but he would also communicate: "Oh, my gosh, more trouble." You know, something like that.

T. As though there were something quite annoying really about being physically ill.

C. Yeah, I am sure that my father has the same disrespect for his own physiology that I have had. Now last summer I twisted my back,

I wrenched it, I heard it snap and everything. There was real pain there all the time at first, real sharp. And I had the doctor look at it and he said it wasn't serious, it should heal by itself as long as I didn't bend too much. Well this was months ago — and I have been noticing recently that — hell, this is real pain and it's still there — and it's not my fault.

T. It doesn't prove something bad about you — .

C. No — and one of the reasons I seem to get more tired than I should maybe is because of this constant strain and so — I have already made an appointment with one of the doctors at the hospital that he would look at it and take an X-ray or something. In a way I guess you could say that I am just more accurately sensitive — or objectively sensitive to this kind of thing. I can say with certainty that this has also spread to what I eat and how much I eat. And this is really a profound change, and of course my relationship with my wife and the two children is — well, you just wouldn't recognize it if you could see me inside — as you have — I mean — there just doesn't seem to be anything more wonderful than really and *genuinely* — really *feeling* love for your own children and at the same time receiving it. I don't know how to put this. We have such an increased respect — both of us — for Judy and we've noticed just — as we participated in this — we have noticed such a tremendous change in her — it seems to be a pretty deep kind of thing.

T. It seems to me you are saying that you can listen more accurately to yourself. If your body says it's tired, you listen to it and believe it, instead of criticizing it; if it's in pain, you can listen to that; if the feeling is really loving your wife or children, you can *feel* that, and it seems to show up in the differences in them too.

Here, in a relatively minor but symbolically important excerpt, can be seen much of what I have been trying to say about openness to experience. Formerly he could not freely feel pain or illness, because being ill meant being unacceptable. Neither could he feel tenderness and love for his child, because such feelings meant being weak, and he had to maintain his façade of being strong and masculine. But now he can be genuinely open to the experiences of his organism — he can be tired when he is tired, he can feel pain when his organism is in pain, he can freely experience the love he feels for his daughter, and he can also feel and express annoyance toward her, as he goes on to say in the next portion of the interview. He can fully live the experiences of his total organism, rather than shutting them out of awareness.

Trust in One's Organism

A second characteristic of the persons who emerge from therapy is that the person increasingly discovers that his own organism is trustworthy, that it is a suitable instrument for discovering the most satisfying behavior in each immediate situation.

If this seems strange, let me try to state it more fully. Perhaps it will help you to understand my description if you think of the individual as faced with some existential choice: "Shall I go home to my family during vacation, or strike out on my own?" "Shall I drink this third cocktail which is being offered?" "Is this the person whom I would like to have as my partner in love and in life?" Thinking of such situations, what seems to be true of the person who emerges from the therapeutic process? To the extent that this person is open to all of his experience, he has access to all of the available data in the situation, on which to base his behavior. He has knowledge of his own feelings and impulses, which are often complex and contradictory. He is freely able to sense the social demands, from the relatively rigid social "laws" to the desires of friends and family. He has access to his memories of similar situations, and the consequences of different behaviors in those situations. He has a relatively accurate perception of this existential situation in all of its complexity. He is better able to permit his total organism, his conscious thought participating, to consider, weigh, and balance each stimulus, need, and demand, and its relative weight and intensity. Out of this complex weighing and balancing he is able to discover that course of action which seems to come closest to satisfying all his needs in the situation, long-range as well as immediate.

In such a weighing and balancing of all of the components of a given life choice, his organism would not by any means be infallible. Mistaken choices might be made. But because he tends to be open to his experience, there is a greater and more immediate awareness of unsatisfying consequences, a quicker correction of choices which are in error.

It may help to realize that in most of us the defects which interfere with this weighing and balancing are that we include things which are not a part of our experience, and exclude elements which are. Thus an individual may persist in the concept that "I can handle liquor," when openness to his past experience would indicate that this is scarcely correct. Or a young woman may see only the good qualities of her prospective mate, where an openness to experience would indicate that he possesses faults as well.

In general then, it appears to be true that when a client is open to his experience, he comes to find his organism more trustworthy. He feels less fear of the emotional reactions which he has. There is a gradual growth of trust in, and even affection for, the complex, rich, varied assortment of feelings and tendencies which exist in him at the organic level. Consciousness, instead of being the watchman over a dangerous and unpredictable lot of impulses, of which few can be permitted to see the light of day, becomes the comfortable inhabitant of a society of impulses and feelings and thoughts, which are discovered to be very satisfactorily self-governing when not fearfully guarded.

An Internal Locus of Evaluation

Another trend which is evident in this process of becoming a person relates to the source or locus of choices and decisions, of evaluative judgments. The individual increasingly comes to feel that this locus of evaluation lies within himself. Less and less does he look to others for approval or disapproval; for standards to live by; for decisions and choices. He recognizes that it rests within himself to choose; that the only question that matters is: "Am I living in a way which is deeply satisfying to me, and which truly expresses me?" This I think is perhaps *the* most important question for the creative individual.

Perhaps it will help if I illustrate with a brief portion of a recorded interview with a young woman, a graduate student, who had come for counseling help. She was initially very much disturbed about many problems, and had been contemplating suicide. During the interviews one of the feelings she discovered was her great desire to be dependent, just to let someone else take over the direction of her life. She was very critical of those who had not given her enough guidance. She talked about one after another of her professors, feeling bitterly that none of them had taught her anything with deep meaning. Gradually she began to realize that part of the difficulty was the fact that she had taken no initiative in *participating* in these classes. Then comes the following portion. This excerpt gives some indication of what it means in experience to accept the locus of evaluation as being within oneself.

CLIENT.   Well now, I wonder if I've been going around doing that, getting smatterings of things, and not getting hold, not really getting down to things.

THERAPIST.   Maybe you've been getting just spoonfuls here and there rather than really digging in somewhere rather deeply.

C.   M-hm. That's why I say — (*slowly and very thoughtfully*) well, with that sort of a foundation, well, it's really up to *me*. I mean, it seems to be really apparent to me that I *can't depend on someone else* to give me an education. (*Very softly*) I'll really have to get it myself.

T.   It really begins to come home — there's only one person that can educate you — a realization that perhaps nobody else *can give* you an education.

C.   M-hm (*long pause — while she sits thinking*). I have all the symptoms of fright (*laughs softly*).

T.   Fright? That this is a scary thing, is that what you mean?

C.   M-hm (*very long pause — obviously struggling with feelings in herself*).

T.   Do you want to say any more about what you mean by that? That it really does give you the symptoms of fright?

C. (*laughs*). I, uh — I don't know whether I quite know. I mean — well, it really seems like I'm cut loose (*pause*), and it seems that I'm very — I don't know — in a vulnerable position, but I, uh, I brought this up and it, uh, somehow it almost came out without my saying it. It seems to be — it's something I let out.

T. Hardly a part of you.

C. Well, I felt surprised.

T. As though: "Well for goodness sake, did I say that?" (*both chuckle*).

C. Really, I don't think I've had that feeling before. I've — uh, well, this really feels like I'm saying something that, uh, *is* a part of me really (*pause*). Or, uh (*quite perplexed*) it feels like I sort of have, uh, I don't know. I have a feeling of *strength,* and yet, I have a feeling of — realizing it's so sort of fearful, of fright.

T. That is, do you mean that saying something of that sort gives you at the same time a feeling of strength in saying it, and yet at the same time a frightened feeling of what you have said, is that it?

C. M-hm. I am feeling that. For instance, I'm feeling it internally now — a sort of surging up, or force. As if that's something really big and strong. And yet, uh, well at first it was almost a physical feeling of just being out alone, and sort of cut off from a — support I had been carrying around.

T. You feel that it's something deep and strong, and surging forth, and at the same time, you just feel as though you'd cut yourself loose from any support when you say it.

C. M-hm. Maybe that's — I don't know — it's a disturbance of a kind of pattern I've been carrying around, I think.

T. It sort of shakes a rather significant pattern, jars it loose.

C. M-hm. (*Pause, then cautiously, but with conviction*) I, I think — I don't know, but I have the feeling that then I am going to begin to *do* more things that I know I should do. . . . There are so many things that I need to do. It seems in so many avenues of my living I have to work out new ways of behaving, but — maybe — I can see myself doing a little better in some things.

I hope that this illustration gives some sense of the strength which is experienced in being a unique person, responsible for oneself, and also the uneasiness that accompanies this assumption of responsibility.

Willingness to Be a Process

I should like to point out one final characteristic of these individuals as they strive to discover and become themselves. It is that the individual seems to become more content to be a process rather than a product. When he enters the therapeutic relationship, the client is likely to wish to achieve some fixed state; he wants to reach the point where his problems are solved, or where he is effective in his work, or where his marriage is satisfactory. He tends, in the freedom of the therapeutic relationship, to drop such fixed goals, and to accept a more satisfying realization that he is not a fixed entity, but a process of becoming.

One client, at the conclusion of therapy, says in rather puzzled fashion:

I haven't finished the job of integrating and reorganizing myself, but that's only confusing, not discouraging, now that I realize this is a continuing process. . . . It is exciting, sometimes upsetting, but deeply encouraging to feel yourself in action, apparently knowing where you are going even though you don't always consciously know what that is.

One can see here both the expression of trust in the organism, which I have mentioned, and also the realization of self as a process.

Here is another statement of this same element of fluidity or existential living.

This whole train of experiencing, and the meanings that I have thus far discovered in it, seem to have launched me on a process which is both fascinating and at times a little frightening. It seems to mean letting my experience carry me on, in a direction which appears to be forward, toward goals that I can but dimly define, as I try to understand at least the current meaning of that experience. The sensation is that of floating with a complex stream of experience, with the fascinating possibility of trying to comprehend its ever-changing complexity.

Here again is a personal description of what it seems like to accept oneself as a stream of becoming, not a finished product. It means that a person is a fluid process, not a fixed and static entity; a flowing river of change, not a block of solid material; a continually changing constellation of potentialities, not a fixed quantity of traits.

CONCLUSION

I have tried to record what has seemed to occur in the lives of people with whom I have had the privilege of being in a relationship as they struggled toward becoming themselves. I have endeavored to describe, as accurately as I can, the meanings which seem to be involved in this process of becoming a person. I am sure that I do not see it clearly or completely, since I keep changing in my comprehension and understanding of it. I hope it will be accepted as a current and tentative picture, not as something final.

One reason for stressing the tentative nature of what I have said is that I wish to make it clear that I am *not* saying: "This is what you should become; here is the goal for you." Rather, I am saying that these are some of the meanings I see in the experiences that my clients and I have shared. Perhaps this picture of the experience of others may illuminate or give more meaning to some of your own experience.

I have pointed out that the individual appears to have a strong desire to become himself; that given a favorable psychological climate he drops the defensive masks with which he has faced life, and begins to discover and to experience the stranger who lives behind these masks — the hidden parts of himself. I have pictured some of the attributes of the person who emerges — the tendency to be more open to all elements of his organic experience; the growth of trust in one's organism as an instrument of sensitive living; the acceptance of the fearsome responsibility of being a unique person; and finally the sense of living in one's life as a participant in a fluid, ongoing process, continually discovering new aspects of one's self in the flow of experience. These are some of the things which seem to me to be involved in becoming a person.

XVI HUMAN NATURE AND AESTHETIC GROWTH

FRANCES WILSON

My purpose in providing art experience for others is to make it possible for each person to explore and learn to use his own *aesthetic sense,* not because the creation of products in art media is of tremendous importance in every life, but because my experience leads me to believe that the aesthetic sense is also the *moral sense,* and the *sense of self — of being.* It seems also to be the person's imagination, taste, and integrity — his source of love and truth. Using the aesthetic sense seems to produce a feeling of being more intensely alive, of feeling significant, of knowing what is liked or disliked, wanted or not wanted by the person, and what is possible or impossible for him. Using it results in greater sensitivity, clearer perception, clearer memory, and a more effective selection of what is needed for growth. Using it results in more successful experience, increased feelings of optimism, confidence, courage, flexibility, stability, freedom, and responsibility. Using it results in a more unique and dynamic integration that permits optimum functioning with the greatest economy of time and energy and resources.

The aesthetic sense here refers to the power of imagination which makes the process of a person a creative one. Imagination, as the aesthetic sense, is very inclusive. Its use results not in contradiction of reality and of rational thinking, but in a more profound kind of thinking, based on a perception of a reality that is nearer the truth because it is perceived not as static and in parts, but as things, forces, tensions, and movements interacting in time and space with the perceiver. Imagination here is the unconscious function which integrates the person-in-a-situation in a dynamic way that allows growth to occur. It provides unconscious awareness of a complexity and of changing relationships too great for the conscious mind. It provides for whole perception, simultaneously perceiving opposites so that elements are not static but become specific only in a particular interaction. It selects from the changing outer situation and from a changing memory those elements, movements, and relationships which are important and suitable for this particular person — on the basis of his changing physical condition, mood, and available energy; his knowledge, skill, his world-view, his experience, and his sensitivity; his self-esteem, self-confidence, his needs, his goals, his values, and his immediate purpose and his unique process and growth pattern.

These functions of imagination, of the aesthetic sense, have become so rare that they are now frequently called unnatural. So many cultural factors inhibit its development that visual art expression is now one of the few experiences in which the aesthetic sense can be coaxed into use, to develop the creative process in richness and variation, to intensify the process so that it becomes increasingly unique, alive, and whole and far-reaching in the areas of space and time in which it can achieve an organic integration. But paradoxically, the art experience cannot be effectively *used* for this purpose or any other. It must be a purposeless activity, as far as we understand "purpose." It can only be an experience in *being* — being a human organism doing what it must and what it is privileged to do — experiencing life keenly and wholly, expending energy and creating beauty in its own style — and the increased sensitivity, integrity, efficiency, and feeling of well-being are by-products.

My picture of what is possible for human beings has been constantly changing, sometimes slowly, sometimes radically. Occasionally I have been privileged to witness a "miracle," when a child, or sometimes an adult, *without conscious knowledge of what constitutes an aesthetic work of art* and without having been taught, effortlessly, but with intense absorption, produces a product of breathtaking aesthetic quality. And the wonder and awe I have felt are intensified by the understanding that what is portrayed in the product is a revelation of the beauty of the person — of his dynamic wholeness at that moment. His behavior, too, is at the moment beautiful and rare. He is "God-like." The experience stamps itself in memory and provides a glimpse into human potential that gives new meaning to all past and future observations and charts the course for imagination and action. The other extreme is all too well known to anyone — the striving, competing, pretending, the discouragement, fear, lethargy, monotony, righteousness, or rigidity, and the products which reflect this state.

The art educator in helping the individual express the aesthetic sense acts on intuition freely, confident that the action will be right for the situation, even if she does not consciously know why but merely recognizes the feeling within of completeness, of wholeness, of an unrestricted movement — a feeling of dynamic equilibrium, frequently called "intuitive knowing." It is not really a mysterious phenomenon and can, with effort, be at least partially brought to consciousness. It is a natural part of using the aesthetic sense to think simultaneously of the immediate and the distant, the specific and the totality so that the solution to an immediate problem involves a reintegration of all that one has experienced and can imagine. If the solution "rings true," if it "fits" with what one knows and imagines so that all is integrated in the present in a wholeness, the solution may be assumed to be the right one. Occasionally the solution may not quite fit and be retained with some tension until a new insight causes the totality — all of memory and all that one imagines — to change to fit the solution. This seems to be the nature of intuition in the creative process. It is in this way that I have formulated my philosophy of human growth as a framework within which I operate intuitively.

What is offered here does not express all the truth that is *known*. And the truth that *is* known unconsciously is in itself still developing as knowledge, experience, and sensitivity increase. The following premises are intended to emphasize a view that is usually overlooked — to paint a picture of human nature and aesthetic growth that focuses on human *potential* as revealed in the experience of an art educator.

1. Change in the universe is constant and complex and follows natural laws which maintain it in a dynamic equilibrium. Because this premise is basic to this philosophy, the philosophy, itself, is tentatively held. These words will change and speak differently to each person who reads them. The experience of forming these words is at the moment changing even the writer, and hence the philosophy.

2. This concept of change according to natural laws is based on a belief that all that *is,* that *exists,* is in a never-ending state and process of simultaneous *being* and *becoming*. It is a constantly changing, interacting totality moving in a vastness of space and infinity of time usually beyond the grasp of conscious human intelligence.

3. The human organism is an integral part of this totality, forming it and being formed by it. Although the totality may exist in and of itself, it also exists for human beings only through human experience. What is experienced outwardly is simultaneously experienced inwardly, each in constant change acting on and being acted upon by the other.

4. Each human organism is related to the totality by the creative process. The same process which forms and integrates all that *is* exists in him simultaneously as the same total process *and* as his own unique process, forming and integrating him and relating him to the larger totality.

5. The process changes constantly from a static to a dynamic in-

tegration and vice versa. When it is dynamically integrated there seems to be an openness to unconscious thinking. Ideas come easily and change rapidly. They are more dynamic, unique, complex, condensed, and more interrelated, They deal less with things and more with the essence or quality, rhythm, movement, and relatedness of things — or with qualities, rhythm, and movement without things (objects). The person is relaxed and alert, feels light (almost bodiless), alive, capable, intelligent, optimistic, lovable, and respectable. His movement is relaxed, purposeful, graceful, and effortless. Perception becomes clearer, color more intense, outlines sharper, space more three-dimensional. Everything seems to be more alive — to be flooded with light. When the integration is static, conscious and unconscious processes seem to separate, and sometimes to work against each other. Ideas become more stereotyped, dealing with things (objects) and not feelings. They are more literal and descriptive of appearances rather than essences. The static person, if he is aware of feeling anything, feels "earthbound," heavy, tense or lethargic, "half-dead," pessimistic, stupid, mean, wary, or frightened. Perception dulls and concentrates on objects needed or feared. The world "closes in"; movement slows or ceases. Things are not seen in a dynamic relationship. His movement is tense and mechanized or erratic — or lethargic and careless.

6. Each human organism is conceived with a potential for becoming a complete human being — as a seed contains the potential for becoming a complete plant. But his becoming may be completed in an infinite variety of ways. What he becomes depends on the integration of his process at conception and then on his unique interaction with the environment (before and after birth) — the love (acceptance, respect, and genuine caring) he receives, the food he eats, the air he breathes, the experiences he has, the ideas he comes in contact with, and the way in which the aesthetic sense selects from, intensifies, and integrates all of this with his total process, including his unique growth pattern and structuring system.

7. Each human process is characterized by a unique structuring system which, in interaction with the aesthetic sense, becomes the person's "style" — his way of forming the structure of his "self." The structuring factor cannot be isolated since it is in constant inter-action, affecting and being affected by such other factors as the person's immediate physical condition and mood, his life-experience, his memory, his art experience, his muscular skill, his openness to his aesthetic sense, and factors in the environment. But even so, the expression of one person over a period of time can be recog-nized by a particular style and sometimes by a lack of a particular style. The style changes slightly with each experience and medium. (A radical change indicates that he is not consistently using his own style.) The style grows and develops; its development in the course of a healthy lifetime can be likened to a simple melody which, as the child grows in experience, skill, knowledge and wisdom to adulthood, becomes a symphony with greater subtlety, variety, strength, and complexity, with an equally dynamic integration.

8. Each person has an integrating system which I call the *aesthetic sense,* (also the moral, social, and religious sense — the sense of self, of being — becoming). It is an integral part of the process and in-separable from the structuring system, growth pattern, and total changing-person-in-changing-situation; but for communication in writing (at the expense of greater truth), I have given it a name and described the way in which it seems to function in the total process of the person. The aesthetic sense functions to integrate the person-in-environment and moves, whenever conditions permit, away from a more static, monotonous wholeness achieved through sameness and toward one with greater differentiation and intensity.

The aesthetic sense is the person's guide in the selection of healthy experiences. When they are right, the person can sense the move-ment toward integration and feels an approaching wholeness and satisfaction; when they are wrong, he might vary from uncomfort-able to feeling intense pain.

Growth becomes painful when the environment is not suited to natural individual growth or when pressures force an experience prematurely. Then the lack of integration is too great, forcing either too rapid an acquisition of knowledge, skills, or insight, or else a pretense of being what one is not in order to escape repercussions from the environment. This destroys confidence in and respect for one's own way of growing.

9. The aesthetic sense makes possible the perception of opposites so that the organism does not move too far in one direction or become monotonous, thus providing stability and liveliness. The more open the person becomes to his aesthetic sense, the more simultaneously the opposites appear, and the more compatible they become, fusing finally into light or life, without either opposite being distinguishable.

10. Natural human growth is determined by the growth pattern, the aesthetic sense, in interaction with the total-person-in-environment. When the unique growth pattern and the structuring system are respected, and the aesthetic sense used, and there is an environment available which meets growth needs, the organism remains dynamically integrated — confident, loving, sensitive, inventive, imaginative, alert, graceful, relaxed, and moral, with an abundance of life and energy to promote life around him. When the natural growth is inhibited, or forced at too rapid a pace or into the wrong experiences, other types of integration occur, varying from those which merely make the person slightly less alive, to what can be called a "negative" integration because it is a deadening condition.

11. The aesthetic sense operates to integrate the person-in-his world whatever its size. Only when the existence of the person is threatened does the aesthetic sense integrate the *person* without equal consideration for all of the life he knows, because in a weakened condition his world shrinks to himself. When the process of the person is dynamically integrated, and he is open to his aesthetic sense, he is sensitive to a lack of wholeness and life, and for his own

comfort moves to bring about a dynamic integration in his world — to protect, maintain, and promote life, to create wholeness. With less sensitivity and skill, he tries to achieve integration through "sameness," by imposing his style of integration on others, by eliminating differences. The more open he is to his aesthetic sense, the more knowledge, skill, and wisdom he acquires, the more he is able to allow for differentiation within the whole, allowing other life to be as it *is* without trying to integrate it in his own style.

CONCLUSION

Considering the forces, apparently intentional and accidental, that inhibit the development of aesthetic sensitivity which is imagination, the sense of self, and the sense of relatedness to all of life — it seems not only miraculous but significant that it persists. The aesthetic sense, which is the power that integrates the opposing forces to create life, resolves, when the person is most open to it, to an awareness only of forces held in a dynamic equilibrium, of vibrant life or light, of a clarity of perception, of a feeling of relatedness with all that is life, of profound knowledge and understanding without knowing what is understood but merely feeling completely satisfied and accepting. The intensification of the aesthetic sense results in an inner perception of the very essence of being — of a unit of energy moving within its wholeness as a simultaneous process and state — a microcosm of the process and state that constantly re-creates all that *is*. Perhaps the aesthetic sense persists in spite of all opposition because it is that part of the human being that is eternal and indestructible.

XVII THE SEARCH FOR GLORY

KAREN HORNEY

Whatever the conditions under which a child grows up he will, if not mentally defective, learn to cope with others in one way or another and he will probably acquire some skills. But there are also forces in him which he cannot acquire or even develop by learning. You need not, and in fact cannot, teach an acorn to grow into an oak tree, but when given a chance, its intrinsic potentialities will develop. Similarly the human individual, given a chance, tends to develop his particular human potentialities. He will develop then the unique alive forces of his real self; the clarity and depth of his own feelings, thoughts, wishes, interests; the ability to tap his own resources, the strength of his will power; the special capacities or gifts he may have; the faculty to express himself and to relate himself to others with his spontaneous feelings. All this will in time enable him to find his set of values and his aims in life. In short, he will grow, substantially undiverted, toward self-realization. And that is why I speak now of the real self as that central inner force, common to all human beings and yet unique in each, which is the deep source of growth.*

Only the individual himself can develop his given potentialities.

* When in the future a reference is made to growth, it is always meant in the sense presented here — that of free, healthy development in accordance with the potentials of one's generic and individual nature.

But like any other living organism, the human individual needs favorable conditions for his growth "from acorn into oak tree"; he needs an atmosphere of warmth to give him both a feeling of inner security and the inner freedom enabling him to have his own feelings and thoughts and to express himself. He needs the good will of others, not only to help him in his many needs but to guide and encourage him to become a mature and fulfilled individual. He also needs healthy friction with the wishes and wills of others. If he can thus grow with others, in love and in friction, he will also grow in accordance with his real self.

But through a variety of adverse influences, a child may not be permitted to grow according to his individual needs and possibilities. Such unfavorable conditions are too manifold to list here. However, when summarized, they all boil down to the fact that the people in the environment are too wrapped up in their own neuroses to be able to love the child, or even to conceive of him as the particular individual he is; their attitude toward him are determined by their own neurotic needs and responses. In simple words, they may be dominating, overprotective, intimidating, irritable, overexacting, overindulgent, erratic, partial to other siblings, hypocritical, indifferent, etc. It is never a matter of just a single factor but always the whole constellation that exerts the untoward influence on a child's growth.

As a result, the child does not develop a feeling of belonging, of "we," but instead a profound insecurity and vague apprehensiveness, for which I use the term basic anxiety. It is his feeling of being isolated and helpless in a world conceived as potentially hostile. The cramping pressure of his basic anxiety prevents the child from relating himself to others with the spontaneity of his real feelings, and forces him to find ways to cope with them. He must (unconsciously) deal with them in ways which do not arouse or increase, but rather allay his basic anxiety. The particular attitudes resulting from such unconscious strategical necessities are determined both by the child's given temperament and by the contingencies of the environment. Briefly, he may try to cling to the most powerful person around him; he may try to rebel and fight; he may try to shut others out of his inner life and withdraw emotionally from them. In principle, this means that he can move toward, against, or away from others.

In a healthy human relationship the moves toward, against, or away from others are not mutually exclusive. The ability to want and to give affection, or to give in; the ability to keep to oneself — these are complementary capacities necessary for good human relations. But in the child who feels himself on precarious ground because of his basic anxiety, these moves become extreme and rigid. Affection, for instance, becomes clinging; compliance becomes appeasement. Similarly, he is driven to rebel or to keep aloof without reference to his real feelings and regardless of the inappropriateness of his attitude in a particular situation. The degree of blindness and rigidity in his attitudes is in proportion to the intensity of the basic anxiety lurking within him.

Since under those conditions the child is driven not only in one of those directions but in all of them, he develops fundamentally contradictory attitudes toward others. The three moves toward, against, and away from others therefore constitute a conflict, his basic conflict with others. In time he tries to solve it by making one of these moves consistently predominant — tries to make his prevailing attitude one of compliance, or aggressiveness, or aloofness.

The first attempt at solving neurotic conflicts is by no means superficial. On the contrary, it has a determining influence upon the further course his neurotic development takes. Nor does it exclusively concern attitudes toward others; inevitably it entails certain changes in the whole personality. According to his main direction, the child also develops certain appropriate needs, sensitivities, inhibitions, and the beginnings of moral values. The predominantly complying child, for instance, not only tends to subordinate himself to others and to lean on them but also tries to be unselfish and good. Similarly, the aggressive child starts to place value on strength and on the capacity to endure and to fight.

However, the integrating effect of this first solution is not as firm or comprehensive as in the neurotic solutions to be discussed later on. In one girl, for instance, compliant trends had become predominant. They showed in a blind adoration of certain authoritative figures, in tendencies to please and appease, in a timidity about expressing her own wishes, and in sporadic attempts to sacrifice. At the age of eight she placed some of her toys in the street for some poorer child to find, without telling anybody about it. At the age of eleven she tried in her childish way for a kind of mystic surrender in prayer. There were fantasies of being punished by teachers on whom she had a crush. But, up to the age of nineteen, she also could easily fall in with plans evolved by others to take revenge on some teacher; while mostly being like a little lamb, she did occasionally take the lead in rebellious activities at school. And, when disappointed in the minister of her church, she switched from a seeming religious devotion to a temporary cynicism.

The reasons for the looseness of integration achieved — of which this illustration is typical — lie partly in the immaturity of the growing individual and partly in the fact that the early solution aims chiefly at a unification of relations with others. There is therefore room, and indeed a need, for firmer integration.

The development described so far is by no means uniform. The particulars of the unfavorable environmental conditions are different in each case, as are those of the course the development takes and its outcome. But it always impairs the inner strength and coherence of the individual, and thereby always generates certain vital needs for remedying the resulting deficiencies. Although these are closely interwoven, we can distinguish the following aspects:

Despite his early attempts at solving his conflicts with others, the individual is still divided and needs a firmer and more comprehensive integration.

For many reasons, he has not had the chance to develop real self-confidence; his inner strength has been sapped by his having to be on the defensive, by his being divided, by the way in which his early "solution" initiated a one-sided development, thereby making large areas of his personality unavailable for constructive uses. Hence, he desperately needs self-confidence, or a substitute for it.

He does not feel weakened in a vacuum, but feels specifically less substantial, less well equipped for life than others. If he had a sense of belonging, his feeling inferior to others would not be so serious a handicap. But living in a competitive society, and feeling at bottom — as he does — isolated and hostile, he can only develop an urgent need to lift himself above others.

Even more basic than these factors is his beginning alienation from self. Not only is his real self prevented from a straight growth, but in addition his need to evolve artificial, strategic ways to cope with others has forced him to override his genuine feelings, wishes, and thoughts. To the extent that safety has become paramount, his innermost feelings and thoughts have receded in importance — in fact, have had to be silenced and have become indistinct. (It does not matter what he feels, if only he is safe.) His feelings and wishes thus cease to be determining factors; he is no longer, so to speak, the driver, but is driven. Also the division in himself not only weakens him in general, but reinforces the alienation by adding an element of confusion; he no longer knows where he stands, or "who" he is.

This beginning alienation from self is more basic because it lends to the other impairments their injurious intensity. We can understand this more clearly if we imagine what would happen if it were possible for the other process to occur without this alienation from the alive center of oneself. In that case the person would have conflicts, but would not be tossed around by them; his self-confidence (as the very word indicates, it requires a self upon which to place confidence) would be impaired, but not uprooted; and his relations to others would be disturbed without his having become inwardly unrelated to them. Hence, most of all the individual alienated from himself needs — it would be absurd to say a "substitute" for his real self, because there is no such thing — something that will give him a hold, a feeling of identity. This could make him meaningful to himself and, despite all the weakness in his structure, give him a feeling of power and significance.

Provided his inner conditions do not change (through fortunate life circumstances), so that he can dispense with the needs I have listed, there is only one way in which he can seem to fulfill them, and seem to fulfill all of them at one stroke: through imagination. Gradually and unconsciously, the imagination sets to work and creates in his mind an idealized image of himself. In this process he endows himself with unlimited powers and with exalted faculties; he becomes a hero, a genius, a supreme lover, a saint, a god.

Self-idealization always entails a general self-glorification, and thereby gives the individual the much-needed feeling of significance and of superiority over others. But it is by no means a blind self-aggrandizement. Each person builds up his personal idealized image from the materials of his own special experiences, his earlier fantasies, his particular needs, and also his given faculties. If it were not for the personal character of the image he would not attain a feeling of identity and unity. He idealizes, to begin with, his particular "solution" of his basic conflict: compliance becomes goodness; love, saintliness; agressiveness becomes strength, leadership, heroism, omnipotence; aloofness becomes wisdom, self-sufficiency, independence. What — according to his particular solution — appear as shortcomings or flaws are always dimmed out or retouched.

He may deal with his contradictory trends in one of three different ways. They may be glorified too, but remain in the background. It may be that an aggressive person, to whom love seems unpermissible softness, is in his idealized image not only a knight in shining armor but also a great lover.

Secondly, contradictory trends, besides being glorified, may be so isolated in the person's mind that they no longer constitute disturbing conflicts. One patient was, in his image, a benefactor of mankind, a wise man who had achieved a self-contained serenity, and a person who could without qualms kill his enemies. These aspects — all of them conscious — were to him not only uncontradictory but also even unconflicting. In literature this way of removing conflicts by isolating them has been presented by Stevenson in Doctor Jekyll and Mr. Hyde.

Lastly, the contradictory trends may be exalted as positive faculties or accomplishments so that they become compatible aspects of a rich personality. I have cited elsewhere * an example in which a gifted person turned his compliant trends into Christlike virtues, his aggressive trends into a unique faculty for political leadership, and his detachment into the wisdom of a philosopher. Thus the three aspects of his basic conflict were at once glorified and reconciled each with the others. He became, in his own mind, a sort of modern equivalent to *l'uomo universale* of the Renaissance.

Eventually the individual may come to identify himself with his idealized, integrated image. Then it does not remain a visionary image which he secretly cherishes; imperceptibly he becomes this image: the idealized image becomes an idealized self. And this idealized self becomes more real to him than his real self, not primarily because it is more appealing but because it answers all his stringent needs. This transfer of his center of gravity is an entirely inward process; there is no observable or conspicuous outward change in him. The change is in the core of his being, in his feeling about himself. It is a curious and exclusively human process. It

* Karen Horney, *Our Inner Conflicts* (New York: W. W. Norton & Company, 1945).

would hardly occur to a cocker spaniel that he "really" is an Irish setter. And the transition can occur in a person only because his real self has previously become indistinct. While the healthy course at this phase of development — and at any phase — would be a move toward his real self, he now starts to abandon it definitely for the idealized self. The latter begins to represent to him what he "really" is, or potentially is — what he could be, and should be. It becomes the perspective from which he looks at himself, the measuring rod with which he measures himself.

Self-idealization, in its various aspects, is what I suggest calling a comprehensive neurotic solution — i.e., a solution not only for a particular conflict but one that implicitly promises to satisfy all the inner needs that have arisen in an individual at a given time. Moreover, it promises not only a riddance from his painful and unbearable feelings (feeling lost, anxious, inferior, and divided), but in addition an ultimately mysterious fulfillment of himself and his life. No wonder, then, that when he believes he has found such a solution he clings to it for dear life. The regular occurrence of self-idealization in neurosis is the result of the regular occurrence of the compulsive needs bred in a neurosis-prone environment.

We can look at self-idealization from two major vantage points: it is the logical outcome of an early development and it is also the beginning of a new one. It is bound to have far-reaching influence upon the further development because there simply is no more consequential step to be taken than the abandoning of the real self. But the main reason for its revolutionary effect lies in another implication of this step. The energies driving toward self-realization are shifted to the aim of actualizing the idealized self. This shift means no more and no less than a change in the course of the individual's whole life and development.

Its more immediate effect is to prevent self-idealization from remaining a purely inward process, and to force it into the total circuit of the individual's life. The individual wants to — or rather is driven to — express himself. And this now means that he wants to express his idealized self, to prove it in action. It infiltrates his aspirations, his goals, his conduct of life, and his relations to others. For this reason, self-idealization inevitably grows into a more comprehensive drive which I suggest calling by a name appropriate to its nature and its dimensions: the search for glory. Self-idealization remains its nuclear part. The other elements in it, all of them always present though in varying degrees of strength and awareness in each individual case, are the need for perfection, neurotic ambition, and the need for a vindictive triumph.

Among the drives toward actualizing the idealized self the need for perfection is the most radical one. It aims at nothing less than molding the whole personality into the idealized self. Like Pygmalion in Bernard Shaw's version, the neurotic aims not only at retouching but at remodeling himself into his special kind of perfection prescribed by the specific features of his idealized image. He tries to achieve this goal by a complicated system of shoulds and taboos.

The most obvious and the most extrovert among the elements of the search for glory is neurotic ambition, the drive toward external success. While this drive toward excelling in actuality is pervasive and tends toward excelling in everything, it is usually most strongly applied to those matters in which excelling is most feasible for the given individual at a given time. Hence the content of ambition may well change several times during a lifetime. At school a person may feel it an intolerable disgrace not to have the very best marks in class. Later on, he may be just as completely driven to have the most dates with the most desirable girls. And again, still later, he may be obsessed with making the most money, or being the most prominent in politics. Such changes easily give rise to certain self-deceptions. A person who has at one period been fanatically determined to be the greatest athletic hero, or war hero, may at another period become equally bent on being the greatest saint. He may believe, then, that he has "lost" his ambition. Or he may decide that excelling in athletics or in war was not what he "really" wanted. Thus he may fail to realize that he still sails on the boat of ambition but has merely changed the course. Of course, one must also analyze in detail what made him change his course at that particular time. I emphasize these changes because they point to the fact that people in the clutches of ambition are but little related to the content of what they are doing. What counts is the excelling itself. If one did not recognize this unrelatedness, many changes would be incomprehensible.

For the purposes of this discussion, the particular area of activity which the specific ambition covets is of little interest. The characteristics remain the same whether it is a question of being a leader in the community, of being the most brilliant conversationalist, of having the greatest reputation as a musician or as an explorer, of playing a role in "society," of writing the best book, or of being the best-dressed person. The picture varies, however, in many ways, according to the nature of the desired success. Roughly, it may belong more in the category of power (direct power, power behind the throne, influence, manipulating), or more in the category of prestige (reputation, acclaim, popularity, admiration, special attention).

These ambitious drives are, comparatively speaking, the most realistic of the expansive drives. At least, this is true in the sense that the people involved put in actual efforts to the end of excelling. These drives also seem more realistic because, with sufficient luck, their possessors may actually acquire the coveted glamor, honors, influence. But on the other hand, when they do attain more money, more distinction, more power, they also come to feel the whole impact of the futility of their chase. They do not secure any more peace of mind, inner security, or joy of living. The inner distress, to remedy which they started out on the chase for the phantom of glory, is still as great as ever. Since these are not accidental results, happening to this or that individual, but are inexorably bound to occur, one may rightly say that the whole pursuit of success is intrinsically unrealistic.

Since we live in a competitive culture, these remarks may sound strange or unworldly. It is so deeply ingrained in all of us that everybody wants to get ahead of the next fellow and be better than he is, that we feel these tendencies to be "natural." But the fact that compulsive drives for success will arise only in a competitive culture does not make them any less neurotic. Even in a competitive culture there are many people for whom other values — such as, in particular, that of growth as a human being — are more important than competitive excelling over others.

The last element in the search for glory, more destructive than the others, is the drive toward a vindictive triumph. It may be closely linked up with the drive for actual achievement and success but, if so, its chief aim is to put others to shame or defeat them through one's very success; or to attain the power, by rising to prominence, to inflict suffering upon them — mostly of a humiliating kind. On the other hand, the drive for excelling may be relegated to fantasy, and the need for a vindictive triumph then manifests itself mainly in often irresistible, mostly unconscious impulses to frustrate, outwit, or defeat others in personal relations. I call this drive "vindictive" because the motivating force stems from impulses to take revenge for humiliations suffered in childhood — impulses which are reinforced during the later neurotic development. These later accretions probably are responsible for the way in which the need for a vindictive triumph eventually becomes a regular ingredient in the search for glory. Both the degree of its strength and the person's awareness of it vary to a remarkable extent. Most people are either entirely unaware of such a need or cognizant of it only in fleeting moments. Yet it is sometimes out in the open, and then it becomes the barely disguised mainspring of life.

Much more frequently the drive toward a vindictive triumph is hidden. Indeed, because of its destructive nature, it is the most hidden element in the search for glory. It may be that only a rather frantic ambition will be apparent. In analysis alone are we able to see that the driving power behind it is the need to defeat and humiliate others by rising above them. The less harmful need for superiority can, as it were, absorb the more destructive compulsion. This allows a person to act out his need and yet feel righteous about it.

XVIII PERSONALITY PROBLEMS AND PERSONALITY GROWTH

A. H. MASLOW

The normal way in which most psychologists would approach this topic would be to list and describe each of the classical psychoses and neuroses and then in the last analysis admit that the sick person can do little for himself. This is also what happens in most books on mental hygiene. They, too, end not with a bang but a whimper.

Supposing we try something different this time. Not only do I feel dissatisfied with the helpless labeling of neuroses but also I and many other psychologists feel excited and hopeful because there is now emerging over the horizon a new conception of human sickness and of human health, a psychology that I find so thrilling and so full of wonderful possibilities that I yield to the temptation to present it publicly even before it is checked and confirmed, and before it can be called reliable scientific knowledge.

Call it an expert guess, if you like, or a set of theories, but remember, I speak for only one school of psychologists and not for all. In any case, here it is!

The basic assumptions of this point of view are:

1. We have, each of us, an essential inner nature, which is to some degree "natural," intrinsic, given, and, in a certain sense, unchangeable, or, at least, unchanging.

2. Each person's inner nature is in part unique to himself and in part species-wide.

232

3. It is possible to study this inner nature scientifically and to discover what it is like — (not *invent* — *discover*).

4. This inner nature, as much as we know of it so far, seems not to be intrinsically evil, but rather either neutral or positively "good." What we call evil appears most often to be a secondary reaction to frustration of this intrinsic nature.

5. Since this inner nature is good rather than bad, it is best to bring it out and to encourage it rather than to suppress it. If it is permitted to guide our life, we grow healthy, fruitful, and happy.

6. If this essential core of the person is denied or suppressed, he gets sick sometimes in obvious ways, sometimes in subtle ways, sometimes immediately, sometimes later.

7. This inner nature is not strong and overpowering and unmistakable like the instincts of animals. It is weak and delicate and subtle and easily overcome by habit, cultural pressure, and wrong attitudes toward it.

8. Even though weak, it never disappears in the normal person — perhaps not even in the sick person. Even though denied, it persists underground forever pressing for actualization.

9. Somehow, these conclusions must all be articulated with the necessity of discipline, deprivation, frustration, pain, and tragedy. To the extent that these experiences reveal and foster and fulfill our inner nature, to that extent they are desirable experiences.

Observe that if these assumptions are proven true, they promise a scientific ethics, a natural value system, a court of ultimate appeal for the determination of good and bad, of right and wrong. The more we learn about man's natural tendencies, the easier it will be to tell him how to be good, how to be happy, how to be fruitful, how to respect himself, how to love, how to fulfill his highest potentialities. This amounts to automatic solution of many of the personality problems of the future. The thing to do seems to be to find out what *you* are *really* like inside, deep down, as a member of the human species and as a particular individual.

The study of such healthy people can teach us much about our own mistakes, our shortcomings, the proper directions in which to grow. Every age but ours has had its model, its ideal. All of these have been given up by our culture; the saint, the hero, the gentleman, the knight, the mystic. About all we have left is the well-adjusted man without problems, a very pale and doubtful substitute. Perhaps we shall soon be able to use as our guide and model the fully growing and self-fulfilling human being, the one in whom all his potentialities are coming to full development, the one whose inner nature expresses itself freely, rather than being warped, suppressed, or denied.

The serious thing for each person to recognize vividly and poignantly, each for himself, is that every falling away from species-virtue, every crime against one's own nature, every evil act, *every one without exception records itself* in our unconscious and makes us despise ourselves. Karen Horney had a good word to describe this unconscious perceiving and remembering; she said it "registers." And it registers *in our books!* If we do something we are ashamed of it registers to our discredit, and if we do something honest or fine or good it registers to our credit. The net results ultimately are either one or the other — either we respect and accept ourselves or we despise ourselves and feel contemptible, worthless, and unlovable. Theologians used to use the word *"accidie"* to describe the sin of failing to do with one's life all that one knows one can do.

This, for sure, is the great personality problem at the root of all personality problems. Let's talk about *it* instead of the derivatives and superficialities. This goes to the root of things. This point of view in no way denies the usual Freudian picture. But it does add to it and supplement it. To oversimplify the matter somewhat, it is as if Freud supplied to us the sick half of psychology and we must now fill it out with the healthy half. Perhaps this health psychology will give us more possibility for controlling and improving our lives and for making ourselves better people. Perhaps this will be more fruitful than asking "how to get *unsick.*"

How can we encourage free development? What are the best educational conditions for it? Sexual? Economic? Political? What kind of world do we need for such people to grow in? What kind of world will such people create? Sick people are made by a sick culture; healthy people are made possible by a healthy culture. But it is just as true that sick individuals make their culture more sick and that healthy individuals make their culture more healthy. Improving individual health is one approach to making a better world. To express it in another way, encouragement of personal growth is a real possibility; cure of actual neurotic symptoms is far less possible without outside help. It is relatively easy to try deliberately to make oneself a more honest man; it is very difficult to try to cure one's own compulsions or obsessions.

The classical approach to personality problems considers them to be problems in an undesirable sense. Struggle, conflict, guilt, bad conscience, anxiety, depression, frustration, tension, shame, self-punishment, feeling of inferiority or unworthiness — they all cause psychic pain, they disturb efficiency of performance, and they are uncontrollable. They are therefore automatically regarded as sick and undesirable and they get "cured" away as soon as possible.

But all of these symptoms are found also in healthy people, or in people who are growing toward health. Supposing you *should* feel guilty and don't? Supposing you have attained a nice stabilization of forces and you *are* adjusted? Perhaps adjustment and stabilization, while good because it cuts your pain, is also bad because development toward a higher ideal ceases?

If this is a startling thought, let me give you a more detailed example. Erich Fromm, in a very important book, attacked the classical Freudian notion of a superego because this concept was entirely authoritarian and relativistic. That is to say, your superego or your conscience was supposed by Freud to be primarily the internalization of the wishes, demands, and ideals of the father and mother, whoever they happen to be. But supposing they are criminals? Then what kind of conscience do you have? Or supposing you have a rigid moralizing father who hates fun? Or a psychopath? This conscience exists — Freud was right. We do get our ideals largely from such early figures and not from Sunday School books read later in life. But there is also another element in conscience, or, if you like, another kind of conscience, which we all have either weakly or strongly. And this is the "intrinsic conscience." This is based upon the unconscious or preconscious perception of our own nature, of our own destiny, or our own capacities, of our own "call" in life. It insists that we be true to our inner nature and that we do not deny it out of weakness or for advantage or for any other reason. He who belies his talent, the born painter who sells stockings instead, the intelligent man who lives a stupid life, the man who sees the truth and keeps his mouth shut, the coward who gives up his manliness, all these people perceive in a deep way that they have done wrong to themselves and despise themselves for it. Out of this self-punishment may come only neurosis, but there may equally well come renewed courage, righteous indignation, increased self-respect, because of thereafter doing the right thing; in a word, growth and improvement can come through pain and conflict.

Supposing we stand by and watch such a person in such a conflict, as students of personality or as therapists or simply as friends? What is our duty? What shall we say? I am afraid that our newer conception means trouble, for it already implies that people who have done wrong to their own nature as human beings or as specific individuals *ought* to feel guilty and if they do not, perhaps we should help them to feel so. What else am I trying to do right now?

Another consequence of our problem can be pointed out. In essence I am deliberately rejecting our present easy distinction between sickness and health, at least as far as symptoms are concerned. Does sickness mean having symptoms? I maintain now that sickness might consist of *not* having symptoms when you should. Does health mean being symptom-free? I deny it. Which of the Nazis at Auschwitz or Dachau were healthy? Those with stricken conscience or those with a nice, clear, happy conscience? Was it possible for a profoundly human person not to feel conflict, suffering, depression, rage, etc.?

In a word if you tell me you have a personality problem I am not certain until I know you better whether to say "Good!" or "I'm sorry." It depends on the reasons. And these, it seems, may be bad reasons, or they may be good reasons.

An example is the changing attitude of psychologists toward popularity, toward adjustment, even toward delinquency. Popular with whom? Perhaps it is better for a youngster to be unpopular with the neighboring snobs or with the local country club set. Adjusted to what? To a bad culture? To a dominating parent? What shall we think of a well-adjusted slave? A well-adjusted prisoner? Even the behavior problem boy is being looked upon with new tolerance. *Why* is he delinquent? Most often it is for sick reasons. But occasionally it is for good reasons and the boy is simply resisting exploitation, domination, neglect, contempt, and trampling upon.

Clearly what will be called personality problems depends on who is doing the calling. The slave owner? The dictator? The patriarchal father? The husband who wants his wife to remain a child? It seems quite clear that personality problems may sometimes be loud protests against the crushing of one's psychological bones, of one's true inner nature. What is sick then is *not* to protest while this crime is being committed. And I am sorry to report my impression that most people do not protest under such treatment. They take it and pay years later, in neurotic and psychosomatic symptoms of various kinds, or perhaps in some cases never become aware that they are sick, that they have missed true happiness, true fulfillment of promise, a rich emotional life, and a serene, fruitful old age, that they have never known how wonderful it is to be creative, to react aesthetically, to find life thrilling.

The question of desirable grief and pain or the necessity for it must also be faced. Is growth and self-fulfillment possible at all without pain and grief and sorrow and turmoil? If these are to some extent necessary and unavoidable, then to what extent? If grief and pain are sometimes necessary for growth of the person, then we must learn not to protect people from them automatically as if they were always bad. Sometimes they may be good and desirable in view of the ultimate good consequences. Not allowing people to go through their pain, and protecting them from it, may turn out to be a kind of overprotection, which in turn implies a certain lack of respect for the integrity and the intrinsic nature and the future development of the individual.

There are many such subtle diseases with which many average Americans are afflicted. They do not think of themselves as sick because everybody else has the same sickness. Where everyone is blind, the sighted man is suspect.

Average Americans do not *really* have fun, and as a matter of fact, do not really know what it is. They do not know how to enjoy themselves, to idle, to saunter. Getting drunk, going to night clubs, watching someone else play games, gambling, insulting women, changing wives at the Saturday night dance are not fun. These are *real* personality problems.

American men and women are not yet friendly enough and respectful enough of each other, nor can they love each other as a rule. The war between the sexes is not yet a partnership. Any man who does not know how to love a woman, fuse with her into a unit, is a cripple, a personality problem. He is not whole and completed. Neither is his wife.

Prejudice and stereotypes are still with us although improvement is in sight. These terrible diseases destroy not only the underdog but the upper dog as well.

Americans are anti-intellectual and anti-aesthetic. Poets, theoretical scientists, painters, sculptors, dancers, cannot easily make a living if they are creative. Their social status is poor with the average American. Good-will ambassadors, selected to represent the best in our culture to other countries, are generally movie stars, the poorer ones at that. More money can be gathered to combat infantile paralysis by television comics than by the greatest researchers. To mistrust your highest intellectual powers, to stifle your creativeness, these are *real* personality problems and not spurious ones. Your own Museum of Modern Art has classes in which your creativeness can be taught to come to life, as I have seen with my own eyes in their television broadcasts, and yet only a few hundred people take advantage of this opportunity to remedy a basic personal defect, the starvation of creativeness.

The lack of meditativeness and inwardness, of real conscience and real values, is a standard American personality defect; a shallowness, a superficial living on the surface of life, a living by other people's opinions rather than by one's own native, inner voice. These are the other-directed men who live, or rather are directed by publicity campaigns, by testimonials, by majority vote, by public opinion, by what other people think. They do not *really* know what *they* want, what *they* feel, what *they,* themselves, think right and wrong. Mind you, when everything goes well these are the adjusted people. They feel fine. They never go to the psychotherapist for help, thinking until it is too late that they need none. And yet they are sick, deep down sick, for they have lost their individuality, their uniqueness. They have become robots.

Loss of the value system is in general a serious *worldwide* disease, not just American. The cynical, the despairing, the disillusioned, the wise-guy, the mistrustful, the swindled ones, the ones who live rootlessly, without zest and without purpose, these too are profoundly serious personality problems even if they do not know they are. The world is too full of them. And they are *very* dangerous, not only to themselves but to others as well. Since every person *needs* a value system and yearns for it until he finds one, these are the ones who can be caught up by an offer of absolute truth, by the lunatic groups, by the fanatics who *know* what's right.

Another widespread personality problem is our conventionality, which is to say the giving up altogether of individual decision and choice. The person who accepts *all* the conventions, not only the sensible ones but the stupid and vicious ones as well, commits himself to stifling his conscience and to inevitable guilt and shame and loss of inner self-respect.

American hypocrisy about the naked body, about pregnancy, about sex, about the bowels, about menstruation, and about the other natural functions is notorious in other countries. Less well known is our fear of our own hostility, of tenderness, of grief and of weeping, of rich emotions, of sentiment. Our embarrassment when confronted by our best impulses — altruism, charity, kindness, honesty, unselfishness, cooperation, love, dedication, devotion, impractical benevolence — is notorious. The response too frequently is "Hm! A Boy Scout!" We have turned our backs on our own nature and it takes its revenge upon us. As Lewis Mumford says, this betrays our fundamental fear of life.

In accordance with this point of view we must think of ourselves as having two kinds of unconscious, the Freudian kind and the intrinsic kind; the Freudian being simply a deposit from the past and a transference from the past to the present situation, and the other one being unconscious perception of one's own original nature, impulses, demands, needs, etc.

This is probably also true for conscience or superego. We may speak again about the intrinsic conscience and the conscience which is only past conditioning. It is only the latter that we have to control or even to get rid of. It is the former that we should cultivate and dig for and reach and get to know, and be controlled by.

Simultaneously with such a position would go some difference in the attitude toward psychotherapy, and particularly psychoanalysis. If we can accept both kinds of unconscious and both kinds of superego, then we need not counterpose the one against the other but realize that they both exist in us and that there are different techniques of handling each of them. I can certainly trust psychoanalysis to soften and correct the Freudian conscience or superego which we do in fact all have. This is the deposition within us of the father, the mother, and of other early forming figures. If they were stupid or bad or evil people, then our superego will have deposited within us all this bad and evil and stupidity. It is this that we have to get rid of. But at the same time this does not mean that we have to get rid of the intrinsic unconscious or the intrinsic conscience or superego. This may be just what we have to make *stronger* and cultivate, to bring out to the surface, to get to know and to approve of more. Perhaps we may consider part of our unconscious conflict in general in our society to be a conflict between the two types of superego and the two types of unconscious. It is as if we had one foreign unconscious and one native unconscious, and one foreign superego and one native superego, and that they struggle within us all the time for mastery.

Though we may give psychoanalysis all the credit in the world for being able to get rid of the sick unconscious and of the sick superego, both of them formed arbitrarily by the past and intruding upon present reality, we must be very aware of the fact that psychoanalysis as it stands now may or may not be able to help the good or intrinsic unconscious and the good or intrinsic superego nor can it help growth in general. Primarily this is because it knows little of either, in fact often denies their existence, and therefore, as nearly as I can make out, might hurt the good superego and the good unconscious. What this means is that psychoanalysis is a therapy, meaning a getting rid of disease, a remover of symptoms, a way of making sick people not sick. It is, however, *not* an intrinsic nature or growth or self-fulfilling kind of regime. It is not adequate for lifting not-sick people to their fullest potentialities even though it *could* become so in principle (as the contemporary development of "ego-psychology" shows). The only word I know so far to describe this is "psychagogy," a word coined by Oswald Schwarz to describe the teaching and the fulfillment of the best potentialities of the psyche rather than the cure of sickness.

One immediate question which troubles me and which is at this moment insoluble is this: Is guilt over dishonesty, duplicity, sneaking, lying, and concealing a product of the Freudian superego or of the intrinsic superego? If it comes from the former, then psychotherapy should make it die out, the guilt should disappear, and the person then should be able to do these undesirable things for the sake of a larger desirability. If, however, these are intrinsically guilt-producing because our intrinsic human nature suffers under them, then psychagogy or growth or fuller development should make the guilt stronger rather than weaker.

Another point is that it is possible to inhibit and to control the intrinsic conscience and the intrinsic unconscious. But this is clearly tiring, fatiguing, and conflicting. It cuts general spontaneity and general freedom and makes the person uneasy with himself. It makes him, in the ultimate sense, split and unintegrated because one part of himself is warring with another part, instead of being partners and going in the same direction toward the same goal — working hand in hand.

Even though the over-all and ultimate problem for each human being is his self-fulfillment and the living up to his potentialities, there are many steps along the path to this goal, many needs which have to be fulfilled and gratified so that he is able to go on to a higher and higher level of living, closer and closer to self-fulfillment. These sub-goals are called basic needs. Each of them represents a special and basic and universal personality problem which must be managed or solved before higher development can take place. In a certain sense these are *the* basic personality problems, and solving them nicely makes possible good healthy growth. Furthermore, when we break them down in this way and separate them out from each other, we can be more practical. We can see more clearly what to do about these problems.

1. Most basic of all are the animal needs, those which we share with most of the other higher animals, the need for food, for water, for sleep, for rest, for sex, for warmth, and so on.

2. Then comes the necessity for safety and for security, for the absence of danger and threat, for being cared for when necessary, being able to be dependent and helpless and weak without feeling endangered.

3. To belong to a group of some sort, and more specifically to be able to love and to be loved, these also are needs in the sense that their fulfillment makes further and higher growth possible and their frustration tends to block it and to make us sick.

4. We need to respect ourselves, to be strong, to have a good sound self-esteem. Generally this good self-esteem rests on three foundations; first, respect and approval from other people; second, actual capacity, achievement, and success; and third, the acceptance of and acting upon our own inner nature.

5. In addition to these needs we also have the so-called cognitive needs and the aesthetic needs. Unfortunately the psychologists do not know enough about these needs to prove their case. But most philosophers, most artists, and indeed also most psychologists are willing to concede the clinical fact that these needs do in fact exist. If they are not satisfied certain forms of sickness result.

The growth of knowledge, of understanding, and the development of a philosophy of values, therefore seem to be necessities rather than luxuries. Fortunately each human being has these possibilities within his own grasp. Creativeness too, especially in the arts, can be fostered and encouraged and taught, it would seem. And I must now agree with the art educators that this is a step in the direction of psychological health, perhaps even a prerequisite or a necessity for full psychological health. My therapeutic recommendations here would be obvious.

The satisfaction of all these basic needs sets the stage for the fullest development of the human being. They are generally prerequisite satisfactions to the full development of the potentialities of the individual. Self-actualization ordinarily implies not only all that has so far been set forth but also several other characteristics that have self-therapeutic implications for each individual.

For one thing, in order to achieve the fullest growth and development of the personality we must develop what Carl Rogers calls the open self. This phrase is the opposite of sensitiveness, or of distorting experiences or rejecting them or repressing them out of fear of what they may do to us and to our picture of ourselves. Most people are not open in this sense. They pick over their experiences and their sensations and perceptions, accepting some, rejecting others, distorting a few, and so on. As examples of this I may cite prejudice, stereotyping, and the like. The healthy person is aware of what actually is happening to him. If he feels pain, he is not afraid to know that he is feeling pain. The same is true for grief or for happiness or tenderness or love or even feelings of weakness and confusion and conflict and guilt. He can accept his own experiences rather than shutting them out of consciousness. This openness of awareness applies both to our inner selves and also to the external world. I have found that healthy people can perceive the external world more efficiently than can other people.

Another characteristic of healthy people which has lessons for us by way of self-improvement is that of spontaneity. Spontaneity means that the behavior of this individual tends to be natural, easy, unself-conscious, and to flow automatically without design and without intent. It comes easily. Perhaps the best example of spontaneity is the behavior of animals. They simply behave without thinking the matter over first, without being self-conscious about it, without being deliberate and designed and planned. One consequence is that the spontaneous person is easy, effortless, and tends to be graceful, well-coordinated, in his motor behavior. The person who is fully integrated behaves in this way quite easily and without design and without planning it to be so. I do not imply that spontaneity can be self-willed. It cannot. I mention it here not as a model to follow necessarily, because this is rarely possible, but rather as an indicator that all is going well within us. When we are in fact spontaneous, we should be pleased and glad and recognize that this is a sign that we are behaving well in the situation. If we feel spontaneous with one person rather than with another, then we can learn from this that we are more compatible, more at ease, less anxious with this first person than with the other.

I want to mention self-knowledge and self-awareness again even though it overlaps much of what I have already discussed. If a person is open to himself and to his self-experiences, then when he looks within himself, not being afraid, he need not distort. Quite easily then, and without effort, he will automatically have more self-knowledge than those people who are afraid to look or who, when they do look, must distort and change and reshape. Self-knowledge either in a conscious or an unconscious form is an ultimate necessary for psychological health. If we are to live with our own inner nature and to fulfill it in its own style, then we must in some fashion or other know what it is and be aware of it. I think for most people that this self-awareness is at an unconscious or semiconscious level. But there is no reason in the world why it should not be made more conscious.

What then can we do about these subtle value illnesses which represent a falling away from perfection, a cessation of growth, a stunting and crippling of our inborn potentialities? For one thing I have indicated that prophylaxis or prevention is far easier than the cure or undoing of already formed illnesses. It is, however, important to point out that the classical neurotic symptoms are another matter altogether. I hope no one will get the idea from what I have said that people can cure their own compulsions or anxiety attacks or depressions. For all practical purposes, they can *not*. What *is* within our power in principle is the improvement of personality, the turn toward honesty, affection, self-respect, intellectual and aesthetic growth, acceptance of our own nature, and turning away from hypocrisy, from meanness, prejudice, cruelty, cowardice, and smallness.

XIX TOWARD THE END

MARIE I. RASEY

Dr. Garn realized that she was coming to the end of the chapter. Which she? she wondered. Was it Marie or was it Dr. Garn? It was then that she discovered that with all this looking backward those two people had been coming closer to each other; that now they had actually merged as does one's shadow with one's substance at noonday. Marie was no more except as she was contained in Dr. Garn. Dr. Garn was no longer an interested spectator, watching a play she had seen before. She was the active participator now.

As an active liver of life, she had two tasks ahead. The play wasn't over. She had next things to plan. In order to do this, it would be necessary to take stock of what she had accomplished so far, both professionally and personally. This inventory would be quite a job. It had always been difficult for her to keep properly separate what one understood, what one knew, and what one merely knew about. She had first learned the distinction from a Tennessee farmer from whom she had inquired about why dogwood and redbud seemed always to grow together. He had said, "Yes, it always is that way. They both grow together, I know that, but I don't rightly understand what I know." Later she had found that Lao-tzu had said similar things centuries before, thousands of miles away.

These were not just words. It was plain that one could give oneself more wholeheartedly to the things one understood. When

247

one only knew, one must keep dividing attention between the doing and the checking of whether what one was doing was right. This kind of doing sucked purpose dry and exhausted one's power to see clearly and to judge unequivocally. And what one merely knew about one had to test at every step.

She would tackle first the planning of next things. The direction was clear even if the details were not, but they would come to light, she thought, as they were put into action. She had lately come into a new knowing about the mechanics of learning. She proposed to understand these matters better. She wished to understand the mechanics of self in order to make the learner's own energy more available to himself. She knew that if she was to understand this in others she would first need to understand it in herself. If teachers were to understand the releasing techniques so that they could help their pupils, they, too, would need to study it first in themselves. For this self-study there were few dependable helps. She wanted to do something about that.

Understanding one's self, she had learned, had a certain tool quality for helping others to understand themselves. With this tool one might unlock new secrets of the working of the self, which would in turn contribute to the solution of problems not yet adequately understood, in spite of all that had been done by professional teachers and research workers in allied fields. She knew that vast masses of unwieldy data had been accumulated concerning what a teacher should help pupils learn — subject matter. She knew that through the years progress had been made in the amount and in the quality of educational materials. Attention had also been given to the preparation of teachers, equipping them both with subject matter and with a plethora of so-called methods. In spite of this loading down of teachers, there were many who decried the inadequate preparation of teachers. It was inadequate. In the nature of the case it must always be. The stupendous task of helping another to

realize himself in the manifold aspects for which each had potential
was of such a nature, in its changefulness and its ever-greater complexity, that no preparation could ever be completely adequate.
Adequacy had more to do with being equal at the moment, with
whatever the moment brought. Preparation could hardly consist of
more than the answers which had been made to earlier problems,
by earlier people. These answers could be no guarantee that what
was yesterday's answer would meet today's needs. The world did
not hold still. It moved not only on but out, and the past could
never catch up with the future.

In spite of all that had been done toward a better understanding
of educational problems, Dr. Garn felt that one area had been
neglected. It was here she wanted to work. She felt that the proverb
of long ago still held the same problem: You could lead the horse
to water, but you couldn't make him drink. We had improved on
the tank and flavored the water. We had learned to lead gently, to
the accompaniment of slow music, but the drinking was not under
control. It was still up to the horse — or the learner. He had to
initiate the drinking process.

She wanted to know how and what could facilitate this release so
that the learner could give himself to the task. She saw this as something other than "catching the child's interest," "stimulation," and
"motivations." It had always irked her to hear teachers sing about
"taught to the tune of the hickory stick." Did they think the use of
the stick had vanished? To be sure, the sticks were less often made
of wood. They did not make visible marks where they hit, but the
scars they could leave on personality were deeper and possibly more
cruel. Actually, motivation — a suave pedagogic term — was little
more than a psychological blackjack. It was used to trap attention
and coerce effort to get children to engage in projects which had
necessarily no intrinsic worth to command the child's interest. She
intended to turn her back resolutely upon these often shabby tricks

of the trade, and search for the cause of that indubitable difference between the intensity with which a child looked at frogs by the stream and the inattention he paid frogs in the textbook.

She intended to start with the analyses which Dr. Horney had presented on several occasions but most fully in her latest book, *Neurosis and Human Growth*. The task would present many difficulties, not the least of which would involve a faithful translation of data and concepts which derive in the field of healing into the field of hygiene. Teachers were now seen to be fairly dependent upon psychiatrists for the basic facts. Teachers got their pupils en masse without the facilities for studying them individually. Psychiatrists saw their patients one at a time and over a period of time. They also possessed the necessary techniques for such studies. Yet the two fields of hygiene and healing were not identical. They were merely contiguous. In spite of the fact that the child is the focus of attention, one behaves differently whether he is engaged in the care of one who has already eaten too generously of green apples or whether he is engaged, before the fact, in trying to help the youngster to avoid the necessity of pain and subsequent ministration.

Teacher or psychiatrist sees the child as a many-faceted jewel. The well-cut diamond may throw off blue from one facet and red from another, but we do not mistake it for two jewels. We know that it is one. Thus the doctrine of multiple selves, arrived at by analytical method, holds the oneness of personality in a single unit.

Dr. Garn had found the concepts of self employed by Dr. Horney in *Neurosis and Human Growth* the most useful of any she had so far found. They served to unify the tasks of growth and guidance of that growth; education and teaching. Out of the clarification they provided, Dr. Garn saw clearly with what tasks she would next concern herself.

Dr. Horney spoke of the idealized self, the actual self, and the real self. The first concerned chiefly the mentally ill and the neurotically inclined. Yet traces were to be found in some areas of the best of us, when the "tyranny" of some particular "ought" or "should" with which we were entangled drove and harassed us. The actual self was conceived as the self at any given moment in its growth, as the individual behavior revealed it. This concept applied to sick and well alike, since we are what we do and we do what we are. The knowledge of the actual self gave one that with which to measure progress and define present state of being. It also pointed next steps for the self to take in directing its own evolvement. This concept of the actual self gave greater significance to Dr. Garn's present studies in behavior as seen in bodily movement.

Finally, the real self, "that central inner force common to all human beings and yet unique to each which is the deep source of growth," gave meaning, significance, and value to the whole human process. It might be viewed as the pregnant, potential, not-yet-differentiated stuff of personality, moving always toward higher integration and fuller manifestation. It gave substance to the description of man "that it hath not yet been revealed what he shall be."

Dr. Garn thought these concepts through again as she realized their always changing and expandingness to her concern for problems of educational growth and development. The individual whose self had become idealized seemed to her to move like one going forward through foggy darkness with the diffused flashlight beam preceding him, distorting objects, half revealing, half concealing them. Such a person, driven by implacable furies of the need for pride and glory, seemed to leap ahead of himself into this chimerical self he had projected. He pulled this shadowy appearance of reality about him until its snug fit convinced him that it was in reality what he agonized to be, aspired to be, but failed utterly to take any steps toward growing to be. The discrepancies between what actually he is and what he believes himself to be might appear ludicrous or pitiful to the most casual onlooker, yet be completely barred from his consciousness. He was cut off from himself, and ultimately and inevitably from his fellows — his only source of help. Such split-apartness was terrible to contemplate. It could be left for the psychiatrists to worry about in their treatment of the sick, except for the awkward fact that sick and well were not thus neatly segregated.

The young child· changes from child to cowboy, horse, wolf with dismaying ease. Nor does fantasy fall out with milk teeth. The best of us are entangled with overgrowth of the best that is in us. Our aspiration and the intensity of our drives and desires betray us into mistaking the sign for the thing signified. "What we strive to be, and are not" by no means "comforts us." This aspect of what might be called the ideal self could also betray us, Dr. Garn mused.

It had to do with the prosaic job of learning. Tied up with it was the difference between a mathematician and a manipulator of digits in the process of collecting right answers. It led in many fields to the mistaking of the sign for the thing signified.

When a learner was coerced into a task, he might produce a problem solved or a report written which was not visibly different from what he solved or wrote when he was requiring his best of himself, instead of having it required of him by someone else. But the difference in the learner was a great one.

The actual self is defined as that which the individual is at any given moment, sick or well, of high or low potential intellectually, with or without any special aptitude. It is, whatever it is, the tool of the self, dull or sharp for hewing away at the job of living. One of Dr. Garn's students had once defined it as "the place where I live." This was a difficult concept to lay hold of, for the actual self was not only the tool but also the user of the tool and the arena in which tool and tool's user operated. This was an important area for the teacher to understand. How well did a self know itself? How well could it know? Did one attain equal skill in recognizing his strength as well as his weaknesses? Could the learner learn to love and nurture his actual self, if and as he came to recognize it? Could the teacher learn to help the student to a self-evaluation, and the requisite courage to look kindly upon whatever he found himself to be, the better to grow himself? Would it be possible to learn to accept oneself as the paraphrase of the old hymn had it: "Just as I am, and asking not to be relieved of one dark blot," understanding that it was he and he alone who could do the relieving? Might not he find the courage for his task in accepting: "Just as I am, without one plea, except that Life has need of me"? *

The actual self had other complications for study. It was subject to change. It changed not only with each new learning. It changed from moment to moment as the individual was caught up in new relationships. While the central core might remain with some constancy, the surface changed, which might be called states-of-being as a fresh situation was interpreted by the self. Since it is at the surface and in the moment that relatednesses are made, it becomes necessary for the teacher to know as much as she can about this aspect of the actual self.

What Dr. Garn wished to study now went deeper than the doing of the actual self. It went deeper than the actualities of everyday doing and being. It had to do with some deep compelling force, at the core of being, "that central inner force, common to all human beings and yet unique to each, which is the deep source of growth." ** This Dr. Horney called the real self. When the real self was overgrown with the demands of the idealized self it functioned feebly. The individual could scarcely extricate himself by his own effort. He had to have help. The frustration and failure which the false claims of the idealized self made upon himself clogged the wellsprings of his being. Dead purposes polluted its stream. Yet this central force was never completely denied. The urge to completion seemed as persistent in the area of personality as in that of proto-

* Truthseekers' version.
** Karen Horney, *Neurosis and Human Growth* (New York: W. W. Norton & Company, 1950).

plasm. This urge was evident in the youngest child and the oldest teacher. Clearing the clogged springs of growth might well be the doctor's function, but helping to keep free-flowing streams to continue to be free and to help the individual avoid the clogging — this was teacher business, and she proposed to learn more about it. It might well be that the real self was in essence what some had thought of as "spirit" — the rushing, driving force of life, the mystery of life, which might prove to lie outside the limitations set by mortality.

The uniqueness which Dr. Horney stressed seemed to be of the same nature as that shared by all that lives. It is the patent to improvement, as change is its dynamic. Uniquenesses are the stuff upon and through which evolvement works. In growth we represent the fulfillment of the trends in evolvement, with Time's arrow always pointing one-way traffic. Perhaps the ancient wise one had such things in mind when he counseled: "Keep thy heart with all diligence," since "out of it are the issues of Life."

It seemed to Dr. Garn that the study of the selves pointed particularly toward a better understanding of the fashion in which the self directed its self in the three major areas — the relation of the self to itself; to the rest of the world; and to the quality of the relatedness.

The culture of the self began to take on a religious aspect. Marie remembered how Dr. Adler had once answered her, when she had commented that psychology and religion used some terms in common. He had said, "The psychology makes a very good religion if one is unfortunate enough to have no other." It seemed true. In a real sense the culture of the real self was a soul-saving business. The description of the paths differed as the goals differed. One individual strove to live up to the best he knew in this life in order to assure himself a longer life in another world to come. Another did the best he knew how, with his eyes upon the here and now, rather than upon the then and there. Some lived each day as well as he knew because he conceived mankind, each as a spark of divinity "fallen" into mortality, clothed on with flesh, in order that it work its slow way up toward the godhood from which he felt he sprang. All three groups have in common the struggle for the good life, here or hereafter. He who recognizes his divinity may see himself as co-worker with God in a creation which was not done once and for all long ago, but as assisting by his present effort the continuing, terribly present task of creation.

These were the things which Dr. Garn felt were immediately before her. As springboard for diving into them, it seemed advisable to work through a kind of inventory of what the years had brought her concerning life itself; people, who were its most interesting aspect; herself as one in the stream of humanity; the profession to which she had given her life; and children, to whom it had been dedicated.

Of one thing she was sure. All life was one. As Marie was contained in Dr. Garn, so also were all its manifestations. She believed that all life was under the same law. As new emergents were manifest, new laws emerged under which they operated. She found security in this recognition. "From the coral too busy to get it a name" to the highest reaches to which humanity had attained stretched a long line of growth, and she was in it and of it.

The urge to grow she understood. Whether the sun played upon the tiny seed to wake it to growth or the sun of love played upon the human child, the urge to grow was the same. It was the urge to become, from the seed to the thousand-petaled lotus to the human spirit, of which the lotus was the symbol for half the world.

She understood also that we were one humanity. She had seen that birth and death, love and labor, were one whatever one's color or by whatever name one named his god. She knew that no one had needed to invent brotherhood. It was inherent in the structure of living. It wanted only to be recognized.

She understood at last the riddle of alone and together. Each man was indeed alone, in a world of his own. He was the axis upon which it turned. He created his world about him in terms of how he saw it. She understood the panic which the recognition of this aloneness could give. She knew how one could be betrayed into hiding his aloneness in sheer proximity to other people. But she also knew the rest of the riddle. One made commonality in one's world by generously sharing oneself with other selves and testing that commonality in the fiery furnaces of cooperative endeavor. She had learned that one's aloneness as person is only as true as is the aloneness of crystal in the rock, or water drop in the sea, or the cell in living tissue. Man gets his togetherness as does a bulb among tulips; a chick among chickens; a man amid mankind, supremely self-responsible and response-able toward all mankind.

She knew that fellow men fed each on the other. The creature aspect lived on bread, but the self not "by bread alone." There were those who knew how to feed and be fed at the table of life. There were those who sat at its well-filled board, and rose and departed hungry. She knew that we fed best from living, breathing related-ness but that we learned also from the static products of art. She knew that equality was also no man's invention but the inescapable concomitant of a biological humanity that nurtured itself upon its self.

She knew that there was no such thing as a type of person. Uniqueness held. What looked like likeness was deceiving. Life was more various than those who led it. Some situations permitted only two choices. One could take it or leave it. The takers had their preference for taking in common. The leavers had their leaving. Those who took in one of the many ways of taking bore resemblances to each other, but it was experiences which determined the appearance of likeness. When a common danger threatened a common value, we found that company in our misery made us seem one.

By this same token she understood that people did not so much disagree with each other as it seemed. They had had different experiences. Words may keep people apart, but dearth of experience divides us more. As we come to know better, we do better. If experience has been so different that hostility has developed, the unhostile one must teach the other cooperation. If the hand of everyman appears to the individual to be against him, it is reasonable that he shall also have his hand against everyman. He can lose his hostility only as he comes to experience its opposite — fellow-manness. He cannot be taught cooperation by a demonstration of a hostility which is greater than his own.

She knew for the most part how to keep up her own courage. She had discovered that it was a matter of two turns of the head. One looked back down the long way one had already come. Seeing what had been climbed refreshed courage. A second turn to view the long procession on ahead, who had won over the obstacles over which she was now passing, renewed purpose. She had a place to go and it was on and up.

Children — they were people beginning to be. The inward process was in progress. Like the children waiting to be born in *The Blue Bird*, each had come with his bundle of assets and liabilities. Because of his uniqueness each was equally precious to life. We learned from children. They learned from us. Their vision was often more single. Ours was often more discriminating. One tried to keep them in the state of expectation of success. Success was basically inborn. Failure had to be learned. She believed that children should be protected from failure in the early years. Time enough to learn the ugly look of failure when success had become first nature.

She knew that everything had its own timetable. Learners must often be waited for. One was not disturbed in October because the tulips were not in bloom. They had their season and their cycle. One waited. It was not even necessary to invoke the virtue of patience.

She knew that no one could make anyone learn anything. The learner had to give consent. This failure to acquiesce was also no mark of original sin. It was a safeguard to one's much needed uniqueness. If every learner drank from the fountains recommended by his teacher, likenesses rather than differences would be served. Emerson had said to a teacher, "You are trying to make the child like you. One is enough."

She had learned not to be distressed that one could not easily see oneself. Actually none has ever seen his own face except by reflection. One learns to observe oneself reflected in those about one, as one learns to see one's face reflected in a mirror. One knows that when one sees a smudge on one's nose it is time to wash the nose and not the mirror. Seeing and correcting one's self as it is reflected in others is a trick done with mirrors too.

She had learned that children were born just babies. They learned to be human or inhuman according to the human beings they found around them. These people were important to their growth not primarily because of their cultural level nor even of their brains. The important matter was what kind of answers they had to the all-important questions of the meaning of life as a whole, their own lives in particular, and the kind of relationship they maintained with their world.

About herself she knew much. She knew her strengths and weaknesses and was biased in favor of both. She had at first learned to make shift with herself as she found herself to be. That had not been as she had dreamed it would be. She had finally come to love herself as she was, and as she loved any other struggling learner. She had learned within herself both the advantages and the hazards of being human. Man's double equipment of thalamus and cortex gave extra advantage but also extra peril. The problem was in fusing the functions of the two. The hazard lay in their separation. Surrender to thalamic behavior was a surrender of one's essential human superiority. Capitulation to reason alone, so often and so justly called cold, cut one off from all but intellectual knowing. One could never understand. One might look at, but could not look with, another.

She was satisfied for herself that with all the frailties of flesh and weaknesses of one and another kind mankind was on its way toward godhood. Or perhaps on its way to being as the gods are. The direction seemed to her plain, though the destination be obscure. Perhaps godhood was inherent in the still-unsolved problem of the nature of life. Perhaps, as had proved true in a number of other things, the sought-for thing already existed. It waited only to be recognized. Perhaps the ancient Mesopotamian tale had its point: When Gilgamesh began his search for eternal life it took him to Utnapishtim, who explained it to him. He said, "Cease your complaints and still your anger. Men and gods are under different laws. Your father and mother created you human. Even if you are two parts god and only one part man, that puts you under the laws of mortality. Life is not decreed to men, and death sets its limit for them. Do we build houses for forever? For lark and nightingale does spring come on forever? When the watchers of the underworld release a soul to be born into the world, the council of gods assemble with the goddess of destiny to decree his fate. They count out with care the days that he lives. The days he is dead they do not count."

Finally, she knew again what she had first learned from her parents. It was perhaps the most important thing she knew. They had taught her to work in gladness, prizing the difficulty as well as the ease with which things could be done, and valuing workmanship above either. They had taught her to laugh. Everything had its funny side, and the hardest thing was less hard with laughter. Yet laughter must never be heedless, for the family proverb ran: "It is easy to be witty and wicked, and hard to be witty and wise." It was easier to live with one's self, if one learned to laugh at one's own discomfitures and blunders. Tears could then be reserved for their single task of clearing vision; and one could live and laugh and learn.

But there was one knowing greater even than these. It was the great necessity to love, to love something. Dogs, cats, flowers, people.

The hardest was to learn to love one's self just as one was, as well as what one would someday be. To design himself, to work toward that end, this was man's supreme privilege — to work out his own salvation. This was a creator's job. It called for purpose and know-how. And it required time. Good that there was eternity in which to do it. She, at least, was surely going to need it. When once one had learned to love oneself, nurture oneself, not only for oneself but for all of life, then the rest of the commandment came fairly easily. One then knew what one had to do to "love thy neighbor as thyself."

She smiled as she remembered one of her dad's favorite sayings, whenever someone whined at what befell him. He always said, "Living is good, hard or easy, and I'm going to let dying be the last thing I do." She intended to follow that, too. And another old man, who was always around the shop, used to say, "I've lived a long time and had a lot of troubles. Most of them didn't happen. But if I hadn't been born, I would have made an awful kick."

XX   GROUNDWORK FOR CREATIVE RESEARCH

ROSS L. MOONEY

Science is grounded in a field of beliefs. It is easy to forget this fact. In our effort to establish findings "beyond doubt" we are prone to wish we were men "beyond beliefs," and, wishing it were so, we are inclined to act as if it were so. This can lead to loss of perspective, lack of humility, and failure to take science as humanly creative.

To offset this tendency, it is important that one challenge oneself from time to time to a statement of the beliefs on which he is acting. This is what I have undertaken here. From statements concerning the social scene, the function of universities, the nature of man, important directions for research, etc., I come into a perspective on research as a creative enterprise.

Institutions are created by a society to serve its needs. Universities are no exception. Their role is to cultivate men who can take leadership in helping the people meet their most critical problems.

The most critical problem today is that of how men are to deal with men — how nations are to treat nations, how groups are to treat groups, how man is to treat himself. We have the physical power to destroy man if we will, or to serve him abundantly; the critical question is what man wants to do with himself.

Teaching men how to deal with men and doing research to improve such teaching is the primary obligation of universities now.

Teaching is impossible without consciously or unconsciously having in mind how one wants to affect the behavior of those who are taught. This requires a view of what one wants man to become. Relevant to any teaching, it is doubly pertinent when the problem is that of teaching men how to deal with men.

Formulating a view of what man is to become requires an assertion of positive values, a definition of what is good in human behavior. There is no escape from this necessity.

The sources for assertions of good are deep within the personal experience of the one who asserts them. They are the product of his total experience as a human being while trying to realize the good in life as he experiences it.

From the ground of the experienced good, a man projects what he wants and, looking at the world of givens about him, he seeks to make things into what he would have them become.

In this respect he is like all living things. A plant reaches out to take chemicals from the soil to compose them into something of value within the living system of the plant. A man, likewise, reaches out to include forms from his environment (internal and external) to compose them into something of value within the system of his life. By such means, living things are able to fulfill their lives.

This is the dynamic of life. It is also the process of creation.

Although natively creative, man can be more or less clumsy in fulfilling his creative potential. There is a lot to a man, a lot to the universe — many levels and orderings. One can compose a little or much; potentially, there is always more. How much one composes depends heavily on the orientation of his conscious behavior.

If he is consciously oriented to the acceptance of himself and others as creative beings and if he seeks consciously to harmonize his deliberate acts with his inherent creative necessities, man can improve the level and quality of his creative performance. If he is asleep to large regions of himself or habitually holds to views which run counter to creativity, he can bungle his creative emergents.

The man I would have us become is the more creative man.

In taking the ideal of the more creative man, I am not alone. Inspection of cultural history reveals that the specimens of men whom our people honor with the·appellation "great" are men who are also called "creative": statesmen, thinkers, artists, writers, teachers, inventors, scientists. Their walks of life are many, but their common quality is their capacity for creation. Deep down, and in the long run, the more creative man appears to be the man our culture idealizes.

This means that Americans have within them a constructive view of the kind of man they would like to see developed. However, this is a slumbering ideal lost in unconsciousness while, for generations, we have given our conscious effort to the conquest of a physical world.

At the founding of our country we were relatively clear and conscious of our ideals for man. We had suffered in foreign lands before we had arrived here, and our ideals had been fired and firmed in the furnaces of personal struggle and affirmation. But as our generations have given themselves to the conquest of the physical environment, our ideals have sunk underground. Now, with the physical environment remarkably conquered, we do not know what it is to amount to — what it is we want the environment to do in the making of man.

As a result we are now oriented more negatively than positively. We know what we are living *against,* but not what we are living *for.* We are equipped for reaction, but not for action. Lacking a realized and meaningful ideal, we lack the means of seeing and composing our environment constructively and integrally.

And yet we also have slumbering within us the ideal of the creative man. We somehow know that the strength of America has come from her creative men.

If we can bring this ideal into prominent and practical focus, can clarify that which is common among creative men, and can show its relevance to the living of the average man, we might be able to aid the positive integration needed. Americans might respond with a welcome sense of self-discovery, a fresh affirmation of the value and meaning of their existence.

A search for what is common among creative men yields fruit when a study is made of the writings of acknowledged creative persons who have attempted to give expression to their experiences when involved in creation.

That which is common among creative men does *not* appear in personality pattern, media used, products produced, or environment provided. Persons can be creative whether introverts or extroverts, naïve or sophisticated, impulsive or steady, recluses or active social participants. They can also be creative whether the medium they use is painting, writing, architecture, mathematics, teaching, administration, or child rearing. They can turn out end-products which are tangible or intangible, abstract or concrete, symbolic or substantial. This work they can do whether their environments are those of the busy city or the isolated country place, the rich man's home or the poverty-ridden hovel. These avenues, while interesting and potentially relevant, are not reaching into the heart of the matter.

Commonness comes when attention is given to the ways in which creative persons relate themselves to facets of their experiencing while creation is under way. The important thing is how the creative person handles himself in relation to (a) the extension of his experiencing, (b) the focusing of his experiencing, (c) the management of his actions during his experiencing, and (d) the derivation of significance from his experiencing.

The creative person seeks to extend his experiencing through holding himself open for increasing inclusions. This is evidenced by an inclination to take life as an adventure and a becoming, a curiosity and willingness to understand what is going on in oneself and in related aspects of the environment, a desire to get out to the edges of conscious realization and to feel a way into the unknown, an interest in new ideas and fresh perspective, a spirit of play and experimentation.

The creative person seeks to focus his experiencing through self-differentiation and self-realization. This is evidenced by a willingness to be different in things that make a difference, an honoring of his own fulfillment even when it runs counter to common expectations of others, a persistent inquiry into the meaning of his own life, a feeling that his individual life has independent roots, an insistence on expression for self-clarification, a feeling that the world is, in important part, his own creation.

The creative person seeks to manage his actions during his experiencing through disciplining himself to serve the extension and focusing of his experience. This is evidenced by an insistence on mastering his materials and tools of work so well that these become a part of his own way of living, an insistence on the privilege of controlling his own work schedule, a willingness to stick with baffling problems over an extended period of time, a capacity to be consumed by his work, a seriousness in selecting work to do which is personally and deeply valuable to him.

The creative person seeks to derive significance from his experiencing through dependence upon aesthetic formings. This is evidenced by an insistence on harmony of form and function, a trusting of feeling to guide his way through an experience, a searching for the simplest structural forms to catch up a whole field of relations at once, an ability to think in terms of patterns of form, a sensing of a profound order in nature and a searching for that order in himself and in the universe, a testing of a solution by the way in which it seems to fall into place without forcing, a deliberate nourishing of aid from unconscious sources, a sensitive awareness to positive and declarative modes of thought.

Inquiry along the dimensions of openness, self-realization, control, and aesthetic evaluation promises further refinements in specifica-

tion so that implicitly creative behavior can be more explicitly de-
noted and identified. With identifications, means are provided for
judging methods and circumstances which are most congenial to
the further development of creativity.

Research in these directions offers three important rewards: (a) a
better conception of man as a creative being, (b) a better conception
of the man we would become, and (c) better ways of ordering
behavior and environment toward the actualizing of the man we
would become.

In this construction, what is *described* in behavior is relevant to
what is *valued* in behavior. The definition of "what is" is functionally relevant to "what might be." Conditions are provided for
creative research.

The research I want is creative research. The science I want is a
more creative science.

Scientific activity is basically creative. The essential characteristic
of science is deliberate hypothesizing and testing. Hypothesizing is
the act of projecting what is wanted, "what might be." Testing is
an effort to compose givens, or "what is," into "what might be."
The effort may succeed or fail, but whatever the outcome, the
effort is to compose givens into something of value within the
system of life of the scientist. This is to create.

If the effort succeeds, the scientist will say that he has "established truth"; "created truth" would be a more accurate term. If
he fails, he will say that he has not yet found the truth. Truth is
that which effectively harmonizes the "is" with the projected and
valued "might be." Truth thus derived becomes a new "is." Truth
is the product of creation, born as a composition of value-in-fact.

Despite the evident creative character of scientific endeavor, scientists seem not to be generally aware of this basic quality in their
work. When asked directly, they may quickly say that scientific
work is creative work; yet, actually, they have not thought through
what this means for themselves or the training of others.

This is evidenced in tendencies to take science as a subject-matter product, neglecting science as an active human process; to fix attention on the scientific truth as already formed, neglecting scientific truth as a continuing creation; to take objectivity as the contending opposite of subjectivity, neglecting the emergence of objectivity as subjectivity clarified; to oppose feeling to thinking, neglecting the integral development of feeling and thinking; to assume an arbitrary separation of fact from value, neglecting the rooting of fact in value; to limit research training to teaching established methods of testing hypotheses, neglecting that half of the research process which has to do with the derivation of hypotheses which are significant for testing; to think of students as means to the teaching of science, neglecting science as means to the teaching of students; to take knowledge as the sufficient goal, neglecting its transformation into wisdom.

Perhaps most revealing of the scientist's frequent failure fully to appreciate his creative necessities is the degree to which he considers his activity to be distinctly different from that of men in the arts and humanities; and yet scientific activity belongs with other creative endeavors, e.g., music, literature, painting, drama, architecture. For centuries, men in the arts and humanities have been giving their attention to creative works and workings. Scientists can profit from association with men in these areas at the point where efforts are made to learn how creativity is to be honored and nourished in its development.

Within the general run of scientists, the leaders are likely to be men who have recognized the role of creativity in their personal work; otherwise, they could not generate the behaviors which are required for making them leaders.

Einstein is an example. He knew that the critical matter was the cultivation of himself as a suitable instrument for creative fulfillment. He paid attention to the content of his subject matter, but he paid even more attention to the quality of his own behavior. By being attentive to the shapings of experience in himself, he came to the development of science. He knew that he could not aim directly at his product because he did not know ahead of its appearance what it was going to be. What he did was to lend himself to creative thought and let his scientific formulations emerge as they will.

Einstein's behavior in his scientific work can be described according to the dimensions elsewhere presented for describing the behavior of any creative man. It is fair to hypothesize that other leaders in science, if able to express themselves on their intimate modes of working, would show similar orientation.

All scientists have a stake in cultivating creativity — for their own self-interest as well as for their service to mankind. However, social scientists more than others have a special reason for being intelligently concerned. Not only do they need to be creative to satisfy their own and society's emergent development, but they need a pattern of inquiry which fits their subject matter. Their subject matter being man, and man being a creative phenomenon, it is necessary that those who study man have creative modes of inquiry to match the requirements of their subject.

The principle that modes of inquiry be fitting for the phenomena inquired into is a stringent requirement acknowledged in science. But if it is stringent, it also offers hope for increasingly rapid development as integration increasingly occurs. It is an axiom in art circles that when an artist finds a way of handling his medium so that it fits the content with which he is dealing, emergent development of creative forms is exceedingly rapid. In addition, the product attains a living quality, having the power that seems everywhere to appear when a living thing is composed.

Social scientists have a challenge, but they also have a possibility of extraordinary richness for themselves and mankind.

The undertaking of research on man as a creative being is likely to bring with it a fundamental shift in the scientist's orientation.

Much of past research on man has been oriented to the under-standing of man not at his best and highest levels of integration, but at his worst and lowest levels of integration. Emphasis has been put upon the identification and treatment of the sick and the ab-normal. This has come about because of a pressure to serve those in need. The motive has been sound, but the consequence, in the absence of a positive definition of good, has been the acceptance of good as the absence of what has been identified as bad. The ad-justed person has come to be defined as one who is not maladjusted, without there being a declarative view of what the fulfilled man may be. By this orientation one's positive guidance is limited to the prevention of bad; it is not toward the accomplishment of a posi-tive state of being which, in the course of its achievement, makes the bad simply out of place.

Orientation to man as a creative being is orientation to the posi-tive, and it marks a shift so profound that few can guess its ulti-mate consequences. It is a whole orientation to life, with life taken not as the absence of death, but as a vital forming so composed that it can be increasingly fulfilled. It is also an orientation to peace, with peace taken not as the absence of war, but as the presence of a vital social harmony, each man fulfilling himself as he aids in the fulfillment of others.

Not only is the scientist's general orientation likely to shift but his more specific ways of working are also likely to change as he gives himself to research on man-as-a-creative-being.

He will soon find that it takes creative behavior to comprehend creative behavior. The identification of creative behavior in others will be found to depend in large part on realizing creative qualities in his own behavior. The primary source for research knowing will thereby come to be in his own experience, with hypothesizing and testing to check for harmonies with the experiencing of others.

He will soon find that he wants a particular kind of association with other research workers. Caught at the frontier of his own attempts at self-growth through inquiry, he will want to meet other research workers who are similarly caught on their own frontiers of self-growth. He will want to share experiences in self-realization and self-management and to find better ways of making research serve this end. For this purpose he will want associations which are informal, freely made, and personally as well as professionally significant.

He will come to value a wide range of disciplines. He will value the arts and humanities for their concern with the creative products of man, looking not so much at the forms of the products as at the formings of the production process. He will value the social sciences for their concern with the behavior of man, looking not so much at the resulting sciences but at the scientist as creatively thinking man.

He will find his greatest difficulty in expression and communication. He will discover that he is trying to use the formings of artists while trying to use the forms of scientists, and he will find that these are not culturally synchronized for his use. With formings and forms split, he will meet a difficult split in himself, and when he speaks, even at his best, he will find that what he says may somehow be hauntingly relevant to both scientists and artists but not clear to either.

He will dislike his clumsiness, but he will stick with his work and its necessities. He will become increasingly convinced that what he is trying to do is something which society, in many ways, is now trying to burst through to do. He will sense that his problem is the cultural problem of getting values clear, of integration, of transcending reaction with action, of establishing a positive basis for peace in the individual and in the world.

XXI SUMMARY: EXPLORATIONS IN ESSENTIAL BEING AND PERSONAL GROWTH

CLARK E. MOUSTAKAS

The central theme of this book has been that the self is the essential being of the individual, substantial as itself yet constantly emerging through actualization of potentials. Certain convictions, implications, and explorations in personal growth comprise the clarifying and elaborating themes. These are discussed separately as essential perceptions of man's personal world and the unfolding of growth, creativity, and health.

INTRINSIC NATURE, BEING, BECOMING

Three central, orienting concepts of self are: *intrinsic nature, being,* and *becoming.* Intrinsic nature refers to the natural, inherent, given, unchanging potentialities, capacities, or proclivities of man. The interest of man is to realize these inherent potentialities, to develop himself as fully and completely as he humanly can. Inner nature is universally noncomparable, absolute, inviolate. But its focus, orientation and unity in any one individual is always unique. There is no such thing as a type of person except for "useful" abstracting purposes. The experience of one's separateness as a human being represents both the necessity and the opportunity for the person to manifest basic tendencies, to develop a personality. The continuing creation of man's uniqueness is guided by values, based upon the unconscious or pre-conscious perceptions of our own nature, of our destiny, or our own capacities, of our own "call" in life, of "man's recall to himself."

The harmony and emergence of one's own life seem to come from the increasing capacity to find in the world that which also obtains within the depths of one's own being. The self emerges in appropriate patterns of experience or being, which incorporates truth, the inherent truth of the organism. Being refers to this concrete, holistic patterning of self in immediate living, as well as the unyielding, absolute, and unique qualities of the individual person. The individual self, or being, is an ultimate core of reality which remains unchanged throughout changes of its qualities or states. To be, a person must be true to himself; not in terms of others, but only to his inner nature, in real experience. The sources for the assertion of human potentialities are deep within the personal experience of the one who asserts them. And one can discover his real self only in true experience, as an autonomous and self-governing entity. Being is good only as itself and can be understood only in itself alone, as a whole; not in terms of attributes. It is an indivisible unity.

True experience is the natural expression of one's inner self in interaction with meaningful people and resources. As such, all expressions in true experience are creative. True experience involves an immanent orientation characterized by the immediate knowing of the world through direct, personal perception. All the undertakings of the past are embedded in the present and cannot be isolated without violating the essence of experience. Expressions of true self are always creative and constructive. They result in social creativity and growth, which in turn, encourage and free the individual to further self-expression and discovery.

The individual is engaged in leading his life in the present, with a forward thrust in the future. This is the concept of becoming, with its implications of change and transformation. Creation is conceived as a continued transition from one form to another. The world, while it is being perceived, is being incessantly created by an individual who is a process, not a product. The individual is not a fixed entity but a center of experience involving the creative synthesis of relations. The central force for this becoming nature of man is a basic striving within the human being to assert and expand his self-determination, to create his own fate.

The organism has different potentialities, and because it has them it has the need to actualize or realize them. The fulfillment of these needs represents the self-actualization of the organism, a constant emerging of self, of one's "nature" in the world. Failure to actualize essential capacities is equivalent to not being. Thus, the goal the individual most wishes to achieve, the end which he knowingly and unknowingly pursues, is to become himself. All reality is this process of becoming, and all life is one, a constant urge to become.

According to his intrinsic nature, the individual develops certain appropriate needs, sensitivities, inhibitions, and moral values. If he can grow in love and in friction, he will also grow in accordance with his real self.

Intrinsic nature, being, and becoming are involved in every true experience. Therefore, all true experience of a real self is healthy and necessary to personal growth. To the extent that painful experiences foster and fulfill our inner nature, they are desirable experiences. Growth in self-fulfilling persons can come through struggle, agony, and conflict, as well as through tranquility, joy, and love, or any other human emotion. The individual becomes himself in true experience in an organic matrix, pattern, or whole, which permits him to be.

THE PERSONAL ORIENTATION OF THE INDIVIDUAL WHO EXPRESSES HIS INTRINSIC CREATIVITY

Every real individual is a creative person. This intrinsic creativity emerges, or is expressed, when the person is free to use his potentialities. Creativity may occur in the context of utter serenity, peace, and absorption in the world, and in such a way that only the individual himself can know the creative worth of his experience. It may be expressed in moments of exhilaration and excitement, the exploration of an idea, the working out of a configuration or pattern in music, art, or science. It may arise in the continued maintenance of tension, which has significance to one's being and makes further ordered activity and discovery possible. Creativity may also be a process in goal-directed behavior. But it always involves the interaction of the real person with the world, and growth as a human being rather than deficiency motivation and competitive excelling over others. The nature and form of creation can have no objectivity or independence isolated from the creating person.

To be creative, the experience must incorporate the personal meanings and values of individual being. The real individual approaches life with an openness of self, a touching, groping, feeling, sensing, reaching, and testing orientation. He perceives all significant experience fully and completely, with sensitivity to a great yariety of internal and external cues. The individual moves toward increased autonomy, and increasingly feels that the locus of direction lies within himself. His development and continued growth are dependent on his own potentialities and latent resources. To express creativity is to be spontaneous, natural, and free in terms of essential being and in interaction with nature and people. It means automatic "self-knowledge" and "self-awareness," though not necessarily fully conscious.

The person who expresses his creativeness has a fresh, naïve, direct way of looking at life. He lends himself to creative thought, and permits truth and scientific formulation to emerge as they will. This giving of oneself to all true experience is accompanied by a vital realization of the immediate experience of living. Preconceived methods and techniques and past histories hold little value. The individual who uses his intrinsic creativity accepts himself as fate-determining, instead of reality as fate. He accepts himself without even thinking about the matter, and accepts his own human nature with all its shortcomings. He accepts all life as worth while and values the absolute integrity of the human being. He has a deep sympathy and identification with all human beings, and finds it possible to learn from anyone who has anything important to teach him. He is loyal to his own individual values, his own being, and regards this loyalty as a source of honesty and integrity. These attitudes of acceptance and respect for human integrity are indivisible. Love for, acceptance of, and understanding of one's own self in experience cannot be separated from respect for, acceptance of, and love and understanding of another individual.

The person who uses his intrinsic creativity acts on conviction and belief. He discovers facts and ideas through his being and his personal unique values, through the process of viewing one's self as relevant to all valid observation and scientific inquiry. He trusts himself to will, without being obliged to justify this will morally or to react with guilt to it. He increasingly discovers that his own being is trustworthy, and a suitable instrument for knowing the most satisfying behavior in each situation.

The person who expresses his unique nature, lives more in the real world of nature than in the man-made complex of concepts, expectations, beliefs, and stereotypes. His unconventionality is essential or internal, in terms of important and basic issues, not trivialities. His code of ethics is autonomous and individual rather than conventional, and is based on fundamental principles and moral values. He acts because of the activity itself, not solely for its effects. He values life and objects because they are *good,* not only because they are *good for.* He enjoys the getting to some place, as well as the arriving. Even when there is a goal, the entire process of pursuing or moving in its direction is important, and as much a value as the *goal* itself. There is a continued freshness, naïveté, and appreciation of life, and a frequent loss of placing in time and space, loss of self, and transcendence of it. There is immersion of self and other, unique and common, individual and universal, in undivided, unified, consistent behavior.

THE INDIVISIBLE NATURE OF INDIVIDUAL AND UNIVERSAL

All true experience involves self and other, unique and common, subject and object, individual and universal, blended imperceptibly and wholly indivisible. Thus to abstract, isolate, analyze human experience in discrete categories is to violate its nature, break it up, and aggress against it.

The world is viewed as a harmonious blending of the personality in all its surroundings. The individual and his world coexist and subsist together. Subject and object are one in true experience. The quality of being possessed does not indicate a purely external denomination between subject and object. To be possessed means *to be for someone*. The possessed object is touched in its being. Thus the bond of possession is a true bond of being. The relationship between possessor and possessed constitutes ideally a unique undivided reality.

The relational world is individual, yet it is universal. If the self were solely the individual's, it could not be true. At the same time, if it were not intimately his, it would not be real. The oneness of each individual realizes itself by uniting with others. There is no concept of man or human nature in which every person is not a part. Love is indivisible between objects and one's own self, and love of one person implies love of man as such, recognizing and nurturing oneself not only for oneself but for all of life. These two elements of selfhood, uniqueness and universality, grow together, until at last the most unique becomes the most universal.

UNITY AND SELF-CONSISTENCY

Personal growth as portrayed here stresses the unity and organization of man. Personality is conceived as an organization of values which are consistent with one another. In all personal transformations, certain persistent and distinguishable characteristics and values remain.

In a real sense there is one whole, the totality of being. Man is a unit in himself, a system which operates as a whole. To view the person in parts or pieces is not only invalid but a denial of the integrity and respect entitled to every human being, a denial of his right to be regarded as himself, as a whole person. Much apparently segmented behavior is the tendency on the part of the individual to remove a condition which interferes with unity and self-actualization.

The individual responds entirely, wholly. He organizes and unifies his perceptions of his immediate personal world so as to have value and meaning appropriate to his personality. The life of the individual is an organized patterned process, a distinctiveness of pattern which constitutes both the unity and distinctiveness of self. All past processes obtain their specific function from the unifying over-all pattern of the individual. The necessity to maintain the unity of the system serves as the universal dynamic principle. Not conflict but unity is the fundamental postulate of personal growth.

MEANING, PERCEPTION, REALITY

Forms of things have no absolute reality. Their truth lies in our personality. The meaning of experience comes from individual, personal perception. These meanings constitute a pattern which *is* reality for the person. Thus personal reality is what the individual *is* in experience. It lies in each unique self. What one perceives to be true is solid and substantial. Attempts to determine reality for another person, to *give* meaning to another's experience, *deny* the self. These other-directed meanings cannot be assimilated. They meet with resistance, which is a natural phenomenon and essential for the maintenance of self. Therefore only those experiences which have significance for the individual person enter his real personality.

Experience may be objectified in terms of measurements, procedures, and regulations. But every true experience changes its essential meaning according to the personality of the individual. The individual is the most constant factor in his experience and he alone can determine the true meaning of his perception.

In essence, the unique patterning of the world is what we perceive it to be. Since each person looks at the world from a characteristic point of view, uniqueness of perception holds. It is upon these perceptions of what is real that people base their actions and decisions. When the individual ignores his own perceptions of reality and the personal meanings of his experience, he denies his own self.

It is possible to *approach* a common or social reality. Such a correspondence of perceptual fields occurs through defining, abstracting, and "objectifying" persons, objects, and events, *more adequately* through empathy and communion, and *most truly* through *experiencing* the reality of another's experience of persons, events, and objects.

THE PLACE OF MOTIVATION AND ADJUSTMENT IN ESSENTIAL BEING AND PERSONAL GROWTH

Motivation implies goal direction, the seeking of a state of equilibrium, the reduction of tensions and drives. The facts taken as foundations for the assumption of different drives and their function in personality are more or less abstractions from the natural behavior of the organism. Striving for equilibrium, release of tensions, and death wishes are erroneous representations of healthy adult behavior.

An attempt to see, seek, and express relations in terms of cause and effect interferes with recognizing the essence and meaning of human experience. Being does not rest on purpose, or previous action, as a basis for behavior. Being is good and true in terms of pattern or unity. *This is the guide.*

What counts in motivation is the satiation, the achievement, the end, not the process or content of experience. In essential being, the creative process itself is important. The person who does not use his intrinsic creativity is *motivated* by compulsive drives to success, competition, and achievement and *adjusts* to unhealthy norms and standards. His life, his entire existence depend upon other persons. In the healthy person autonomy, self-direction is the guide, not adjustment and popularity.

Adjustment is not a *positive* assertion of self; it does not indicate what we are living for, but points toward a giving in to external pressures, of leading a life apart from intrinsic nature and moral values. Adjustment leaves us without a positive expression of what is good, only the acceptance of good as the average or the absence of bad.

The tendency to maintain an existent or "safe" state is characteristic of sick people, a sign of anomaly and decay of life. The tendency in healthy life is toward self-expression, activity, and progress. While adjustment and stabilization are perhaps good because they cut pain, they are also bad because development toward higher ideals, ordering, and creation ceases.

Motivation too often is used to trap attention and coerce effort, to get people to engage in projects which have no intrinsic worth. Since essential being and personal growth are concerned with pattern, organization, and unity, the concept of motivation is rarely necessary to an understanding of behavior and self.

SELF-IMPAIRING FORCES: ANALYSIS, SELF-DENIAL, SELF-DEROGATION

One can never come to the reality of creation by contemplating it from the point of view of destruction. Analysis breaks up the individual self in experience and objectifies what is unyieldingly personal and subjective. It attempts to derive from external sources knowledge of self, which is, and remains, destructive with all its content of "truth." Significance and meaning are grounded not on the objective truth of behavior but on reality experience. Knowledge contains a self-interpretation which is opposed to experience. Thus the neurotic person needs no more self-knowledge, only experience, and his capacity for it yet may be able to save him.

A science which objectifies and views behavior externally as symbolic or in categories tries to do away altogether with the real person, the central personality. It sets up impersonal and unalterable *standards of creation*, and eliminates the *personality of creation*. It deals with elements of sameness rather than the unique, idiosyncratic, and peculiar qualities that exist in being. It abstracts until eventually persons and things become nothing at all. A flower is nothing when we analyze it and abstract its characteristics and qualities, but it is *positively* a flower when we enjoy it in absorption with nature. Joy is real because it is personal. The reality of the flower and the personal creation of the individual can never be known or truly experienced, in analysis and abstraction. These approaches give us a false view of the world, an element of sameness and commonness, a basis for scientific prediction, but not the essence of truth and reality. The reality of the world belongs to man in *exact experience*, not precise measurement, in wholeness and not in splitting.

Another impairing and destructive approach to the essence of being is self-derogation, a feeling of inadequacy, and a feeling of being unloved. Self-derogation leads to an impairment of self-determination and a stifling of the capacity to love. All criticism, "judgment," comparison, and evaluation imply self-derogation and interfere with being and becoming. These approaches create superordinate and subordinate relationships which minimize and deny the self-directing, self-fulfilling nature of man.

Love can never be experienced through analysis and evaluation; only through self-interest, self-regards, and respect for one's real self. Self-love does not mean selfishness but its opposite. Only if man can love himself can he love others; as he values his own sheer being he values others. Self and other are one, distinct, yet indivisible in real experience. Every violation of self is an attack on all human beings everywhere. Every alienation from self is a departure from virtue and truth. When the individual is alienated from himself he needs something that will give him a hold, a feeling of identity.

The worship of success, reward, and accomplishment, the striving for external symbols and gains, the attempt to sell oneself effectively, and impressively to become the expectations of others, alienates man from himself and fails to satisfy man's ineradicable striving to be himself. Conformity to imposed standards and values, responding in conventional ways which are not based on principles of integrity and personal growth, impair man's essential creativity, his will to explore and actualize. The lack of meditativeness and inwardness, of real conscience and real values is a standard personality defect.

Self-significance must not be "I am what I possess," or "I am as you desire me," but "I am true to myself."

EMOTIONAL CLIMATE CONDUCIVE TO SELF-EXPERIENCE AND SELF-GROWTH

The life of any living person or thing is its own. All that man can do is affect the environment in which potentialities can be fulfilled. Materials and resources can be provided which may enrich experience, and man can be valued as sheer personal being, but the individual alone determines his direction and his reality. To value the person, every person, as sheer personal being is to love him. Brotherhood is inherent in the structure of human living. It needs only to be recognized and felt. Tenderness, care, personal warmth, all affect the development of individuality, expression of one's being, and enhancement of self. Relations must be such that each person is free to express, experience, actualize, and affirm his own uniqueness.

To proclaim the value of self-fulfillment means unalterable belief in the potentiality of each person and what he is trying to do in life. It means a climate where the individual is trusted. It means the person is assumed as honest and insightful until proven otherwise. It means trusting that what the individual expresses of himself is true and valid and need not be examined, interpreted, or looked into for possible hidden dynamics.

In an emotional climate conducive to growth of self, the individuality of the person is completely accepted, a reality in which doubt is impossible. There is an effort to understand the true nature of the individual's experience in his own terms, in communion, through empathy. The individual's own point of view is regarded as substantial, as the most real and valid way of knowing him. In such a setting, the meanings that experiences have for others are listened to with warmth and "objectivity," *seeing* another's experience through his own personal perceptions. There can be no real love without this understanding of the other person, without a deep perception of the core of the essential nature of the person. To recognize and accept the otherness of a person means to respect him as a valuable being in his own right, in his autonomy and independence.

In such a setting, the individual is completely free to be himself, to express spontaneously his intrinsic nature. Work expresses one's life so long as one's infinity can be expressed in everything around him. Helping to keep free-flowing streams to continue to be free, and helping the individual avoid the clogging — these are significant values in every growth experience.

It is within the power of man to treasure his personality, to strengthen and value his individuality, to turn toward honesty, affection, self-respect, and intellectual and aesthetic growth, to accept one's nature, and to turn away from destructive analysis, self-derogation, alienation, hypocrisy, cruelty, cowardliness and smallness.

CONCLUSION

The self in this book has been discussed in many variations of one central theme: Man has an intrinsic nature which must be recognized and treasured. Man's inner nature is the key to human joy, happiness, and fulfillment. In interpersonal experience it is expressed in warmth, empathy, cognition, acceptance, tenderness, and love. Respect for man's essential creativity is the declaration of each man's true worth, of his uniqueness as a human being, unmatched, unparalleled, and unmeasured; the proclamation of the dignity of the individual and the incommensurable nature of his existence.

Man's inherent being is embedded in every fiber of his experience. To turn away from one's true existence as a human being is to violate one's nature and to threaten and impair human dignity everywhere. Man's innate potentials are good when free to function naturally, as utterances, expressions, and self-assertions, not solely driving forces maintaining tension but expressions of ourselves, basically and fully, in what being human means. Man's being may be experienced in contemplation, absorption, and immersion in the world. It may be expressed in serenity, calmness, and complete inner peace. It is known in the deep love and empathy of significant relationships. Self-exploration may also involve a maintenance of tension, struggling with values, ideas, and the exciting discovery of significant meanings in perception and experience. Rarely is self-exploration simply a tension-reducing and goal-seeking device.

To express and affirm one's inner nature, to be courageous and honest to all that one truly experiences, this is essential to personal growth. Realization of one's being is man's real fate and the *only* realization which permits the emergence of individuality and uniqueness as well as universal growth.

The concept of personal growth is a positive affirmation, not the absence of symptoms nor the presence of the striving to fulfill conventional standards and norms. It is an understanding of health in its truest form, the expression of one's creative nature in true experience, the exploration of one's being in nature, in individual projects and vocations, in interpersonal relations.

Thus the thesis of this book has been that each man has a personal destiny, a personal self. Within this self lies the essential equality of all human nature. The personal self is focused in unique expressions and individual variations and comes to form the personality of man, substantial in its being yet forever in transformation and in becoming. It is man's duty and responsibility to nurture, cultivate, and find expression for this inner nature and potentiality.